DENIS HEALEY

AND THE POLICIES OF POWER

DENIS HEALEY

and the

Policies of Power

BRUCE REED

and

GEOFFREY WILLIAMS

SIDGWICK & JACKSON

LONDON

ISBN 0 283 48464 0

Made and printed in Great Britain by
William Clowes & Sons, Limited
London, Beccles and Colchester
for
Sidgwick and Jackson Limited
1 Tavistock Chambers, Bloomsbury Way
London, W.C.1

Contents

Introduction

IN the six years between 1964 and 1970, Denis Healey supervised some of the most profound changes ever to have occurred in British defence policy.

The reduction in spending and the decision to withdraw from being a world power and concentrate on Europe should have been easier for a Labour Government than a Conservative one. The Labour movement has always preferred social to military advance, so its leaders please the Party when they reduce defence spending.

Denis Healey introduced a policy of cuts and realignment in defence policy, yet he kept the confidence of the armed services, and the respect of those with a professional interest in defence. Few politicians understand defence – not even the retired Conservative admirals and brigadiers who understand the Services.

Healey was the first 'meritocrat' to have so completely dominated the Ministry. 'I believed in controlling the Ministry absolutely,' he said. The way he dominated the department, probing down to junior staff officer level, and reorganizing it to make it more professional, justifies his assertion.

Healey has had a remarkable political career. With Britain standing today on the threshold of membership of a political and economic community, the like of which has not been seen in Europe since the end of the Holy Roman Empire, it is particularly worth surveying the life and politics of the man who was in power at the time of the fundamental change in Britain's defence policy. Healey's work in European defence has done much to give Britain the chance of successful entry to the European Economic Community.

The young Healey was a Communist, yet he became Secretary of State for Defence. He began work for the Labour Party as an extreme left-winger, but in his six years at Transport House he helped Social Democrats escape from Eastern Europe where the Communists were taking over. He also wrote anti-Communist pamphlets, and a large part of the modern charter of the Socialist International – a movement begun originally by Karl Marx in 1864.

His dramatic selection for a Leeds constituency and his turbulent relationship with his Left-wing constituency workers did not hamper his independent position on the Right of the Party. He played an active part in shaping the Labour Party's foreign and defence policies before entering office in 1964.

As Minister of Defence he supervised drastic cuts and drew up new policies. Like Haldane before the First World War he overhauled the Ministry of Defence, making it a more efficient fighting machine.

But as a Minister in Wilson's Government he and his colleagues had to struggle to master the economy. Their failure to control the economy and the series of set-backs at home and abroad which they faced forced them to adopt a new defence policy – dictated more by events than by choice.

*   *   *

In compiling this book we have interviewed a large number of people in politics, diplomacy, academic life, journalism, the services, and the Civil Service. We are unable to reveal the names of all of those who helped us, but we would like to thank them for their observations and advice, as well as others named in the text who gave us their valuable time and comments.

We would also like to thank Denis Healey for his assistance, and the Ministry of Defence for their co-operation in the preparation of this book. While we have made every effort to check the facts presented in this book we acknowledge that a definitive account of the Labour Cabinet's discussions and decisions will not be possible until the Cabinet papers are published between A.D. 1994 and 2000.

We would like to thank Southampton College of Technology and Southampton University for allowing us time to undertake the research, and for their help. We would also like to thank Bay Hasseler in the research department of Transport House, and the librarians there, our typists Brenda Clark and Eve

Taylor for their efforts, Bryan Reed for his editorial assistance, Sue Ashton for compiling the index, and our wives for their patience and encouragement. We also want to thank Alan Lee Williams for his advice and assistance.

We ourselves, however, accept full responsibility for the views which follow.

BRUCE REED
and GEOFFREY WILLIAMS

November, 1970

Chapter One

The Setting Sun

'*His Majesty's dominion, on which the sun never sets.*'
CHRISTOPHER NORTH (1785–1854) in 'Noctes Ambrosianæ'

'*Britain has lost an Empire, and has not yet found a role.*'
DEAN ACHESON, former American Secretary of State,
5 December 1962, at West Point

Chapter One

STAYING the other side of Suez made sense for Britain only if it could be achieved this side of solvency. In January 1968 the British Government finally realized this was no longer possible and Denis Healey, Secretary of State for Defence, announced that by the end of 1971 Britain's permanent garrisons East of Suez would be wound up.

Victory against Hitler and the Japanese hid Britain's economic exhaustion from her leaders. The politicians, especially, suffered from a hangover of the Gladstonian view that Britain had somehow a more moral idea of world order than other more selfish powers, and therefore had both a greater duty and greater right to act as a world policeman.

For almost five centuries Britain had had strong imperial and commercial commitments East of Suez. She had also been a liberal in international affairs, and had felt a responsibility for what was happening to people, even those on the other side of the globe with an entirely different history and culture. When war ended in 1945 the new Labour Government in Britain, with its firmly-rooted belief in the international brotherhood of man, could not simply stop caring.

Neither could Denis Healey, the Party's International Secretary in Transport House. He firmly supported the efforts of Foreign Minister Ernest Bevin, the rotund former boss of Britain's biggest union, the Transport and General Workers, to build a world union – drawing on American economic and military strength while he did so. As it happened, Bevin's realization in 1947 that Britain did not have the economic resources to play policeman in Greece and Turkey had helped nudge the Americans into the role of European guardian, via the Truman Doctrine. The myth that Britain was still a Great Power, however, refused to die.

Denis Healey was a back-bench Labour M.P. in 1956 when Anthony Eden, confused by illness into thinking that a nuclear power like Britain must not make the same mistake she had made against Hitler at Munich in time of military weakness, attacked Suez. But Egypt's Colonel Nasser was not just another upstart dictator of the sort Eden had faced as a Foreign Minister in the 1930s. Nasser represented a 'Third World' of developing nations, struggling to throw off old ties of imperialism and domination by European powers.

The United States, which had never regarded its own activities in the Philippines or Latin America in the same imperialistic light, in a fit of righteous pique at not being informed or consulted about the British adventure, started selling sterling through the Swiss financiers. Chancellor of the Exchequer Harold Macmillan realized that Britain could not afford to go on losing some £400 million a day from its reserves to prop up the pound, and counselled caution. As a result, when Britain called a halt her allies, the French, were disgusted at her weakness under American pressure. The British White Man, defeated by international pressure, had been unable to impose his version of a 'just' solution.

As Healey saw, in 1956, Britain was impotent in the face of opposition from her superpower protector, the United States. He savagely attacked Government policy in the House of Commons and throughout the nation – an unpopular attitude for people who yearned for a sign that Britain was still the Great Power, that her word could not be questioned, that her actions could not be queried and her deeds not thwarted. The mass of the people, caught in a rapidly changing environment where every standard and attitude was being questioned, desperately wanted the Government to show who was really master.

Events have shown that Eden's temporary aberration was also ill-conceived, and created more problems than it solved. Since the Second World War, however, Britain has had her military successes. Whether in Malaya or Kenya fighting terrorists, in Korea and Borneo, holding bigger fish, or propping up regimes in Kuwait or East Africa, there were enough successes to persuade the Government that it was doing a useful job as an international fireman, helping to douse the flames that might lead to larger conflicts.

The role of providing a fire brigade for the world's trouble spots was one with immense appeal for the Labour Government of Harold Wilson when it assumed office on Friday, 16 October 1964. Buying time for small nations, so that they could build up their economies and forces to a point where they could look after themselves, appealed to the 'internationalists'. The realization that Britain's contribution to international security could no longer be reconciled with its economic circumstances was slow to dawn – until 1968.

When the Wilson Government came to office Britain still had traditional ties and defence burdens around the globe. British troops were in the Far East, the Indian Ocean, the Middle East, and East Africa, as well as in the Caribbean. Her defence policy, however, had gradually shifted to more of an alliance policy, working with the U.S.A., mainly through the North Atlantic Treaty Organization (NATO), and nominally the South East Asian Treaty Organization (SEATO), and the Central Treaty Organization (CENTO), which had more political than military significance.

Some strategists, especially those who wanted Britain to join the Common Market, argued also that she should concentrate on making a major contribution to the defence of Europe. And politicians like Sir Alec Douglas-Home, then leader of the Conservative Party, held that Britain had a 'place at the top table' because she possessed the nuclear deterrent.

So Britain dissipated her military energies for several ends, and in several places. Gradually the Labour Government began to realize that it was not worth the effort, and also that it was an effort we could no longer afford.

The Dwindling Empire

By 1968 a number of factors suggested that it was time Britain rethought her policy of policing the world. Rhodesian independence, and Britain's inability to do much about it, together with a declining imperial position within the Commonwealth, began to disillusion even such strongly pro-Commonwealth men as Prime Minister Harold Wilson.

Doubts about whether peace-keeping only preserved the *status quo* at the expense of postponing the inevitable (as the United Nations peace-keeping force, UNEF, had done in the Middle East until the Six Day War of 1967) questioned the very *raison d'être* of policing.

The decline in the intensity of ideological rivalries, especially in the mid-sixties within the Communist bloc with its new idea of 'polycentrism' – having many centres of power instead of being just part of one united international conspiracy – encouraged the West to think it had less to fear, and also to assume that states that did go Communist would not necessarily join in support of the Soviet Union. Indeed not. The Sino-Soviet dispute, which began in ideological terms, had now become a public political conflict between two intensely nationalist great powers, each pre-occupied about its role in world politics, its influence in the Communist movement, its power in Asia, its frontiers and its economic strength.

There were doubts among the liberals that unstable, corrupt and autocratic regimes, which seemed to abound throughout the 'Third World', were worth fighting for. The Middle East June war of 1967, when oil supplies to the West were cut off for a few months, showed Britain that her presence did not protect British oil, and that the Arabs could block her route to the Far East. A role East of Nasser seemed less viable than before. The Six Day War showed that the Mediterranean was no longer an exclusively Western preserve. Yet whatever the degree of Russian penetration in the Middle East, Britain was in no shape to challenge single-handed its present or potential course.

East of Suez itself the changes were causing Britain to question whether it was worth-while staying: in Vietnam, Indonesia, and North Korea there were increased assertions of national independence. When the ill-conceived Malaysian Federation broke up, Britain was powerless to prevent it; just as she was powerless to do anything in the Indo-Pakistani conflict of 1965, and in South Arabia. The example of Vietnam showed that, given the right conditions and the will to fight, a small nation could hold even a superpower like the United States. The British Government could be thankful that the Indonesian Army and President Sukarno did not commit all their forces against the Malaysians; and more than one senior British general was grateful when that conflict came to a halt. Had it become Britain's Vietnam it is doubtful whether Britain could have coped. But with China's Cultural Revolution producing internal upheaval, and the increased tendencies of countries like Australia and

New Zealand to prepare to defend themselves – with the aid of the United States – the need to stay was on the wane.

As Prime Minister Wilson said in the Defence Debate of July 1967, by keeping a 'military capability' rather than a 'military presence' Britain could go on providing the sophisticated support necessary to deter a sophisticated aggressor. Surely, that was enough to ask of us?

Factors nearer home, however, were decisive in the final conversion of Denis Healey and the Wilson Cabinet to announcing that Britain would be pulling out. The growing disillusion with a world role came during a crisis of confidence among the British people and leaders of political, academic, and popular opinion. The decision to reapply for admission to the Common Market, agreed to by a majority of almost 500 M.P.s, one of the largest ever in the House of Commons, was given all-party backing on 10 May 1967. It was seen, politically, as a chance for Britain to play a new and larger role in world affairs through her membership of a vital, dynamic, and expanding force.

The decision to search for a new identity in Europe came slowly. Britain's politicians did not want to be accused of scurrying out of world-wide commitments in unseemly haste.

When Duncan Sandys, as Tory Defence Minister, announced the end of conscription in 1957, Britain had almost 700,000 men under arms. In the course of the 1960s the number dropped to 400,000. But commitments were retained in spite of the cuts. According to an Opinion Research Centre poll taken at the end of the decade, 50 per cent of the British public thought Britain underrated her own importance as a power, while only 31 per cent thought she overrated it. The poll showed that the younger the people questioned, the more likely they were to think that Britain's role in world affairs was played out. Fifty-seven per cent of the over-55s still believed, nostalgically, that the country's power was underrated.

After the Second World War, however, the major change in Britain's status had been economic, not strategic; and success in many fields served only to disguise the fact. But the message of the continued and increasing balance of payments deficits (buying more goods and services from abroad than were sold in return) finally got home, and on Saturday, 18 November 1967, Britain was forced to devalue the pound to make goods cheaper to foreigners and eventually push up the standard of living at home.

Faced with the growing payments crisis in the 1950s and 1960s Britain had refused to accept economic and political realities. The cuts in defence spending were piecemeal. They had not attacked the cause of Britain's economic sickness; they had merely been temporary alleviations of one of its consequences – an aspirin for the headache. But eventually the fog of nostalgia gave way to a more pragmatic and realistic approach. Britain had become a second-class power, whose future strategic interests seemed to lie in Europe. It was now impossible to protect her world-wide trade and financial interests by military means.

Britain's defence policy has always reflected her national ambitions as much as her necessities. With an economist, Harold Wilson, at the helm, and a Government committed to growth as a means of financing the socialist revolution, arguments for becoming a European-oriented, rather than a world-oriented power, seemed economically strong. Before the Second World War Britain had financed her usual deficit on trade with other nations by selling the rest of the world services such as shipping and insurance, and by earnings from investments. In the war the merchant fleet had suffered huge losses, and much of Britain's overseas investments had been sold.

In spite of this, Government spending overseas outstripped the economic recovery of the nation and her ability to finance British statesmen's desire to play major parts in the world. In 1952 overseas spending had been only £52 million, and by 1957 it was still only £144 million. It trebled between then and 1964 when the Conservatives left office. In the first four years of the Labour Government it rose another £30 million to a peak of £446 million in 1967 – the year of devaluation. Defence spending accounted for roughly two-thirds of the bill.

Apart from the tremendous cost to the balance of payments, politicians realized that spending on defence was a major cause of Britain's economic weakness, diverting precious resources of manpower, skills, and capital, and resulting in a slower rate of growth. Competitors in world markets had not made the same mistake. In 1967, according to the Institute for Strategic Studies, Japan devoted only 0·9 per cent of her gross national product (the amount of goods and services produced by the nation) to defence expenditure. Germany spent 4·3 per cent on defence. Britain spent 5·7 per cent, exceeded in Europe only by Portugal, another imperial power, heavily engaged with her African colonies.

Britain had decided to come home again to Europe after almost 500 years. She no longer intended fighting lone battles thousands of miles away. The world had changed; Britain clearly lacked the resources to be in the same league with the superpowers.

Challenge in Europe

Adventurers and statesmen gave Britain her Empire. While Pitt financed Prussian armies, British soldiers and sailors were securing vast dominions in America and India. Pitt won Canada because Frederick's efforts tied down the armies of Europe. By the reign of George III Britain's maritime power was at its peak of success, and Britain had the role of trading, civilizing, and converting the natives to the superior British way of Christian life. The Empire was founded.

Britain's imperial crown was shattered by the Second World War. Countries such as India and Ceylon achieved their independence in a new Commonwealth which served to link an assortment of races, colours, and creeds.

When Harold Macmillan won the 'Never-had-it-so-good' election in 1959 he asked the Civil Service to carry out a review of British interests. Its conclusion, that Britain's future lay in Europe, encouraged him to apply for membership of the European Economic Community on 10 August 1961.

Labour politicians, led by Hugh Gaitskell and encouraged by Healey, initially looked towards the Commonwealth for political and economic substance. Gaitskell pointed out that in 1961 only a modest 16·7 per cent of Britain's exports went to Common Market countries, while her exports to the Commonwealth amounted to 39·5 per cent. He emphasized that gains in Europe were doubtful, while trade with the old Empire was known, and was substantial.

But in the sixties the facts and mood of the nation changed. The percentage of British exports going to the Commonwealth countries fell by 1966 to only 25 per cent. Imports similarly declined. When Harold Wilson announced on 10 November 1966 that he and George Brown were to sound out European opinion about entry into the Common Market, the writing was on the wall. Public opinion polls carried out in 1961 and 1969 by the *Daily Telegraph* showed that the British people thought the Commonwealth had declined in importance, compared with Europe and America. In September 1961, 48 per cent had thought that the Commonwealth was more important. By January 1969 only 34 per cent thought so. Meanwhile the 18 per cent who had thought Europe of most importance to Britain had swollen to 26 per cent.

This swing in opinion reflected economic realities. Trade with European countries was expanding, and even Commonwealth preferences declined steadily. However, economic reality was no guarantee that Britain would walk into the European Economic Community.

Macmillan's attempt to join was rejected. His mistake lay in assuming that it did not matter whether General de Gaulle approved of the British application or not. So the debate about entry began before London had cultivated a close link with Paris or Bonn. Negotiations, which began in November 1961, dragged on until the French finally decided to end the charade in January 1963. De Gaulle said 'Non', and Britain was firmly out in the cold.

It was a cold made bearable only by success at Nassau in December 1962. At that meeting Macmillan had won from the Americans an offer of Polaris submarines and missiles to replace the strategically-obsolescent Skybolt stand-off missile which had proved too costly. The Nassau meeting, which re-affirmed close Anglo-American links, gave de Gaulle the excuse he needed to keep Britain out and leave him to dominate the Market.

When Britain re-applied to the E.E.C. in 1967, however, the argument that her political, economic, and strategic policies should all be in line had won influential supporters. They questioned whether it was possible for Britain to be committed to Europe and have a 'special relationship' with the United States, yet still remain East of Suez. To join Europe it would have to be all or nothing; which might mean, as Edward Heath, the Conservative leader, pointed out, some kind of Anglo-French nuclear co-operation.

Europeans were conscious that Britain's leaders had not

always been enthusiastic 'Europeans'. De Gaulle also recalled the words of earlier British leaders in his memoirs, *Le Salut*. In June 1944 Churchill had told him 'Here is something you should know; whenever we have to choose between Europe and the open sea, we shall always choose the open sea. Whenever I have to choose between you and Roosevelt, I shall always choose Roosevelt.' De Gaulle further remembered that in a moment of anguish in Algiers during the war Harold Macmillan had said, 'If General de Gaulle refuses the hand stretched towards him, let him know that Britain and the United States will abandon him completely – and he will be nothing any more.'

In spite of enthusiastic pro-Europe speeches by Churchill, Eden, and Macmillan in the late forties, the Conservatives had cooled in the 1950s. Britain had returned to her 'open sea' policy of a world role, which most of her people firmly supported. So, when Britain was invited to send a delegation to the Messina Conference in 1955 to examine the possibility of European integration, she disdainfully refused. A British official who helped to prepare the draft of the Spaak Report considering the political implications of a customs union was withdrawn when the Government realized the direction Europe might take. The enormous political and strategic implications of any move towards Europe, for a country with such a great maritime tradition, must be emphasized.

Britain has been a great trading nation in modern times. She had a great ship-building industry and a huge merchant navy. Her overseas investments were also considerable, penetrating the social and industrial infra-structure of the embryonic nation states of the multi-racial Commonwealth. Moreover, military bases and coaling stations, acquired for imperial strategic reasons, became closely involved in the politics of their areas.

Bases were essential in the conduct of the wider strategy on which the Empire depended. The Middle East, for example, was more important to Britain as a half-way stage on the road to India, than as a supplier of an important raw commodity such as oil. In the Persian Gulf the British were gradually ensnared in a web of commitments, constituting a patchwork of protectorates. Early in the nineteenth century gunboat diplomacy was established as protection was offered to Kuwait, Bahrein, Qatar, the seven Trucial states, Muscat and Oman, the East Aden Protectorate and the sixteen protectorates with Aden Colony. Protection, given to thwart piracy and tribal feuding which might have disrupted the trade routes, could always be backed up because the arrival of a British gunboat meant that the might of the Royal Navy was just over the horizon.

The Indian Ocean was a British lake. For more than a hundred years its perimeter was British (or British-dominated) territory. From South Africa, Tanganyika, Kenya, Somaliland, Aden and the Protectorates, to India, Ceylon, Burma, Malaya, Singapore, and Australia, the might of Great Britain reigned supreme. The Royal Navy patrolled the sea with ease and confidence. The greatest naval force in world history was unchallengeable, and as yet undefeated. The Empire seemed secure. Yet the fear of attack from other nations with imperial ambitions was very real, so Britain carefully controlled the key points. A few critically placed troops held the strategic focal points at the Cape of Good Hope, the Suez Canal, the Persian Gulf, the Malacca Straits, and Cape Leeuwin at the south-east end of the Indian Ocean. When needed, garrison troops from India were ready and eager for service anywhere.

The English had ceased to run a country with limited dynastic ambitions. A maritime tradition had produced strategy based on naval power defending imperial and commercial interests. The continental strategy, with the basis of helping allies defeat the sovereign's enemies in Europe, was an addition to Britain's real interest of controlling imperial lines of communication.

A balance of power in Europe and a dominant naval role outside it were the essence of Britain's national survival. In the two world wars the strategies were combined – although during the First World War the Dardanelles Expedition, insufficiently supported by a divided War Council, failed to relieve troops bogged down in the mud of France. The two schools of thought – maritime and continental strategies – were merely alternative methods of beating the monarch's enemies, whose land armies had to be defeated in battles where sea power could play only an indirect part.

Although it is possible to speak of maritime and continental strategies as theoretical alternatives, capable at times of being combined, there were many in the War Office and Admiralty who took a different view. Sailors wanted a sweeping maritime strategy. Soldiers wanted a full-blooded continental strategy. Both groups of protagonists thought that an all-or-nothing approach would avoid the danger of failing to support one or the other adequately. But the fact remains that in every war with European enemies British leaders thought it best to regard maritime and continental strategies as complementary options which must be effectively combined. As naval historian Professor Ranft has observed: 'In the one war where we depended on sea power alone we lost the American colonies.'

The existence of these two opposed ideas of strategy, however, confused and embittered discussion of how Britain could best achieve national objectives. Inter-service rivalry, together with political squabbles between ministers of the different departments, grew bitter in time of war, disfigured rational thinking about strategy, and disturbed the peace after the Second World War. The position was radically altered by Britain's commitment to NATO in 1949. Defence policy became alliance policy. The old idea of relying on a traditional maritime strategy gave way to 'interdependence'; which was officially recognized as an adequate description of alliance integration in 1957.

The debate between 'maritime' and 'continental' strategists became the problem of whether the security of Western Europe could be guaranteed by the 'Atlanticists' or the 'Europeanists' – by working with the Americans in a world role, or by throwing everything into Europe. The essential question was how to achieve the best national contribution to a multi-national and integrated alliance. Britain was committed to NATO Europe, but still had obligations outside it. She was required to keep a large army in Germany, but her leaders still judged the need to keep forces East of Suez on an even larger scale to be vital in the national interest.

A World on the Never-Never

In the first decade of the post-war world Britain was stretched far beyond her economic and military resources. Her overseas commitments and the defence requirements of Europe were further complicated by the development of an independent nuclear force. Competition for scarce resources worsened inter-service rivalry. Defence planners cast around for easy solutions. The illusion that a solution had been found soon emerged.

It was mistakenly thought that if Britain concentrated her efforts in two fields, she could maintain her influence on events with fewer men. The components were to be the Strategic Reserve (a mobile fire brigade operating anywhere from Malta to the Malacca Straits at a moment's notice – first referred to in the Defence White Paper of 1954 and established by 1957) and the small force of nuclear weapons. The nuclear force, decided upon by a small Cabinet Committee under Attlee, and later agreed to by his full Cabinet without a murmur, was at the height of its effectiveness by the mid-fifties. The 20,000 men of the Strategic Reserve were complemented on the naval side by a naval task group – again perhaps thought an adequate substitute for the maintenance of large numbers of men abroad.

Yet the true position soon became clear, and the Sandys decision to end conscription by 1960 only aggravated the situation. The air-lifted Strategic Reserve and the commando ships did not displace the need for large permanent bases overseas, because neither force could otherwise be deployed in sufficient strength. Further, European defence needed the same general types of forces as were deployed overseas. And, of course, the strategic nuclear capability was almost entirely irrelevant to the solution of internal security problems, perhaps the major threat to peace in the 1960s and 1970s.

Defence problems arising out of over-stretch, and the increasing burden of costly military equipment persisted to the period when Healey became Secretary of State for Defence in October 1964. The 1964 deficit on Britain's balance of payments – more than £750 million – was the largest in Britain's peacetime history. Three-eighths of it could be accounted for by defence expenditure.

The slow growth of British exports, combined with the sharp rise in the import of manufactured goods, was made worse by the large outflow of private capital. Only drastic measures seemed capable of solving the balance of payments problem. Piecemeal deflationary measures at home and an import surcharge were unpopular, and did nothing to tackle the fundamental problems. By such means the Government hoped to buy time; but time ran out. The British economic malaise had its roots in its sluggish industrial production growth rate. With prices rising relatively fast in comparison with the products of her competitors Britain's grip on world markets was steadily weakened, and her share of markets for export manufactures steadily fell. In 1950 Britain had accounted for a quarter of the total; by 1962 for less than a sixth.

Gross overseas defence expenditure in 1964 was running at more than £250 million, and the Wilson Cabinet were determined to reduce it drastically. Defence costs had risen for two basic reasons: escalating equipment costs, which turned defence production into a field of declining productivity, and the mounting cost of stationing troops overseas – which, in a protracted struggle like Vietnam, would have resulted in an unacceptable defence bill.

International Brotherhood

Denis Healey, as Labour's Defence Minister, had to examine the need to reduce commitments, manpower, and equipment. A cut in commitments could mean a denial of one of the fundamental beliefs of the Labour Party: in the universal brotherhood of man. The reduction of commitments to keep the peace and safeguard Commonwealth brothers and sisters went against the grain. This was not an imperial link (as Attlee had demonstrated when he began the process of disengagement with the granting of independence to India in 1947) but the politicians understood that Britain had played an important and constructive part in establishing and preserving conditions in which the emergent Commonwealth countries could achieve genuine independence.

Healey in particular regarded Britain's handling of the Malaysian Confrontation operation as a model for counter-insurgency which the Americans could have profitably emulated in Vietnam, although he thought that the Vietcong were a tougher proposition, with more popular support than the Indonesians. The Labour Party in general believed that 'peace-keeping' in Africa and the Middle and Far East was an important contribution to international security.

The new Commonwealth also allowed the Labour Party room for its idealism. It was different from its pre-war predecessor, mainly a small group of English-speaking peoples with a common cultural heritage. This cosy family club of former 'white' colonies had, after their peaceful acquisition of independence, eagerly elected to keep their membership of an association which gave them the expectation of mutual co-operation in trade, finance, and defence. When independence was granted to India, Pakistan, Ceylon and, later, African and Caribbean territories, new nations with different tongues, races, religions, and cultures transformed the Commonwealth into a heterogeneous body bound loosely together by ill-defined ideals.

The Labour Party had always shown sympathy for the emancipated masses, and for those yet to achieve emancipation. It was proud of the fact that in its period of office of 1945–1951 the number of people over whom Britain exercised direct sovereignty declined from 457,000,000 to 70,000,000. It believed it had conscientiously applied its principles: belief in the equality of man in one international brotherhood, and racial equality. This was further backed by a commitment to economic development which would determine a standard of living with improved medical and educational opportunities, resulting, in the long run, in viable new nations. Perhaps, also, for many in the Party, commitment to the coloured 'Third World' members of the Commonwealth purged them of the taint of Cold War alignments represented in Britain's membership of NATO, CENTO, and SEATO. The howl of anger which burst out in India, Pakistan, and Ceylon when Britain and France invaded Egypt in 1956 was echoed in the anguish and almost manic ferocity with which Healey and Gaitskell expressed themselves.

Labour leaders had believed that the meeting of uncommitted nations at Bandung in 1955 might help to encourage a thaw in East–West relations. Britain's links with its former colonies could help to bring peaceful initiatives, and restrain the recklessness of American policy. What threats there were in the new countries came from the nationalist revolt against European domination, and the Labour Party thought it understood this reaction to white control, and felt confident that it was trusted by the new Commonwealth countries to behave in an enlightened and progressive manner.

There was also the question of China, quickly recognized by Attlee's Government in 1949, and venerated by back-benchers and the constituency party members in a way the Soviet Union had been before the 1940s. The idealism was transferred to a country where the masses no longer starved, and the admirable discipline and dedication of the Chinese Communist leaders and peasantry had shown in their long and bitter struggle. Britain and America disagreed. America refused to recognize the Communist Government of China.

For Conservative and Labour politicians alike it was obviously necessary that Britain should remain one of the great powers, determining the outcome of international problems and disputes. Labour's left wing supported Churchill's love of summit diplomacy, believing it gave Britain a chance to disagree or even oppose America on great moral and political issues. Attlee's hurried visit to the United States to dissuade President Truman from using the atomic bomb in Korea was seen by Labour's left wing to be solid justification of Britain's right to sit at the top table. Churchill's similar advice to the Americans not to back the French in the crucial battle of Dien Bien Phu in 1954 again justified the wisdom of having a voice in the key arenas of the day.

With the Cold War at its height, and the issue of German rearmament, the European Defence Community and the growth of NATO, as well as the great arms race, well under way, the Attlee Government was defeated at the polls in 1951. It was thirteen years before another Labour Prime Minister was in Ten Downing Street. That man, Harold Wilson, believed in Britain's world role, and personally admired the statesmanlike activities of Clement Attlee and Winston Churchill. Wilson also personally believed in a maritime strategy, and thought Asia to be strategically as important to British interests as the European commitment to NATO. The policy of the Wilson Cabinet was that of a world power, with a world-wide mission and close links with the United States. America was supported over Vietnam while Wilson tried to emulate the Conservatives' 1954 efforts in bringing about a peaceful solution at Geneva.

Revolution in Defence

Under Denis Healey, however, dramatic defence decisions were in the making which were completely to reverse the Labour Government's attachment to the world role, the Commonwealth, and even its attitude to membership of the Common Market. NATO Europe became top priority, and the belief grew that the unique nature of the Anglo-American alliance was a declining asset to London compared with the need to agree with Bonn how best to keep America committed to the defence of Europe.

These changes were momentous. Attlee had given India her independence in 1947, and brought to an end an era in British colonial history. In 1968 the Wilson Cabinet decided to pull out of the Persian Gulf and South East Asia, and to concentrate on Europe. It was a watershed in British history. Britain had announced that she would no longer try to act as a world power in the way her statesmen had done for five centuries. A new era was about to begin.

This fundamental change and, in particular, the part played by the Rt. Hon. Denis Healey, M.P., P.C., Secretary of State for Defence, in bringing it about, needs to be explained.

Britain's present defence policy, its credibility and relevance to today's problems, have all been determined under Denis Healey in his six years at the Ministry of Defence. The record of the Labour Party in the period before it came to power in 1964 must be understood in order to grasp how its new foreign and defence policies emerged. Several men played their part in that struggle. Of these, Denis Healey was one of the most important.

He was a young man when Britain failed to check Hitler in Europe with the policy of appeasement, and the League of Nations showed its impotence in dealing with the international crimes of Japan and Italy. The great British Empire was still apparently a great force. Britain symbolized a diplomatic tradition of reasonableness, of pragmatic compromise, avoiding overtly reckless acts, with belief in a balance of power and acceptance of the need for orderly change. But in the 1930s British power was already declining. The passing of the Great Power was at hand. The struggle with the dictators was about to begin.

The generation that survived Hitler's War is now in power, moulded and transformed by its experiences. But the changed political and strategic situation that now confronts those whose responsibility it is to govern the nation lies deep in history. Recent decisions have only emphasized, and perhaps accelerated, an inevitable process.

Chapter Two

Communist and Patriot

'I became a Marxist while I was at Oxford – but I never believed in it.'
DENIS HEALEY
'Denis was always full of mischief and tricks.'
ARTHUR SPENCER, a schoolboy friend

Chapter Two

O NCE upon a time, says the Fleet Street fable, a young
man joined the Communist Party at university, and decided to bring his country to its knees by undermining its
armed forces.

The young man entered politics, and became Minister of
Defence. Then, as chief of the country's armed forces he used
a devious policy to weaken the nation's fighting ability. He said
one thing, and did another. He spoke of 'efficiency', and made
drastic cuts. He stressed the need for 'economy', and made more.
He talked of 'interdependence' and 'rationalization' and further
reduced the number of men under his command, and their
equipment.

Armed with the jargon of 'feasibility studies' and 'cost-benefit
analysis' he chopped and pared to the bone. He cancelled aircraft and a submarine with nuclear missiles as soon as he came
into office. He ordered replacements from America, but regret-
tably cancelled again. He spoke of the need for more men in
the British Army of the Rhine while he withdrew them to reduce overseas spending. He told sailors that the aircraft carrier
was the corner-stone on which the modern navy was founded,
but then refused to build another. In a bid to overcome the cancellations at home he set about joint procurement of aircraft
with European neighbours. One by one the schemes collapsed.
Forces' morale fell to an all-time low. More successfully than
any spy he had reduced the country's ability to wage war to a
point where it was defenceless.

This elaborate tale was devised by a right-wing journalist
critic of Healey and the Labour Government. The chronicle of
the university Communist who reduced the armed forces when
he became Minister of Defence is, perhaps, the story of Denis
Healey's career. The sorry tale is told by his enemies with glee.

This neat piece of character assassination gets its pungency, however, by selecting its facts very carefully. A full examination of the evidence produces a different story.

The Commies

Healey joined the Communist Party while at Balliol College, Oxford, soon after the beginning of the Spanish Civil War. His first term, at the end of 1936, coincided with the successful but desperate battle to save Madrid. The aid given to the city by the U.S.S.R. convinced him that only the Communists were serious about wanting to stop the Fascists; so he joined the Party.

'I became a Marxist while I was at Oxford,' said Healey. 'I read all the basic books, but I never believed in it. It was more of a reaction to Nazism.'

The war broke out while he was cycling round Germany in the holiday between school and Oxford.

'It was obvious there was going to be a European war, but nobody was doing anything about it,' he said.

His German holiday had shown him at first hand what was happening under Hitler:

'The really big issue was the rise of Hitler and the coming war. Any young man who was interested in stopping the war became a Communist at Oxford, whether he joined the Party or not.'

Many of his Oxford friends who are now pillars of the Establishment were also members of the C.P. at Oxford. One close comrade, now an important Foreign Office official, remembered how he was fined for putting a banner across Oxford's High Street, emblazoned with the words 'Save Spain, Save Peace'.

'Pug' Healey, as he was affectionately nicknamed by his friends, did not fight in Spain though, because his feet were firmly on the ground and he was uninterested by ineffectual romantic gestures. The Communist Party students, having made no real impact in the universities until the slump, had been told at the 1935 Seventh World Conference of Comintern to get haircuts, shave, and look like bank clerks. They then infiltrated the Labour Clubs and ran them. The University Labour Federation was dominated by Communists. As Healey recently observed, many of his colleagues have not been so open about their pasts.

He became chairman of the Oxford Labour Club, then with a record membership, when he was chosen by the C.P. to keep out another man who was considered politically unreliable. That man is now a settled international Communist bureaucrat working in Britain as a representative of a Communist Front organization – Tom McWhinnie, of the World Federation of Trade Unions.

Healey was an intellectual Communist, with no deep attachment to the cause. As Lord Fulton, then his tutor in political philosophy, drily remarked: 'He never had a nervous breakdown over any cause at home.'

The clash between middle class background and the espousal of a working class ethic didn't bother him because he never became enamoured of the working class either. But he was attached to the cause of anti-Fascism. He can remember in minute detail the weeks leading up to Munich. And proudly talks of the large overflow at the Oxford meeting when Attlee addressed the Labour Club during the crisis.

Healey parted company with the Communists in 1940.

By that time international communism had adopted a seemingly indifferent stance to the Fascists with the Nazi-Soviet Pact of August 1939. Also, as he explained:

'I didn't like the Finnish war, and I was opposed to their line on the fall of France.'

He ignored C.P. advice, and enlisted as a private to fight for his country against the menace of Hitler's Germany.

The Artist

Politics was a small part of his life at Oxford, however. Julian Amery, a Tory Minister in Heath's first Government, remembered:

'He was more interested in painting than politics. My recollection of him was more in the literary field – I thought his interests were marginally political. I think of him as a gentle, shy creature who enjoyed talking about pictures, poetry, and that sort of thing – an artistic dilettante.'

Healey has said that inside the Labour Club he was regarded 'as the culture boss rather than a politician'. His home life and school had fostered a wide range of artistic interests.

'It was rather a bore to me when I got to Oxford and found

that nobody was interested in the arts. There wasn't even an Oxford Arts Society until I formed one in 1938.'

It was exciting in Oxford, and especially at Balliol where Doctor, later Lord Lindsay was Master. He was the first liberal socialist Master of an Oxford college, and set the tone, making it the most left-wing college in the University.

'Balliol went through an extraordinary transformation during this period,' recalled Lord Fulton. 'It had been dominated by Etonians before, but Lindsay brought the grammar schools into one of the strongholds of privilege. He was carrying out a social revolution; he set the pace for modern Greats (Philosophy, Politics, and Economics) – and he was hated in Oxford for doing so.'

At Balliol, during 1924–50, Lord Lindsay helped to educate more than 600 men and women who later became university professors around the world.

Healey remembered Lindsay's impact: 'He had a big influence on me of a profound but indirect nature. He was my tutor in Greats – in philosophy – and he got me to read people like Kierkegaard and Chestov, the Russian mystical writer; then, later, Nietzsche and twentieth-century theologians like Berdgebeo and Niebuhr. They influenced my political thought.'

Lindsay's outlook communicated itself to his students, especially those with whom he took trouble. Lord Morris, Vice-Chancellor of Bradford University, and formerly one of Healey's tutors, said: 'He was probably the biggest influence on Denis – he was always nice, friendly, and easy to get on with. Lindsay liked him, believed in him, took trouble with him, and got him to read things. You had to be intellectual because you didn't get on well at his weekly meetings if you were not good enough. Healey was lucky to have Lindsay keeping him alive.'

Lindsay dissipated his energies but his ability to think fast and his dynamism influenced dons and students. One idea, for example, was for all freshmen to write a weekly essay on a general subject, with a prize – the Powell Essay Prize – to be awarded to the best student at the end of the year. Healey won it.

Lindsay figured in the biggest political event of Healey's time at Oxford: the by-election of 1938. Patrick Gordon-Walker, the official Labour candidate, reluctantly stood down to allow

3

Lindsay to stand against Quintin Hogg. Lindsay was supported by Communists, Liberals, and anti-appeasement Conservatives in a united popular front who were determined to show what they felt about the recent Munich settlement between Chamberlain and Hitler.

There was a widespread feeling that Britain had abrogated her responsibility in the world and those on the Left had a deep sense of guilt and shame about the Munich settlement. The by-election was a chance to overcome the frustration and inaction of pacifism, and grammar school boys like Healey and Edward Heath united in their support for Lindsay.

'Denis and Ted both worked hard for Lindsay in the election,' said Lord Fulton, who was the Master's agent for a short period.

Healey maintained the friendship with Lindsay until his death. According to a friend, Healey was regarded as one of the family, almost replacing Lindsay's son, who had died tragically.

Although his relationship with the Master of Balliol was probably the most important in his time at Oxford, Healey had a wide range of pursuits. He was remembered by Lord Fulton as 'a very able man of great intellectual power with a cutting edge that came out in tutorials and in his general impact on the college.' Besides being efficient and well-organized he remained to the Rhodes Scholar, Phil Kaiser, 'a very bright, gay young man – a lively guy, warm, with a twinkle in his eye. In some ways he has changed the least of all the people I knew at that time.'

Healey followed Kaiser and Heath in being selected by his fellow students as President of the Junior Common Room. Yet, despite his political, artistic, and social activities he left with the highest academic distinction possible – a Double First in Mods and Greats. He had shown that he was a born leader. As his father, William Healey, said: 'He wouldn't go in for anything he couldn't be boss of – he always wanted to lead.'

Healey at Home

In the examination of every important and interesting man there is a place for the origins and early ideas and attitudes that helped build him into a formidable force. In Healey's case it is possible to trace his development as a politician and expert on foreign affairs even from his infancy. Moulded by his home and school environment it was natural that he should lead; just as it was natural that he would have a keen and enquiring interest in the arts.

He was born to William and Winifred Healey on 30 August 1917, in Mottingham Nursing Home at Eltham in Kent.

'I wanted a girl,' said Mrs Healey, 'I had chosen her name, so when he turned out to be a boy I told my husband to choose the name.' Mr Healey called his first child Denis Winston Healey; the second name was a sentimental choice by Will Healey, because Winston Churchill was his hero – despite the failure of the Dardanelles expedition.

Will Healey married on the day the First World War broke out. A political romantic, he identified himself with the Irish struggle for freedom: his father had been a Sinn Feiner before he came to England. From teaching at technical college he moved to Woolwich Arsenal during the war, before going on to the Regent Street Polytechnic and then, in 1923, becoming Principal of Keighley Technical College in Yorkshire – the county where he had been brought up.

'Pa' Healey (as he was known to Denis and their second child, Terry, born three years later) was regarded very much as a radical when he went to Keighley in his thirties. Regarded as a breath of fresh air, he also acquired a reputation as a good administrator, orderly and tidy. His approach was typified by his action on arriving at the college.

'The first thing I did,' said Mr Healey, 'was look in the cupboard in the Principal's office where I discovered the records going back to 1863. I had them all burnt and started afresh.'

He was a firm disciplinarian, with a fund of comic stories and a domineering personality; but he encouraged tolerance.

'I argued a lot with my parents – about everything,' said Denis Healey. His mother said: 'We had healthy argument all day in our house – we all seemed to think differently. Denis was good at argument from the start. The others couldn't answer him.'

The sons were isolated from their father, however, by his job. Most of his time was given to work in the college and the community. There was always a closer relationship between mother and sons; only his mother, for example, knew that Denis had joined the Communist Party. 'Pa' would have objected rather violently, so he was not told.

Pa Healey, although trained as an engineer, and Principal of a technical college, was attracted to the arts. He met his wife on a tennis court, bought her a basket of over-ripe strawberries which they greedily consumed before he serenaded her with 'The Road to Mandalay'. 'It was a different world then,' he said. As a young man he also wrote poetry – a taste for which he passed on to his children – and was part-time drama critic for a South London newspaper.

'Ma Healey', a close friend said, 'was active and intelligent, really interested only in intellectual achievements, and extremely ambitious for her family.' She was the dominant force in her son's life. When she first met her husband she was a teacher of English and gymnastics from Gloucestershire, with a Liberal political bias. Her tremendous drive, inherited by her eldest son, took her continuously to WEA classes in modern English literature or politics and she became a Labour supporter in the thirties. She set a high standard for her sons.

'My mother was terribly keen that I got on with my work and went to Oxford,' said Healey. 'She would have liked me to become a don.'

She has admitted that she was 'rather thrilled by the possibility of him becoming a don,' adding, 'I never thought of him going into politics, although I was not disappointed.'

It was largely because of his mother that the young Healey developed his enthusiasm for the arts: 'She was a great influence when I was a boy in encouraging my interest in painting. She stimulated my interest in modern poetry, drama, and music.'

'The London companies,' explained Mrs Healey, 'tried out drama and opera in Leeds, and if there was anything I was keen on seeing I would take Denis and Terry. If it was an opera I thought they could follow, or a play, we would go in the cheap seats. Sometimes we would go to Bradford or Leeds every night of the week for different productions.'

Healey remembers that apart from having a week at Filey when he was eight the family never went away together for a holiday.

'But every now and again we used to have an orgy – which was a long weekend in London, when we went every afternoon and evening to the theatre. I remember one weekend where we went to an opera, a ballet, a play, and two films.'

Unlike his younger brother, who was boisterous and gregarious, Denis had more of his mother's self-discipline and control. The two boys were encouraged to go their own ways.

'We encouraged them to do things independently,' said Mrs Healey. 'Denis knew exactly where he was going. When you asked him what he wanted for a present he always said "books". Three walls of his bedroom were lined with them.'

'Almost the most impressive incident of my early life – it's extraordinary even now when I think of it,' said Healey, 'was on 3 September 1939. Mother came clattering up the stairs, burst into my room where I was reading Kant and said "Denis, you can put away your books – war has been declared." The first part of the sentence was more surprising to me than the second.'

His parents paid fees for five-year-old Denis to go to the Drake and Tonson primary school, a prep school for Keighley Boys and Girls Grammar Schools. When he was eight, in the junior department of the grammar school, he first met Arthur Spencer – later head boy of Bradford Grammar.

'We were the villain and archvillain of Thornhill (the prep school),' Arthur remembered. 'We used to get up to simple pranks like pinching apples. Denis was always full of mischief and tricks, and generally speaking we were two ringleaders.'

Healey's reputation as a practical joker, which he still has, was well deserved. At home he would climb into the wardrobe in Terry's room, close the door behind him, and then burst out after his brother had put the light out and got into bed.

His father recalled a more elaborate prank.

'We were playing bridge with the local bank manager in Keighley when a man with a foreign accent came to the door. He said he was starting a business in Keighley and needed money. It was Denis, who had dressed for the part, playing a joke. The bank manager, who was very stuffy, was livid when he found out – not the least bit amused.'

Unlike his brother, Healey had no love of fighting.

'Terry fought every day, and always used to come home with a lost cap or torn mac, or something wrong,' said Mrs Healey.

Denis never became Terry's protector, although he was three years older. When he was eleven Terry went to Pangbourne, where he trained for the merchant navy. He later became master of a bulk carrier.

The Young Learner

At Bradford Grammar School, Healey, with his West Riding County Minor Scholarship, found himself in a forcing house for bright boys. With a tradition dating from its fourteenth-century endowment, and a reputation for sending at least a dozen boys a year to Oxbridge, it has encouraged many boys who later made their marks. Composer Frederick Delius, Sir Mortimer Wheeler the archaeologist, historian Alan Bullock, and David Hockney the artist, are just a few of them. A former master said: 'We used to think of Bradford Grammar as the Yorkshire equivalent of Manchester Grammar – only better. Very few of the masters married, and they married late; they didn't have the time to do so earlier.'

Healey stood out in a very competitive field. 'I remember Healey as a leader even when he was twelve,' said former school-friend John Farrar.

In 1930 Healey carried off first prize in the Under-14 section of the National Book Council Essay Competition. The following year he won the Senior Section. He was prominent in literary, debating, and dramatic activities. Commenting on his July 1936 performance as the woodcutter in Molière's *Le Médecin Malgré Lui,* the school drama critic wrote: 'Healey acted with a natural artlessness and a familiar ease which made the play his.'

Another commentator, writing of his performance in the literary society debate in March 1936, noted his ability to detach himself from lesser mortals:

'Healey sadly remarked that his definition of morality was incomprehensible to others, and hence discussion was futile; he contented himself with a counter-attack against Brooman's attack on Tolstoy. Spencer and the Hon. Sec. nodded significantly and said nothing. A puzzled frown remained on every brow when the House finally broke up.'

On other occasions he enthused about his favourites of the moment: Chesterton, Masefield, Eliot, Auden, Spender, Day Lewis. His mother noted that from the age of six or seven he was a compulsive reader of 'good' books.

'I'd read most of the classics by the time I'd reached the sixth form, but none of the "modern" English novelists. But then we had a master who was keen on the authors favoured by Leavisite intellectuals – Forster, D. H. Lawrence, and Virginia Woolf, with Aldous Huxley thrown in for fun. These were the writers who enlarged my sense of things around me – flowers, scents, colours, objects, scenery, and, of course, people.'

The precise mixture of intellect and feeling of such a work as Woolf's *To the Lighthouse* he found especially appealing. So is Yeats to him now.

He developed other artistic interests at school. One Easter he practised Bach so much on the piano that he nearly drove Pa mad, until he agreed to practise only when Pa was out. Before exams he would break off for an hour's playing as an aid to concentration. He was particularly concerned about the formal exams – 'My life was dominated by them to a great extent, and for years after I left Oxford I used to have examination dreams. I loathed sitting them.' He could handle them, however, as his Keeling Classics Prize and his Domus Exhibition for Classics award at Balliol later indicated.

He was lucky enough to be taught by gifted teachers. Masters such as Hall, Glassey, Lewis, Bottom, Arthur Farrell, and 'Gus' Shepherd each contributed something important. The classicists – a particularly strong suit of the school – developed important relationships with the young Healey, and profoundly influenced his development.

Glassey, himself described by a former student as being 'especially good on nuts and bolts and on opening one's eyes to things' remembered Healey as 'one of those types who always make their presence felt without trying obviously to impress. He was the clever boy whose cleverness made no enemies, but earned him admirers.'

Although he taught him only until the sixth form he thought that: 'I possibly influenced him in the Literary Society by reluctantly allowing him to influence me. As a man of mature years who had read all the English and French poetry of acknowledged greatness I was not prepared to admit that modern poetry of the incomprehensible, cacophonous, unscannable type was worth the trouble. Denis taught me otherwise, and in the course of the relentless argument Denis may have learned something *with* me, though not *from* me.'

Healey was no 'yes-man', as his relations with other masters showed. Arthur Farrell, a classics master of excellent scholar-ship with an acute mind, often used to argue with Healey.

'Denis was rather dogmatic in debate,' explained a school-friend. 'He used to have rows with Farrell, who got icy and would say "The fact is, Healey, that I have a First in Philo-sophy, but you have not yet."'

Healey won the Debating Society Cup.

Then Healey, who became head of his house in 1935, re-signed from the Officers Training Corps. By being in the O.T.C. he had escaped games one afternoon a week. Although he liked camping, walked on the moors with his mother and Terry, cycled, swam, and played tennis and golf, he hated team games. He also hated wearing First World War puttees for the O.T.C. He was, according to his mother, 'one of the worst-dressed cadets you ever saw.' So, when he was sixteen, he resigned.

'I had become a pacifist. It started in the early thirties when the whole anti-war movement was gaining strength, and I be-came disillusioned when the invasion of Abyssinia in 1935–6 showed how useless it was. When I resigned I simply thought that killing people was wrong – and I was also bored stiff with the O.T.C.'

'I think Denis became politically conscious when he was about fourteen or fifteen,' said Arthur Spencer.

'There was the Japanese invasion of Manchuria in 1931–2, the futility of the League, Hoare–Laval, the Italian invasion of Abyssinia, and Hitler coming up on the outside.'

In July 1935 Healey won the school's Political Science Prize.

When he entered the classical sixth he encountered Leslie Shepherd, the history teacher who, with Lindsay at Oxford, was most responsible for moulding his political outlook. Shepherd, known to his pupils as 'Giggling Gus' because of his apologetic laughter and nervous giggling, was a young man not long down from Cambridge who says he 'nourished the kids on Leavis and the Marxist view of history'. He joined the Communist Party in 1942–3, when it became socially acceptable to do so, but says 'I have always been interested in revolution.'

'Denis adored him, and he had a terrific influence over the boy,' said his mother. Arthur Spencer agreed that 'Gus' was a formative influence on everybody, mainly because he would argue and 'let chaps talk'.

Shepherd devoted himself to mastering his job and coaching a hundred boys in the sixth form for their three-hour essay and General Paper for Oxbridge.

'I had to work like hell just to keep up. I did things like Leavis's *Mass Civilisation and Minority Culture* and his pamphlet, *Standards in Literature*, with Denis, who was brilliant throughout. The only essay I ever remember by anybody was one by him on courage.

'I never pulled my punches with the kids, and when I thought something I shared it. Marxism was an approach rather than a solution.

'It was obvious that Denis was extremely able, and I would not have been surprised if he had become a don or a literary critic. It never occurred to me that he would become a politician, because it was not a thing our kids did.'

But Healey was becoming extremely interested in politics in the late 1930s. He formally joined Keighley Labour Party in 1937, after he had started his studies at Oxford. He also began to speak in public – and to demonstrate. He spoke at an open air meeting in Keighley, which his parents didn't attend.

'Mrs Kirk, the headmistress of the girls' grammar school went, and told me she would have been proud had it been her son,' said Mrs Healey. 'It was the first public meeting he ever addressed.'

He did not demonstrate alone. He often had the support of his girlfriend, Pat Walker, a dark-haired, plump-faced daughter of a Keighley doctor. They were photographed together leading a demonstration in Trafalgar Square. In February 1939 Healey led the procession at the Youth Pilgrimage in London. At Oxford he had a number of girlfriends, as a fellow student remembered:

'He and Jack Dawes, who later became an investment consultant, used to hunt together for women in left-wing circles. There was much better talent there – better than the "county" women.'

One friend was Stella Zilliacus, daughter of Communist M.P., Konni Zilliacus. Another piece of 'talent' who was a member of the Communist Party at Oxford was Edna Edmunds, later to become Healey's wife and mother of his three children – Jennifer, Timothy, and Cressida.

Edna went up to St Hugh's College, Oxford, to read English. She came from a modest home, where her mother brought up five children after Edna's father, a crane driver, died when she was fourteen. The influence of the Baptist church and the mining community of Coleford in Gloucestershire formed the ethical basis of her socialism. Her first attempts to produce a play, to teach, and to speak in public were all made at the village church.

She was the first girl from her school to go to university, and she made the most of it. It was the first time she had had a room to herself, a proper bath instead of a tin bath in front of the fire, and a library.

'I never had the chance to work in a library before, and I used to sit in the Bodleian, sending down for books with sheer joy – some of them I didn't even read.'

She also joined all the political parties before finally opting for the Labour Club because of its attitude to the Spanish Civil War.

'That war was my political birth. I think I joined the Communist Party because most of my friends were in it. I came in on Spain, and went out on Finland.'

Although Secretary of the Labour Club, Edna did not get to know Healey properly until after she left university.

'My first teaching post was in Keighley, where I met up with him again, and we started going out together.'

At the grammar school she joined two young teachers from Aberystwyth, Beryl and Peggy Jones. Beryl had joined the Keighley Left Book Club, which Healey had started while he was a student at Oxford. 'He had a whole bookcase full of Left books – he was terribly keen on Gollancz,' recalled his mother. Later, when *Who's Who* asked him for his club, he told them 'Left Book Club'. The Saturday night meetings of the club, often held at the Jones's, gave Denis and Edna a place to meet and talk.

Healey had known Beryl for about two years before Edna went to Keighley, although she remembered him as a nine-year-old prince in a Christmas play at the Drake and Tonson school.

'He ran his whole kingdom with great confidence and charm, giving a wonderful performance. I then first tipped him as a

future Prime Minister. In the late thirties he began coming to
Labour Party meetings, taking a rather left-of-party line, much
the same as my own – I was then an undercover member of the
Communist Party.'

She was also a member of the Fabian Society and the Peace
Pledge Union. Healey found her especially stimulating because
her knowledge of English literature outrivalled his own. (She
later gave evidence in favour of *Lady Chatterley's Lover* at the
book's famous 'trial' in 1960.)

Army Days

In 1940 Healey joined the Army. 'He was so patriotic,' said
his mother. 'We agreed that he and Terry were right to volunteer straight away.'

By joining up, Healey dropped the idea of going to America
to study. 'I would have gone for a Commonwealth Scholarship
and spent a year there,' he said. 'A lot of people used to do this
after taking their degree, and I think I could easily have got
one.' Instead he became a private.

'It was murder to begin with. I was very opposed to discipline, and totally opposed to drill and having to do things in an
orderly way. But one of the great benefits I got from army service was to learn that there are advantages in doing some things
fairly automatically, so you free your mind to do the important
things rationally.'

He did his inaugural 'square-bashing' with the Field Training Regiment at Harrogate. But he didn't enjoy early training.
His encounter with gritty Yorkshire stoicism provided him with
a favourite story:

'We went out on a hike, and I noticed in the middle of it
that one of the men was limping very badly because his boots
were two sizes too small. So I said to him "Jim, when I get back
to barracks I am going to take you down to the Quartermaster's
stores, and get you a proper pair of boots."

'"Don't do that," he said. "From the barracks there is not a
pub within five miles, and there is not a girl within ten miles,
and taking off these bloody boots is the only bit of pleasure I
get." '

His basic training was cut short after a few weeks, when he
ruptured himself. He went to the military huts at Harrogate

Hospital for repairs, where he shared the ward with wounded soldiers from Dunkirk. One nurse who became quite fond of him, and looked forward to going on duty to see him, was Mrs Janet Clark.

'He was rather reserved, more academic than the ordinary soldier, nearly always reading, but a good patient – always willing to have a joke and fun. From his conversation and arguments with the other patients I gathered he was keen on politics.'

The winter of 1940–1 was spent at the Gunners' Depot in Woolwich. He grew accustomed to nightly air raids, and remembered a 5 a.m. parade held after a stick of bombs fell in the barracks.

'They found a thousand missing – but they hadn't been killed. They were chaps who normally spent the night out with girlfriends or families, and came in only during the day, or on paydays.'

Then he went to Swindon, addressing envelopes and collecting statistics at the railway station. His job 'was to meet every train and count the number of troops getting off, getting on, and getting on-and-off'. Such totals as he didn't invent on the spot he got from the ticket collectors until, after a few weeks, he discovered that they made them all up as well. Ever since then he has been sceptical about statistics, and statistical surveys.

'I just want to see a thing proved. I think the fallibility of basic data is something always to be borne in mind.'

His time at Swindon broadened his outlook in another way.

'At school he had little contact with working people,' said his mother. 'In Swindon he lived in a working-class house, in a very working-class district. It made him extremely miserable.'

Healey accepted the offer of a commission, went to Scarborough, joining a group of actors in the Artists' Rifles, before being trained for Movement Control at Derby with 'the weirdest group of people you ever met'. They included a male opera singer from Covent Garden who sloped arms on the wrong shoulder at the passing-out parade, and a group of gallant French officers whom the army hadn't yet sorted out. In July 1941 he received his commission in Movement Control, and spent several months in Hull and Sheffield as a Rail Traffic Officer.

'I learnt something from that,' he said. 'First, I can read a rail timetable faster than anyone I know. Second, if you go out to load a lot of tanks on the moor take a pencil and a piece of paper with you. They didn't teach us that sort of thing at Oxford.'

His next move was to Troon and Prestwick in Scotland after he had volunteered for 'exciting work'. Here he was trained in Combined Operations before going out to North Africa with 21 Beach Group as a Movements Landing Officer with the rank of captain.

'He had a very vital job,' said Lord Glendevon, formerly John Hope, then a senior officer and a Conservative Cabinet Minister in the 1950s. In a Brains Trust held on board ship going to North Africa he had accused Healey of being bound up with suspect 'isms'. Healey retorted, 'Well, sir, what about patriot*ism*?' There was tumultuous applause.

Lord Glendevon thought Healey was easy to get on with, pleasant, stimulating, naturally friendly, and the possessor of a tremendous sense of humour. There was a visit to a restaurant stuffed with blackmarket food in the hillside suburb of La Bouzarea in North Africa with a few friends and a number of Frenchmen in May 1943. At the end of dinner Healey, like his companions, full of cheap Algerian wine, stood on one of the tables outside to sing a song.

'He started singing a bloodthirsty revolutionary song about hanging the marquis from the lamp post, in flawless French,' recalled Glendevon. 'He was having a bit of fun, but when he got into the song he was desperately serious. He was carried away by its revolutionary fervour. We and the French all laughed like anything.'

Number 21 Beach Group moved up North Africa to Tunisia, joined Montgomery's 78 Division before landing in Sicily on the third day of the invasion, 13 July 1943. Healey then prepared to land at Salerno with General Mark Clark's mixed American and British troops. He was taken away from 21 Group at the last minute.

'I was furious when he was taken away from us,' said Glendevon. 'I knew what it was like to fight battles, and help one's men when one is whacked and tired after forty-eight hours. You can't do more than bet on who is going to be good, and I never had any doubts that he was the sort of man who would be good if we got into trouble on the beach. I would trust him anywhere, anytime.'

He joined 231 Infantry Brigade and landed to the north of Salerno on 8 September 1943, the day Italy's signing of the armistice and surrender were announced.

'It didn't make any difference to us,' said Healey. 'The Germans were retreating northwards on to the point where we were landing, and we had a very lively day on the beach.' He had been told not to bother about loading ambulances as they would probably not be needed, and craft were short. 'But I managed to get them all in, which was very lucky. It was the first opposed landing since Dieppe in August 1942.'

The German counter-attacks were held, however, and by October Naples was in Allied hands.

Healey went to Taranto, was in and out of Combined Ops, and was the Beach Landing Officer for the British First Brigade, Second Division, for the landing at Anzio in 1944, when he gained a mention in despatches.

He was proving his worth in many spheres. Brigadier Reggie Fellows, who was on General Alexander's staff looking after Movement Control Organization, later remembered Healey as 'a very able chap with a quick clear brain: he didn't get rattled.' Of Healey's section of the Anzio landing: 'This was a very sticky assignment, as the whole small area was always under shell fire.'

He was appointed to the Movement Branch of H.Q. Allied Armies in Italy as Staff Captain and later Deputy Assistant Quartermaster-General (Movements).

'He proved a most efficient staff officer, cheerful, unflappable, a strong character, but with a delightful sense of humour, and most pleasant to work with,' said Brigadier Fellows. 'He was popular with seniors and juniors alike, and got on particularly well with Americans.'

A senior officer with him in 231 Brigade, R. L. E. Lawrence, remembered Healey as very well-read and earnest. He also thought him a good professional soldier: 'He was efficient and took everything seriously: rather a contrast to the somewhat swashbuckling attitude of the old hands from the Western Desert.'

Sir Val Duncan, also sorting out the priorities of what should move where, remembered Healey as 'a good planner, with the ability to get the co-operation of various arms of the fighting services, and to handle certain elements of the civilian population.

'Denis was well-suited to that sort of job. I think the fact that he bothered to learn Italian pretty rapidly showed this, as it was something most of us didn't bother to do.'

His old schoolmaster, Glassey, pointed out that he had been 'so very good' at Latin and Greek that if the occasion had arisen he would have found no difficulty in picking up modern related languages.

Lord Jack Donaldson, who commanded the detachment Healey was posted to in Naples remembered him as 'the most intelligent man in the unit when it came to dealing with military and personal matters – or indeed most things.' In letters home to his wife he wrote: 'Denis Healey is great fun. He's got the same interests as I have, but a much better brain, is much better read, and is also ten years younger. I find conversation with him stimulating.'

He spoke of Healey's efforts to improve relations with the local populace. His rapidly improving Italian helped; although Healey mastered languages easily and used them whenever he could – as his wartime broadcasts to France for the B.B.C. showed. Healey, admitting that he 'learnt Italian quickly – it's a very easy language' – used to go off into the villages to talk to people whenever he had any spare time. Colonel Jack Donaldson hinted at one use to which Healey put his Italian when he wrote to his wife: 'B——, T——, Denis and R—— all have permanent girls who are in and out of the mess all day.' Healey later confirmed that he had had 'one Italian girlfriend who was very nice'.

To Edna Edmunds he wrote warm, informative, but not passionate letters home. His mother, explaining that in his weekly letters he never showed emotion, only writing the facts, recalled that Edna once replied to the question of whether she had heard from Denis by saying, 'Oh yes – but I could pin the letter up in my classroom!'

Healey had other outside interests to keep him busy. He arranged concerts, by local musicians, for the eight-strong Officers' Mess and also stumbled on something to further his interest in fine art. At Oxford he had been Secretary of the

Leonardo Society, and a member of the hanging committee which chose paintings for Balliol's Junior Common Room. His idol was Heinrich Wolfflin, a nineteenth century art historian who categorized art into the classic and the baroque. In Italy Healey had a chance to discover Renaissance painting and architecture for himself, and he found a number of art books in a bombed building. He brought them all home with him.

Healey, who in 1940 had the chance of taking up a Harmsworth Fellowship at Merton College, Oxford, in the philosophy of aesthetics was beginning to have doubts about it by 1945: 'During the war I discovered that I thought much better, even about such problems as aesthetics, if I was under external pressure and doing something else, rather than if I was in an academic vacuum.'

He revisited Merton in August 1945, to see his tutor about the fellowship at a time when the news of the atomic bomb was announced.

'This struck him at once as revolutionary', said Edna, who was with him. 'It was tremendously important.'

'In the evening after dinner, when he was supposed to go for this interview, it began very lightly raining. The tutor rang up and said "Since the weather is a trifle inclement, do you not think that we might perhaps postpone our discussion until tomorrow?"'

To a young soldier, just back from the front, the remote, unrealistic, ivory-towerish world of Merton seemed light years away.

Into Politics

The world that did attract him was one he had discussed endlessly with fellow officers – politics. Lord Glendevon remembered many stimulating arguments with him – heightened by Glendevon's own interest in entering Parliament.

'He [Healey] was still very left-wing in his views, even though he had lost his sympathy for Russia. I would have put him very far to the left of the Labour Party; he pretty well told me that he would still have been a Communist had there not been the Nazi-Soviet Pact betrayal. But I had not the slightest doubt that he was the man I wanted more than anybody else. He was patriotic and utterly reliable.'

R. L. E. Lawrence recalled a discussion between himself, Healey, and Winston Field – another M.L.O. and later Prime Minister of Southern Rhodesia – where they all decided to go into politics. Donaldson, a Labour Party member, found Healey's outlook similar to his own. He thought that he had moved more towards the right wing during his time in Italy. Healey told him that he intended to enter politics as soon as the war was over. He soon had a chance to do so.

Ivor Thomas, his local M.P. in Keighley, wrote a letter to him in Florence at the end of 1944, saying: 'From conversations with your parents, and knowing your views, I thought you might be interested to go on to the Labour Party panel of potential candidates.'

Pudsey and Otley, in Yorkshire, was without a candidate, and they asked him to apply for it.

To Leonard Rawson, Chairman of Pudsey Constituency Labour Party 'it was a very unusual selection conference because one of the candidates could not get to the meeting – he was still serving with H.M. Forces.'

Sam Mason, a friend of the Healeys, and an active member of Keighley Labour Party spoke on his behalf.

Mrs Ethel Green, later his secretary for the campaign, and then in her forties said: 'We wanted the fire and enthusiasm of youth. We were tired and we wanted youth to help us; we were waiting for them to come back. We saw that Denis lived in Keighley, and from his university and war record he had done well.'

Rawson added: 'We had a photograph of this very handsome young man in officer's uniform which, I think, swung some of our lady delegates, and when the votes were counted Denis Healey was chosen.'

Mrs Green wrote to tell him of his appointment.

By the time of the selection conference, Healey had been awarded the M.B.E. for services in Italy, and, in March 1945, was promoted major.

He was diffident about his awards. Of his mention in despatches he had said to his mother, 'You know, mother, it doesn't mean anything. It's all a matter of luck.' He considered that his only really worthwhile contribution had been made when he was with 231 Brigade:

4

'We landed in a tiny port immediately under a 3,000-feet mountain side where the Germans had a couple of batteries of 88mm. mortars. These things were coming over all day long. It was really frightening and tiring that night, trying to catch a few minutes sleep wedged between concrete blocks on the beach. Twice I was dive-bombed.'

He got no award or honourable mention – it was just part of the job.

'I think what happens is that they make marks against people's names, and when you've got enough marks they put you up for something.'

Sir Val Duncan agreed: 'When you are a staff officer doing a job like that you don't go and charge up a hill and capture a lot of Germans – you make a consistently meaningful contribution over a period.'

As the war ended, Healey was planning to lead a landing to help Yugoslav partisans. Developments there and elsewhere led to the plan being dropped. Healey was allowed home as a prospective candidate for the election. The date was announced on 27 May, Parliament dissolved on 15 June, and polling day was 5 July.

'I arrived on Friday night from Italy, and was told at Transport House that the Party Conference was on in Blackpool the following week, and that I ought to be there. I went without any intention of speaking, but I got more and more concerned as I chatted to people that we were going to have a very right-wing foreign policy, so I decided to try and speak in the foreign affairs debate.'

His short speech, given on 23 May, was highly successful.

'There are two most important facts which are not very clear to people who have been living in England during the last five years,' said Major Healey, speaking in uniform.

'One of them is that the socialist revolution has already begun in Europe, and is already firmly established in many countries in Eastern and Southern Europe. The crucial principle of our own foreign policy should be to protect, assist, encourage, and aid in every way that socialist revolution wherever it appears.

'The Labour Party must be extremely alert and vigilant in judging its friends and enemies in Europe,' he continued. 'It is quite easy for a person like myself who has spent the last three years in Europe to tell who are our friends and who are our enemies. The upper classes in every country are selfish, depraved, dissolute, and decadent. There is a very great danger, unless we are very careful, that we shall find ourselves running with the Red Flag in front of the armoured cars of Tory imperialism and counter-revolution.'

He spoke of the 'hard, cruel, bitter, merciless and bloody' struggle for socialism in Europe, and ended: 'If the Labour Movement in Europe finds it necessary to introduce a greater degree of police supervision, and more immediate and drastic punishment for their opponents than we in this country would be prepared to tolerate, we must be prepared to understand their point of view.'

He sat down with tumultuous applause thundering in his ears. He had caught the mood of the conference, and of the nation. The official representative of Pudsey and Otley reported back that they had a wonderful candidate.

Charles Pannell, the Member for Leeds West, remembered that the conference was attended by many enthusiastic communists, adding that – 'Denis's speech stamped him as a more-than-able man, and he was noticed by the Party Executive.'

Three people in particular were impressed by his speech: Harold Laski, Hugh Dalton, and Philip Noel-Baker. Each of them, independently, told Healey that the job of International Secretary of the Party was coming up, and advised him to apply for it. Although he little realized it, the speech had been one of the most important of his life. It had accurately reflected his views.

'In Italy I saw an old society, overripe and dying. And I saw a whole new society of technicians and workers ready to take over, but unable to do so. I was very interested in what was going on in the world at that time, and had great sympathy for partisan movements on the Continent and for some of their chaps, whom I'd met. I also thought that upper class people I'd met were dreadful.'

The Campaign for Pudsey

In his election campaign he stuck to Party policy, and spoke in favour of friendly relations with Britain's wartime ally, the Soviet Union. Foreign Affairs was his speciality, as Ethel Green remembered: 'He was great on foreign affairs, and after our first meeting Councillor Mrs Mary Johnson said, "There is a future Foreign Secretary."'

Healey later admitted:

'I knew the answer to every question. I didn't have to think twice about anything, but as far as Party politics was concerned I knew nothing – like most ex-service candidates who had been away for a long time.'

Pudsey and Otley was a large constituency about twenty miles across, in the shape of the letter 'H'. It had bits left out of constituencies in Leeds, Bradford, and Shipley. The only solid working class area was near Pudsey, which was Liberal. Farsley was strongly pro-Labour, but in most of the constituency the Labour Party organization was run down. The Conservative majority in the previous election was 21,425. It was regarded as a safe seat.

Opposing him Healey had two other soldiers: Colonel Stoddart Scott, the sitting Conservative Member, and Army heavyweight champion Brigadier Terence Clarke, the Liberal candidate, who disappeared for a week during the campaign to receive tuition in Liberal Party thinking. He later became an extreme right-wing Conservative M.P. in Portsmouth. Healey's agent was a Quaker conscientious objector, Jack Pritchard, later a councillor and President of Leeds City Labour Party. Ethel Green was their secretary.

The campaign was blessed with beautiful weather and Healey with well-attended meetings.

'It was a lively campaign, and Denis Healey made a great impression from the beginning,' said Pritchard. 'He was a very good speaker, and in places like Otley and Ilkley, which were regarded as solidly Tory, and where Labour would normally have had a furtive meeting, we were crowded out. On the second time round his reputation had spread, and we were turning people away. People came forward after hearing him speak at the first round of meetings and built up the Party organization.'

It was a hectic programme. Healey hired a car for five guineas a week, and spoke at three or four meetings every evening, with an occasional afternoon meeting as well. On the last night he made eleven speeches in four hours.

The organization of the campaign was left to Pritchard, ably assisted by Ethel Green.

'Denis never bossed us around,' she said. 'He would just say, "Where am I tonight?" and we would tell him.'

Issues of policy were decided by Healey, although his line was strictly orthodox.

'He had a reputation for being a bit leftish, but he was certainly moving away from such connections at that time,' said Pritchard. 'He did not work with the Communists, and you would not have detected any leftish leanings in his speeches.'

Buoyed by the response to the speeches and questions of his meetings in a campaign he described as 'the best I've ever had', Healey half hoped he might pull it off. Even in the safe Tory areas he was getting a response.

'There was an enormous area where we had never had political meetings. But we would take a loudspeaker down to the village green, and although nobody would come out because they did not want to be seen at a Labour meeting, they sat behind their windows and listened. You could see windows open slightly, curtains twitch – and that was all.'

His mother saw that he tuned his speeches to the audience.

'You wouldn't know Denis. He knew exactly how to speak to every audience – and there was always a bevy of girls in the front row.'

The count was on 26 July, to allow for the return of ballot papers from soldiers still overseas. Stoddart Scott and his wife picnicked on the lawn outside the hall in Pudsey where the count took place. Initially the votes for Healey mounted faster than for his Tory opponent. Then they levelled off. Results began to come in from the rest of the country, and it became obvious, as one Conservative Minister after another lost his seat, that Britain was rejecting Churchill, the acknowledged great war leader.

'Stoddart Scott was very worried. The result was a great shock to him,' said Pritchard. 'We had thought we would do well, but we didn't expect to do as well as we did.'

Scott won – but only just. His majority of 21,425 was cut to 1,651. The farming area votes had tipped the scales, but he admitted to the Labour candidate's mother that he had never been so scared in his life. The poor performance of the Liberal candidate was perhaps decisive; but the result was good enough for Hugh Dalton to describe it to a friend as the best result in the whole election.

It was a good result for Dalton for another reason, apart from Labour's improved performance. It meant that his protégé, Denis Healey, could become head of the International Department of Transport House. Brigadier Fellows arranged for him to return from Italy (with the section of the war history of Italy he had written) at the same time as the interview for the job was being held. He was chosen, in preference to more than seventy other applicants.

'I took it the day my Class B release for me to return to Merton came through,' said Healey.

He was adopted as Secretary of the International Department on 29 November 1945. He married Edna who was wearing a pale blue suit, black hat, and carrying orchids in St Peter's Church, Mayfair, with his brother Terry as his best man, on 21 December. They spent their honeymoon, at Christmas, in the loft of a cottage at the Buck Inn among the Yorkshire Dales. It was a marriage long delayed – a delay he regretted all the more as he could have had £1,500 saved from his pay as a married officer, instead of which he began his £350-a-year job at Transport House while they lived in a bedsitter in Spanish Place.

The reason for the delay in marrying was, Edna said, because 'he never would make a decision unless he'd considered all the possibilities, and, being a young man going off to war he couldn't see ahead to commit himself. He couldn't guarantee that he would return or that he would come back fit.' His mother also knew that he had been very moved by the Somerset Maugham play in which a young wife has a difficult life when her soldier husband returns to her as a complete invalid.

Edna was an ideal choice. Tougher, less naïve in worldly matters, and ambitious, she has also provided him with a secure home background against the difficulties of political life. He is fond of quoting Hugh Gaitskell, who observed that 'often people want the love of the world when they're not getting the love of one person.' Edna succeeded in her avowed aim to try to remove all friction, and to provide him with a happy married life.

Chapter Three

Backroom Boy

'*A younger generation trying to kick the older generation into the twentieth century.*'

MICHAEL MIDDLETON

'*We felt like Socialists against the world.*'

VILEM BERNARD

Chapter Three

'IN 1945 I had a choice,' said Healey. 'I could either have become a full colonel, and written an official war history, or gone to Merton to study the philosophy of aesthetics, but I rejected both alternatives and chose the Labour Party instead, because I wanted to get back into real life.'

His six years as Secretary of the International Department of the British Labour Party, which began in January 1946, gave him a good understanding of politics and politicians.

'When I started the job I didn't have much idea of the realities of power in politics. The speech I made at Blackpool represented hopes and aspirations. At Transport House I came slap up against the unpleasant realities.'

The new Labour Government were also coming to grips with reality. The Second World War had left Britain victorious, but exhausted. Some of the limitations of British power had become apparent on 15 February 1942, when more than 100,000 Allied troops had surrendered to a Japanese force less than half its size at Singapore. This Far Eastern stronghold had had £60 million spent on making it impregnable – but its 15-inch guns pointed out to sea. It was ill-prepared for the landward invasion.

The war had made worse Britain's relatively declining economic position. The problems of major industries in danger – engineering, shipping and textiles – and the demands of new light industries for skills and capital were worsened by crowding competition from developing nations and the rapid pace of change. Britain's capacity to trade and manufacture were hit. She lost almost a third of her merchant shipping; more than five million houses were destroyed or damaged; much of her overseas investment had been sold to pay for the war effort. Victory over Hitler and the Japanese hid the reality of her economic exhaustion.

The new mood of the nation, however, eager for changes towards greater social justice and economic reconstruction, gave Labour a landslide victory, with 393 seats to the Conservatives' 213, and a mandate for their Five Year Plan.

Ernest Bevin's foreign policy was dominated by the need to find new sources of power, to drop any responsibilities considered inessential, and to encourage the United States, as an ally, to pick up the burden. Healey watched from close range.

'I saw a lot of Bevin because I really had two big jobs to do. The first was to interpret Bevin's policy to the Party, and the Party to Bevin. I had to go round the country, standing up for Ernie, explaining what he was doing, because he found it difficult to explain it himself.'

Without a Foreign Office brief Bevin was not a good speaker, and at Party Conferences usually got his way through his appeal to loyalty in a movement reared on loyalty. Healey was Bevin's sweetly reasonable voice. Bevin did things. Healey provided the intellectual rationalization.

Back to Europe

His second main job was to reorganize the Socialist International, which had fallen into disuse, and this took him all over Europe. Through this Healey built up friends and contacts like Willy Brandt, Chancellor of Germany, whom he first got to know in 1947.

'He knows foreign affairs and the people involved in a way that would have been impossible if he had not had that job,' said Healey's wife.

When Healey first entered the square room on the sixth floor of Transport House, his windows overlooked a dismal courtyard and a fire escape. It was a desolate setting, made more so by the near collapse of any organization. Willie Gillies, the previous Secretary, had resigned a year earlier. Gillies recognized the nature of German and Soviet imperialism in the 1930s, and written *Solar System* and *Finnish War* to expose it. Idealistic left-wingers like Laski never forgave him.

At the end of the war Laski published a pamphlet which saw the Workers' International built on the twin pillars of the British Labour Party and the Soviet Communist Party. The National Executive suppressed it. Healey's speech at Blackpool attracted Laski, and helped him get the job. But Healey was too independent a man to remain subservient to the Party Chairman. He was unlikely to be accused, as Gillies was, of embracing too readily the Vansittart belief in the eternal evil of the German race – which had caused Gillies to neglect German Socialist refugees.

The moribund department, manned by Miss Howie and a raw 16-year-old, Pat Evans, had a chance to move forward on the crest of popular enthusiasm.

'The International Department was Denis, Miss Howie and a junior secretary,' Pat Evans remembered. 'It gradually changed after 1945. Before then Transport House's staff was small – either not very good, or very good indeed with a few well-to-do idealists who didn't need the money.'

One man who also joined them in 1946, Michael Middleton, now director of the Civic Trust, said: 'We had the feeling of being a younger generation trying to kick the older generation into the twentieth century.'

Healey, ably assisted by Pat Evans, built up the department and began to assert his influence as a backroom boy who knew where he wanted to go, Tom McNally, current Overseas Secretary, put it succinctly: 'Denis created the department.'

Transport House had a healthy contempt for M.P.s whom they regarded as being 'Lobby fodder', voting for the Party's policies with their feet by walking into the Government Lobby. Transport House staff thought themselves 'professionals' with time to help mould policy. The bright boys could stay for low pay – Healey's annual salary slowly rose from £350 to £750 by 1952 – but they had a chance to exert influence. As he confided at the time to Brigadier Fellows, his job was far more influential and interesting than a back-bencher's.

Lord Longford, in 1947–8 Chancellor of the Duchy of Lancaster, with special responsibility for German affairs, found Healey 'more important than I had suspected when I came from Oxford. Bevin would use him, and often send round for him. I remember him as brash and bursting with life.'

Alice Bacon, on the National Executive, and later chairman of it, emphasized that Healey was not in Transport House merely to do what he was told.

'He showed initiative in producing the policy in immediate post-war years that was to form the basis of the Party's international policy. He produced memoranda and documents for the Executive, and fought hard for the things he wanted.'

In 1945 Healey had told his mother: 'I want to do some good for the country.' In his new position he got that chance.

As a boss Healey was efficient and pleasant to work for but he was intolerant of fools. For the same reason he ignored cocktail parties and social occasions – which he thought a waste of time – although he enjoyed dinner parties, where he had a chance to get to know people much better. Diplomatic journalists working at that time confirmed how much they respected him.

His uninhibited enthusiasm, a love of spur-of-the-moment excursions and boyish pranks, and his refusal to dissemble – 'brutally frank', said one politician who had been on the receiving end – all made him seem essentially awkward in sophisticated society (although he himself seemed unconscious of the fact). He was accepted as being tough, brash and earthy. His command of choice four-letter words hid a sensitive, if self-centred, personality. Michael Middleton, art critic of the *Spectator* (1946–52) as well as Transport House colleague, remembered when he visited Healey's home 'Denis being very apologetic about the rows of art books.'

Friends spoke of his ebullient and dynamic character, which always seemed to be pushed by controlled energy, and his sense of humour. Critics spoke of being irritated by his incessant smiling, and his practical jokes. He was always mimicking people on the phone, sometimes throwing the office into confusion with an Eastern European or Yorkshire accent. He went round pulling funny faces.

'Once or twice he startled sober visitors he did not know were there,' said Pat Evans. 'But this jolliness was just on the surface. Underneath there beat a heart of stone. He was not a man whom lame ducks would have limped towards. He did not alienate people, but neither did he strike a responsive chord.'

Through his contact with the political realities of Europe Healey gradually moved towards the right wing in the forties.

'I have a vivid memory of meeting him in the forties,' said Leslie Shepherd, 'and thought he was right outside the Party – on the extreme left. I often wonder what made him change his politics.'

But change he did. Pat Evans recollected: 'His 1945 Conference speech incurred a lot of criticism among Party stalwarts – but I never heard him say anything like it after he got his new job. He defended Bevin right down the line with a straight bat.'

Francis Mennell, who shared the sixth floor office with Healey for a time, said, 'He really knew nothing about foreign policy when he made that speech, except what he had seen in Italy. But he learned the political facts very fast.' So fast, in fact, that by 1947 to Middleton 'Denis seemed much to the right of centre especially on such things as relations with Eastern Europe.'

The move towards a 'hard line' position had begun earlier. Just before the 1946 Whitsun Conference, as Healey said, 'The Executive were worried that the Communists might get a majority for affiliation to the Party. So I said, "Why not amend the constitution so that other parties can't affiliate to the Labour Party?" It had never struck them.'

Morgan Phillips took up the idea, and the amendment was carried, ending more than a decade of wrangling and Communist hopes of taking over the Labour Party.

Eastern Europe – Poland

As part of his job to re-establish links with European socialist parties, and to help form a new Socialist International, Healey toured fraternal conferences in West and East Europe till the Iron Curtain came down.

'I was committed to the Social Democrats in Europe,' he said. 'As soon as I came into contact with the problem I began to see the difference between them and the Communists. I thought at first that we could do business with the Soviet Union, but I became more and more depressed – particularly in 1947 and '48 when the Socialist parties in Eastern Europe were being eliminated.'

At the Yalta Conference in February 1945 the Western Powers had recognized Soviet predominance in most of Eastern Europe for a short period after the war, until freely elected governments could be set up. Initially, governments of national unity were established which included a few Communists – but often in key posts.

'In many Eastern European countries the Social Democrats had to work with the Communists because they were a real political force,' explained Blazej Vilim, a former General Secretary of the Czech S.D.P. who spent five and a half years in German prisons because he was secretary of Czechoslovakia's largest trade union before the Nazi take-over.

'We tried to get them out of the Ministry of the Interior in 1946, but we did not have enough support from other parties.'

Social Democrats in Eastern Europe were faced with the same problem Laval had to surmount in France when the Germans invaded. They had to compromise, or adopt a position that could only lead to exile.

In 1946 some countries presented problems for Healey in deciding which was the true faction of Social Democrats. In Poland, for example, Joseph Cyrankiewicz became General Secretary of the 'official' Party (P.P.S.), which was closely allied to the Moscow-dominated Communists. Members of the authentic P.P.S. followed him because they were personally attracted to the man himself – not realizing that he had decided to 'collaborate' with the Russians. The long-delayed elections were rigged, but as this did not entirely remove authentic P.P.S. members they were suppressed by arrests and mock trials. After a time the official Party broke with the Western Socialist Parties and fused with the Communists. Cyrankiewicz was duly rewarded with a job of ministerial rank. He remained Prime Minister until the Polish Baltic Port riots of 1970.

The Polish position was complicated for Healey by the over-hasty recognition of the Polish Provisional Government of National Unity, formed on 28 June 1945, and based on the Lublin Committee. Bevin had also met Cyrankiewicz for an hour on a train passing through Poland, and the leader of the P.P.S. had promised that: (a) the P.P.S. would keep a separate existence, and (b) Poland would keep an independent position in East-West relations, similar to that of Finland. He impressed Bevin, who thought him sincere. Cyrankiewicz was lying, but this made Healey's position difficult when it came to dealing with Adam Ciolcosz.

Ciolcosz, who became a Polish M.P. in 1928, was imprisoned by Pilsudski in 1930, and in 1933 sentenced to three years hard labour. He was a member of the Executive of the P.P.S. from 1931. In 1940 he escaped to France and became representative of the Polish underground abroad. He is now Chairman of the

Polish Socialist Party in exile. He has described his dealings with Healey in the 1940s: 'I explained the position in Poland to him in 1946. I wanted him to invite some Socialists to the International Conference and recognize them as a faction, but it was all in vain. He was very polite, but he had a preconceived idea that the salvation of Polish Socialists lay in the hands of Cyrankiewicz.'

But how could the Labour Party recognize both the Polish Government and the exiled Socialists?

Healey conceded that 'one couldn't really write-off people in Poland like Ciolcosz – who was chained to the walls of a dungeon for eleven months – as not being Socialists.' He was polite, but firm. A few years later, said Ciolcosz, 'he called Cyrankiewicz a crook – an apt description.'

Hungarian Dilemma

With Hungary, Healey was faced with two parties in exile. Both claimed to be the true Socialists. Which should he recommend the National Executive to recognize?

There was no doubt that the right-wing splinter group, led by Karoly Peyer, was determinedly anti-Communist. At the February 1947 Congress of his Party he was defeated. But Communist agents and crypto-Communists were already infiltrating the Socialist Party. The election of August 1947 was rigged by the Russians, and the results manipulated so that the Communists, with 22·5 per cent of the vote, became the majority party. Arrests and trials of Social Democrats were followed by a fusion of the Socialist and Communist parties. Between March and June 1948 the persecution, according to Antal Ban (who spent two years in a Nazi concentration camp, became deputy Secretary-General of the underground, and then Minister of Industry in 1945) developed into a manhunt. Ban himself fled to the West in February 1948. One of his supporters, Mrs Imre Szelig, wife of the leader of the trade unions, has maintained: 'We were the true representatives of the Social Democratic Party in England.'

Lajos Lederer, a follower of Peyer, rightly accused the Labour Party of failing to recognize the nature of the Communist plot when he reviewed *The Curtain Falls*, a book published in 1951 about the Eastern European Socialists and edited by Healey.

'Instead of pointing out that Communist policy was to destroy Socialism by alliance with it, it was official Transport House policy to support the Eastern European Socialists' policy of alliance with the Communists,' Lederer wrote. Socialists like Peyer, he continued, who had opposed this policy, received short shrift from Labour Party officials.

Both Hungarian groups – Peyer's and Ban's – were undoubtedly anti-Communist, and both asked for recognition. Peyer had gone into exile before Ban and Szelig. Healey broadly supported the official Socialist group. 'I think you can argue that Peyer had collaborated with Admiral Horthy, who worked with the Nazis, and was really a "yellow dog" socialist,' said Healey.

But the question was not resolved until 1949, after the Baarn Conference in Holland.

Rumania was more difficult. As in Poland and Hungary, the pre-war left-wing tried to work with the Communists, while the right was not allowed to organize. Some of them, having gone abroad during the war, stayed away. There were also two groups inside Rumania. Daniel Norman (formerly Nuselovici-Moldavanu), who left Rumania in 1938 to avoid imprisonment, fought with the French, spent four years as a P.o.W. and became a free spokesman for the Party in exile has explained the situation:

'When I arrived in England the national Socialist Party was split in two. One group was in the government coalition – with Communist parties and other parties. The other was led by the President with a few supporters. I was in favour of going it alone without the Communists, but the majority decided to go with the Communists – it was a question of tactics, not principles. I was not alone, however, as I was with Serban Voinea – the Rumanian Laski.'

Norman arrived in England for the first meeting of the Socialist parties, held in Clacton. He went straight to Transport House and asked for the International Secretary. Healey struck him as extremely gifted, serious, and reliable. They spoke in French and had one of those strange conversations, full of political nuance, where one man is feeling out the reliability of the other, and where obvious commitment can too easily seem a cover for another belief.

'Denis asked me, "Which party are you?" and I said, "What a question! I am a democrat; I am not with one man or another." He then asked what I would do if the President decided to go it alone with only a handful of men against the Party. "What would you do as a democrat?" he asked. "I leave it to you" I said. "You answer." It was clear to me that I was a democrat, and that I would abide by the decision of the majority. He sent me to see Harold Laski. Harold asked the same question, and we had the same dialogue. So, I went back to see Denis.'

Neither of the Rumanian factions had been invited to the conference. It had seemed impossible to decide which one to support. Norman told Healey that his faction, led by Serban Voinea, would be there. Healey told him to wait for the Executive's decision, expected that evening. Norman told him, 'I am going down in any case, because I have a mandate from the Party to be there. If you prefer me to wait outside and tell the Press you have refused entry to a genuine socialist, I don't mind.'

Norman went to Clacton.

'At nine o'clock I arrived, and contacted him. He said it was O.K. for me to come down. I told him I was already there. "Do you want me to sleep in the station?" I asked, and he laughed.'

Norman was a man after Healey's own heart. Voinea arrived, and was one of the main speakers against the Communists. He admits that it was difficult for Healey to distinguish between 'true' Socialists, and those who would collaborate with the Communists.

'I gave Denis the whole story about the collaborationist groups, and he was grateful for my help and advice, which guided him later.'

'A Real Bashing'

In 1946, when attending the Italian Socialist Party Conference he almost went too far. Saragat, who was President of the Constituent Assembly in 1946, and already moving to the right and towards a break with Nenni, who had close ties with Togliatti's Communist Party, attacked the Labour Government for being imperialistic, and supporting the Communists and Nenni.

'I answered this at the Conference in Italian,' said Healey. 'It

made a great sensation in Italy, and Saragat complained to de
Gasperi (the Premier). He in turn complained to Mallet, the
Ambassador, of interference in internal Italian affairs.'

When Bevin sent for Healey the latter had already been
forewarned by a Foreign Office friend – who represented the
orthodox doctrinaire Foreign Office view of rejecting the more
left-wing groups – and told that he could expect 'a real bashing'.
Healey, who still thought he was right, sent Bevin the text of
what he had said, and a letter explaining why he had said it.

'In fear and trembling I went along the next day, because
Ernie was a formidable fellow to row with. I was ushered into
his big room, and he asked me to sit down before sending his
private secretary out of the room. Then he said to me in his soft
Somersetshire voice, "Well, Denis, I've read your letter, and the
speech you made. Have you anything else to say about how you
behaved?" I said No, I don't think so, and he said "All right,
then. I'll tell Mallet to stop whining." My devotion to Ernie
after that was even less bounded than before.'

Healey was also at the January 1947 Congress of the Italian
Socialist Party where the Party split, Saragat seceding with the
right-wing S.D.P., leaving Nenni leader of the Italian Socialist
Party (P.S.I.). It was another split about whether to work with
or against the Communists, and gave Healey the usual problem
of which group to recognize – although in Italy's case the country
was not under Soviet control. It is possible to date Healey's
changing attitude by studying his relations with the P.S.I. At
the March 1948 meeting of the Committee of International
Socialist Conferences (COMISCO) Nenni's group withdrew
and Saragat's was accepted as the true representative of Italian
socialists.

As Adam Ciolcosz, who was at the meeting, said: 'Denis and
Morgan Phillips were instrumental in expelling them, together
with the collaborators in Poland and Czechoslovakia. This was
Denis's first concrete act after the takeover of the Communists
in Prague in February 1948.'

The Czech experience was the turning point for Healey, as it
was for a number of other socialists who had believed that 'Left
understands Left' – the slogan coined by Bevin at the 1945
Labour Party Conference.

Outside the Cabinet Labour politicians were trying to find

5

some form of 'socialist' foreign policy; possibly linking European socialists with the Commonwealth to form a third force with America and the Soviet Union. Even the Labour leaders thought they would get on better with the Russians than their Tory opponents, and there was some feeling that Russia had to be admired for her achievements – the belief of the Webbs that they had at least a competent bureaucracy. In December 1945 Bevin offered to extend the twenty-year Anglo-Soviet treaty of 1942 to fifty years.

But gradually Bevin had to abandon hope of a *modus vivendi* with the Soviet Union. In Germany the occupying Allies came into conflict over the policies they should pursue, and in the foreign policy discussions of the great powers Molotov said 'No' to almost everything. In the Soviet zone of Germany the Russians eliminated party leaders, and organizations not subservient to them, during 1946. In a series of superbly-timed moves Bevin enticed the United States away from her growing isolationist position to help in the defence of Greece and Turkey – the Truman Doctrine of 12 March 1947 – and into the Western security system.

Cards on the Table

Bevin's growing disillusion was aptly reflected in Healey's pamphlet of May 1947 – *Cards on the Table*. It was a pamphlet that nearly split the Party, for it went much further than Bevin was able to go publicly, although, as Healey's colleagues said, it was his idea, and not Bevin's. He was well in touch with Foreign Office opinion at the time, however, having frequent contact with Bevin and Hector McNeil, his Minister of State, as well as the civil servants.

Cards on the Table argued that Britain had to reduce commitments because of her declining resources, yet in an orderly manner so as not to lose control over the process, or her power and initiative. It savagely attacked the way Russia's 'attempt to destroy Britain's freedom of initiative was double-edged' and clearly argued that the Soviet Union represented the biggest danger to Britain, while America – seemingly unwilling to shoulder the burdens and responsibilities of power – had to be encouraged to give up her desire for isolationism.

The Left especially were horrified at the clear tones in which

Healey stated that 'Britain could not under any circumstances adopt a policy which might lead her to war against America,' and added 'we can only be grateful if America is prepared in any way to make it easier for us to defend our security.' The pamphlet greeted the way Bevin had encouraged the Americans to help the British prop up certain regimes in Europe as a triumph – a presence which the left did not appreciate. Between capitalist America and communist Russia, he asserted, 'democratic socialism will only survive as an alternative if Labour Britain survives as a world power.'

When *Cards on the Table* was put before the Executive at the Margate Party Conference there was tremendous opposition, led by Laski, supported by Dick Crossman. As Francis Mennell said: 'Although Laski and Denis thought in similar terms in 1945, by 1947 they were arguing about almost everything.' The problem was compounded by the prejudice among some leading Labour Party politicians who thought that the research department for international affairs was a waste of members' money. This in itself made it difficult to put through documents on foreign policy. But, as Pat Evans said: '*Cards on the Table* produced a greater split in the Party than had been expected.'

The problem arose because of Hugh Dalton, then Chairman of the International Sub-committee as well as Chancellor of the Exchequer. Dalton, as Healey said, 'wasn't an easy man to argue with; because he was a great bully; on the other hand, if you argued back, he didn't bully you very long.' When *Cards on the Table* was presented, however, his disloyalty was almost Healey's downfall.

'I showed Dalton *Cards on the Table* and said that I had just produced it for the Party, and did he agree that I should publish it. He said "Yes". Then there was a terrible row at Margate, and it was savagely attacked. The Executive held meeting after meeting, and it wasn't until almost the end of the last one that Dalton, under repeated prodding by Shinwell, admitted that he had cleared it for publication. Up to that point he let it appear that I had done this entirely off my own bat without consulting anyone.'

Alice Bacon, who was on the Executive, remembered that

'Denis stood his ground pretty well at that time – quite effectively'.

Cards on the Table is important, for it shows how Healey was changing attitudes.

'The big issue was what the Russians were up to in Eastern Europe – the takeover of power, and steady elimination of anybody who disagreed,' he said. 'At first I had the feeling that the Russians had made an unfortunate mistake, and only needed to be told to be sensible. But it soon became apparent that the Soviet system was very different to what its pre-war sympathizers had thought it to be.'

Czechoslovakia

By November 1947, when Healey went as fraternal delegate representing the British Labour Party to the Czechoslovak Social Democratic Party's Congress, it was apparent that the Russians were starting to put on the pressure. The offer of American aid under the Marshall Plan had first been accepted by them, and then rejected in July 1947, on Russian insistence. In October the Russians set up their answer to it – COMINFORM. Blazej Vilim, who was General Secretary of the Czech S.D.P. during 1945–8, explained that 'after the rejection of the Marshall Plan in Paris I knew that we had lost in Czechoslovakia. It was only a question of time.'

Vilim was worried about Healey coming to Brno as he thought it would make his job of removing the leader of the Party, Sdenek Fierlinger, more difficult.

'Vilim was rather embarrassed by my presence because of my reputation as a well-known "social-fascist", which made me a great figure in Soviet demonology at the time,' said Healey.

Healey had arrived in Brno at a time of crisis. Following the free elections of May 1946, where the Communists under Gottwald gained thirty-eight per cent of the votes, there had been co-operation between the parties in a coalition government until the rejection of Marshall Aid. The Communists, who were losing popularity, and feared the result of the elections due in June 1948, began to put the squeeze on non-Communists, and to terrorize non-Communist workers in the factories. Fierlinger, chairman of the S.D.P., who it was later learned had been working for fusion with the Communists since 1942, tried to force his Party into an alliance with the Communists. The Brno Congress was the opportunity to rally the rank and file in a bid to remove him.

'The Brno Congress was held at the decisive moment of a dangerous political crisis in the country as a whole,' explained Vaclav Majer, who was Minister of Food. 'The congress was carefully watched by public opinion throughout Czechoslovakia and also abroad. The Social Democratic Party held a key position for the country's future.'

At the congress Fierlinger was ousted, the pro-Communist wing was heavily defeated, and the resolutions passed supported an independent socialist policy. It was a daring decision, rejecting the idea of alliance with the Eastern bloc.

Healey's presence was important, as Vilem Bernard, Chairman of the Foreign Affairs Commission and head of the International Department, said:

'The presence of Western European socialist parties was a demonstration of solidarity. It showed the unity of social democratic parties East and West of the Iron Curtain. Among all these the British Party was perhaps the most important of those present for it represented the victorious nation of the Second World War, one of the most stable in Europe, and it was a party in power translating into reality a radical programme of economic and social reform.'

There were two huge flags on the platform at the Congress – the Czech flag and the British Union Jack.

Healey, then aged thirty, made a speech in which he said the economic crisis which Britain was going through arose from the decision of the British people to win independence of foreign aid. 'We want to create good relations with all the big powers,' he said, 'so that small states can live in freedom. One cannot agree that Europe must be divided.'

The British Labour Party wanted sincere co-operation with the Soviet Union, he said, but 'it must be based on mutual respect and democratic tolerance'. The text of the speech was published in the Czech daily paper *Cin*, and other papers.

Vilem Bernard told of the impact of the speech:

'When he stressed the egalitarian aspect of the British socialist policies it had a particularly important effect in the atmosphere where we were under the heavy pressure of propaganda.

We felt like socialists against the world, needing support from other parties of social progress. Denis emphasized the meaning of political freedom – he answered the Communists back. We saw eye to eye; we were fighting for the same thing. He reassured us that we were part of an international movement.'

Healey was struck by the defeated Fierlinger's appearance. 'I have never seen such a display of despair and savagery on anybody's face as I did then,' he said. It boded ill for the Social Democrats.

Blazej Vilim remembered that after the congress was over 'Denis came to me and congratulated me because he knew it was my job to chop off Fierlinger, and he said "I am a bit afraid that you will come under stronger pressure from the Communists now." But I knew that we had already lost, and that we were not saving Czechoslovak democracy in that hall – only the honour of our Party. I told him that in the Spring I would be in London.'

Vilim was not forgotten by the Communists. In the White Book published by the Communists to explain their invasion of Czechoslovakia in August 1968, he is accused of being a major British agent, more than twenty years after dropping out of active politics.

Bernard also met Healey to discuss the S.D.P.'s problems.

'Denis certainly knew our problems, and perfectly understood the restrictions and tactical considerations we had to take into account,' he explained. 'Almost any contacts with the West were regarded as high treason, and we had to move cautiously. The British didn't want to make our position too difficult – Denis's policy showed real political wisdom, and was based on his personal experience of our countries. What I admired at the time was his detailed knowledge of other parties, and understanding of the people concerned.'

His knowledge of the facts and his interpretation of them made him realize that the end was near. He discussed frankly the implications of a delicate situation.

'When he was taking leave of me in Brno he was very worried,' Bernard admitted. 'He asked me what was going to happen to us, and said "How are you going to resist? Will you be able to preserve this decision and this policy? What will happen when stronger methods are applied against you?" I told him we could not say, or give any safeguards.'

With the Communist penetration of the state machine and their control of the Ministry of the Interior, which ran the police, the end was in sight. As Vaclav Majer explained, they used 'police, militiamen, and armed Communist thugs to break down Social-Democratic resistance'. This was followed by the usual persecutions, imprisonments, and deaths. On 20 February 1948, the twelve moderates resigned from the Government, hoping for a dissolution of Parliament before the Communists could arrange for the elections to be rigged. But the left-wing Social Democrats supported the Communists, and they remained in office with a new Cabinet.

Converted

'Denis was right,' Bernard admitted. 'My Party, while making its position clear, was unable to prevent the Communists from seizing full power.'

The end came swiftly. The Czech coup was soon followed by tremendous pressure on the Poles and Hungarians. Those who resisted were at best imprisoned, and at worst killed. The lucky ones escaped and made their way to friendly states.

'On 29 March I illegally crossed the Austrian frontier,' Bernard stated. 'From the French zone I wrote to Edith Loeb – running the COMISCO office in London at that time – and she approached Denis. I came to England with Denis's help.'

Healey arranged visas and facilitated the exiles' passage to England. Bernard explained that 'the same was done for six more Czechoslovak Social Democrats, Executive members, and Parliamentarians, as well as for four Hungarians and their families.'

Mrs Imre Szelig, who escaped from Hungary with her husband, said: 'We were treated very well by Denis Healey and the British Labour Party, who gave us guarantees so that we could come to England where we were given political asylum.'

The refugees came via Switzerland (where they were given British visas) to England. Bernard remembered his first day in England:

'I went with my wife to see Denis and he invited us to lunch. Then he took us to the Tate Gallery. It was not our main con-

cern; our problem was more prosaic, apart from the political
position it was to find accommodation, and so on.'

Daniel Norman confirmed Healey's willingness to help the
refugees:

'If you went to Denis for something and it was a matter of
helping, it was done immediately. You can rely on his word,
and you can be sure that it will be done in the minimum of
time. He was always frank, direct, and practical.'

The Czechoslovak *putsch* was the turning point in Healey's
attitude to the Communists. Adam Ciolcosz explained: 'The
coup made him change his mind – he didn't like being deceived,
nor did the Labour Party. After the fall of Prague he saw the
light, and turned from Saul into Paul. He finally saw the Soviets
as imperialist power men.'

Healey had become disillusioned slowly. As Bernard put it:
'At first he hoped for some sort of socialist reconciliation in
Eastern Europe – a socialist transformation, even through harsh
measures. He was disappointed by the realities of Soviet power.
Throughout 1947 he was a worried man, and the February coup
in Prague confirmed his worst fears.'

Today Healey bluntly states: 'Stalin was going mad at this
time.'

The fall of Czechoslovakia brought a change in the Labour
Party's attitude to the Soviet Union and the menace of Communism. Healey did not succeed in getting a much more active
policy adopted by Labour Party leaders, who became bogged
down in the Korean War in June 1950. To compensate for this,
perhaps, he edited *The Curtain Falls*, which was a clear condemnation of the Soviet Union and its methods of taking control
in Eastern European states.

He had difficulty in persuading Aneurin Bevan to write the
introduction, for, although he was extremely anti-Communist
and had many friends among the refugees, he had just split
with the official leadership of the party, and needed the support
of the Left, who were more sympathetic to the Soviet Union.
Bevan didn't mince his words, however, and wrote: 'It is a grim,
depressing narrative . . . The Communist Party is the sworn
inveterate enemy of the Socialist and Democratic Parties. The
Communist does not look upon a Socialist as an ally in a common cause. He looks upon him as a dupe, as a temporary con-

venience, and as something to be thrust relentlessly to one side when he has served his purpose.'

The Anti-Communist

Healey's explanation of the techniques of Communist take-over in *The Curtain Falls* is a clear condemnation of Soviet be-haviour. As Daniel Norman said: 'He recognized the menace of the Russians; being an ex-Communist he knew what to expect from them, and that they could not be disposed of, but were a reality that had to be taken into account.'

In his concluding sentences Healey wrote: 'This story of hopes frustrated, idealism betrayed, and freedom in chains does not make pleasant reading.'

His final break showed the shattering of earlier faith: 'One of the most seductive arguments of Communism,' he said, 'rests on the false assumption that in any crisis Communism is the only alternative to Fascism. The post-war history of Eastern Europe disproves this utterly.'

Healey set to work with renewed vigour for the Eastern Euro-pean socialists and against the communists. Dr Rita Hinden, editor of *Socialist Commentary*, suggested to him that Trans-port House needed a 'Colonial Secretary' to help combat the menace of communist propaganda among African and other overseas students.

'Denis agreed, and suggested I should draw up a memoran-dum. I did, and he sponsored it.'

A colonial officer was appointed, and Healey's own interest in the under-developed countries widened. He got Dr Hinden and Michael Young to write *A World of Peace and Plenty*, about aid to the under-developed countries.

The major contribution made by Healey, however, was for the international organization of socialists. Before the war there had been the Socialist International – a descendant of the First International of Working Men's Associations, which Marx had helped set up in the 1860s – led by the German S.D.P., which the Czechs quit after the Munich Settlement.

'We could not join the Socialist International again,' Vilim stated, 'but we had to have some kind of international body for socialists.'

So COMISCO was established in 1946.

In 1948 the question of relations with the Soviet Union, and the membership of different parties, all claiming to be the true Socialists, topped the agenda at Clacton on 19–20 March. On 2 March the Executive had issued a statement in which they said 'Communists consider as enemies all those who do not surrender unconditionally to their slightest whims: slave or enemy – there is no third way.'

It continued, however: 'Communists cannot achieve their aims without support from a minority within the camp of democratic socialism', and listed Czechoslovakia, Hungary, Rumania, and Bulgaria as places where – 'Socialists by permitting or abetting Communist attacks on democracy, have connived at their own destruction.' The results for the common man, it warned, would be dictatorship indistinguishable from that of Hitler or Mussolini.

The highlight of the meeting was the speech made by Blazej Vilim who arrived as the meeting was sitting, having been brought straight to England in a special plane from Germany following his escape from Czechoslovakia, and then by car from the airport.

'I presented a report to the meeting, and after that a resolution was made. It was the start of a new policy towards European socialist parties that were co-operating with the Communists.'

When the resolution was agreed Nenni's delegation left the hall.

The resolution stated categorically that 'Communist Parties have been ordered to destroy democratic socialism'. It continued by outlawing the S.D.P.s of Rumania, Bulgaria, and Hungary – 'absorbed into the Communist movement by an arbitrary decision of their leaders', and the S.D.P. collaborators in Czechoslovakia – 'this Committee cannot accept the present leadership of the Czechoslovak Social Democratic Party as representative of Socialism'. And it warned 'the Polish and Italian Socialist Parties, which are at present following the same path to absorption'. It appealed to them to reject the road of co-operation with the Communists. Healey played a key part in the formulation of this new policy.

He also played a vital role in the talks leading to the resolution at the COMISCO meeting the following December, 'concerning Eastern European Socialist Parties in Exile'. This

meeting, at Clacton on 3 December 1948, tried to arrive at a
formula to accommodate the S.D.P.s of Eastern Europe. A sub-
committee was established with three functions: (a) To attempt
reconciliation of the rival groups of Hungary and Rumania, or
failing reconciliation, to choose between them; (b) to assist the
six Parties of Eastern Europe in forming a joint organization;
(c) to draw up proposals governing the relationship between
COMISCO and the East European Parties in exile.

The meeting, held in Baarn, Holland, on 13 May 1949, considered the sub-committee's report, and recommended the setting up of a common centre in exile for the East European
parties, so that they could send delegates to full meetings of the
International Socialist Conference and to committee meetings,
with the right to speak, but not to vote.

'The status of the exiled parties was a problem because we
were too many,' explained Bernard. 'The Baarn resolution came
at a time when the subject of relations with Communist-domi-
nated East European countries was under steady debate. What
was to be done? Thus, this decision to disassociate itself with
the Communists, declaring these continuing links with the
socialist parties, was a great one.

'Denis was the key man, the most important in all that, and
I think the major part of the resolutions was his working. The
final settlement was based on his proposals.'

The centre, named the 'Socialist Union of Central-Eastern
Europe', was established in July 1949. The decisions taken at
Baarn remain in force.

Aims and Tasks

Healey also played a vital part in drawing up the *Aims and
Tasks of Democratic Socialism* the importance of which, as one
prominent socialist philosopher stated, 'can be compared only
to the Inaugural Address of the International Working Men's
Association in London in 1864'.

The International Socialist Conference held in Copenhagen
on 1–3 June 1950, set up a sub-committee to prepare a declaration on the basic principles of democratic socialism common to
all party members. The sub-committee had representatives of
Austria, Belgium, France, Germany, Britain, Scandinavia, Switzerland, and Eastern Europe, and was nominally under the

chairmanship of Guy Mollet, although Solomon Grumbach, another Frenchman, exercised this role in practice. It met in Paris
in October 1950, in London in March 1951, and in Strasbourg
in May 1951, before a final meeting in Frankfurt in June 1951.

Four drafts were elaborated before the final one was submitted to the Socialist International, meeting at Frankfurt during 30 June–3 July. Two of the five sections were written by
Healey. He wrote the preamble, and, when Grumbach's draft
for the section on 'International Democracy' proved inadequate, he wrote that too. The full meeting of the foundation
Congress of the new Socialist International unanimously accepted the 'charter' that Healey had done so much to mould.

In the Declaration, Healey wrote of the evils of capitalism.

'Socialism aims to liberate the peoples from dependence on
a minority which owns or controls the means of production,' he
said. But he also attacked Communism, which falsely claimed a
share in the socialist tradition. He continued:

'Communism has split the International Labour Movement
and has set back the realization of Socialism in many countries
for decades. It has distorted that tradition beyond recognition.
It has built up a rigid theology which is incompatible with the
critical spirit of Marxism.

'Where Socialists aim to achieve freedom and justice by removing the exploitation which divides men under capitalism,
Communists seek to sharpen those class divisions only in order
to establish the dictatorship of a single party. International
Communism is the instrument of a new imperialism.'

Socialists who built their faith on Marxist and other methods
of analysing society, he wrote, 'all strive for the same goal – a
system of social justice, better living, freedom and world peace'.

The final section emphasized the international nature of the
socialist movement, and thundered: 'Absolute national sovereignty must be transcended.'

After speaking of the need for socialists to help overcome extreme poverty, illiteracy, and disease throughout the world, he
continued:

'Democratic Socialists recognize the maintenance of world
peace as the supreme task in our time. Peace can be secured
only by a system of collective security. This will create the conditions for international disarmament... The struggle for world

peace is inseparably bound up with the struggle for freedom. It is the threat to the independence of free peoples that is directly responsible for the danger of war in our time.'

The Soviet threat to economically weak nations was the major preoccupation of Western statesmen in the late forties. Bevin set about drawing the United States into an alliance that would protect the integrity of the West European states. Healey supported him ardently. His strong pro-Americanism dates from 1948.

Like many of Healey's firmly held beliefs it was not emotionally conceived. As Ciolcosz stated: 'He is not that kind of man. He simply does his sums and puts two and two together.' He added: 'I think Denis contributed very much to the military thing against the Soviets. If they were not to be trusted, then you had to defend the rest of Europe – and the U.S.A. was necessary for the defence of Europe.'

Healey confirmed that 'basically I was an Atlantic Community man from about 1948'.

For Transport House the Cold War dated from the coup in Czechoslovakia, and the flood of refugees who came in and out all day long. Bevin saw the essential problem, Healey explained, 'as committing the Americans to the protection and economic support of Western Europe before we accepted any more responsibilities in Europe'. He added: 'The only time we went ahead of events was with the Dunkirk Treaty, but that was definitely the sprat to catch the whale of NATO.'

The Dunkirk Treaty, concluded between Britain and France in March 1947, was for mutual defence against aggression by Germany – occupied at that time by the Allies. It symbolized the re-emergence of France as a European power, and led, in March 1948, to the Brussels Treaty, which promised 'all the military and other aid and assistance in their power' to any of the signatories (Belgium, Britain, France, Luxemburg, and the Netherlands) if they were the object of armed attack. When the arrangement ended in May 1955 it was replaced by the expanded Western European Union, which included Italy and the German Federal Republic.

Francis Mennell explained Healey's attachment to this when he said: 'Denis became convinced that an economic union and a NATO build-up were necessary to stop the threat of communism. He rallied support for W.E.U. Without that it might never have got off the ground.'

The Marshall Plan

Healey watched while Bevin, 'a master of timing', which he learned as a trade union negotiator, brought America out of isolation and into the defence of the free Western European states. The Marshall Plan, to give economic aid to the struggling democracies, was perhaps the highlight of the period. On 5 June 1947, George Marshall, the American Secretary of State, had talked of 'a programme designed to place Europe on its feet economically', and added, 'The initiative, I think, must come from Europe.'

Bevin welcomed the proposal eight days later, on 13 June.

'He had been looking for a chance to catch the Americans on that,' explained Healey. 'The Americans themselves didn't regard the speech made at Harvard as much more than waffling aloud, but Ernie seized on it as an American "offer" that Europe should respond to.'

The report and plan drawn up by the Europeans for the European Recovery Programme were given to Marshall on 22 September 1947, and the Organization for European Economic Co-operation (O.E.E.C.) was set up to administer it.

The plan, together with the Brussels Treaty and the stationing of American B29s with atomic bombs in East Anglia in 1948, led to the formal NATO alliance, established on 4 April 1949. This was the first post-war alliance linking the two North American powers to the defence of the Western democracies. Bevin had taken the cold dregs of wartime collaboration and cemented them into a big power relationship. Britain's freedom to act was curtailed by her need for an American prop. Her influence in the world would prosper only if she could milk the special relationship with the United States for all it was worth. With the coming of the superpowers the old idea of 'balance of power' diplomacy gave way to 'alliance diplomacy'. It was a new form of diplomacy which Healey could see at close quarters from its inception, and which he was to practise in the 1960s.

One Healey contribution to the general spirit of construction was his pamphlet *Feet on the Ground* (discussed in Chapter Six). It was another important foreign policy contribution – he never spoke or wrote on domestic affairs, although friends advised him to go and look at drains if he wanted to broaden his outlook and further his career.

It was much in line with the thinking of Dalton, to whom he was very close on matters of policy – with the exception of Germany and German rearmament. Dalton was very anti-German and pro-French. Healey, who saw the need for the Germans to join the Western allies after the war, was himself 'anti'-German big business and cartels, but he played an important part in encouraging German socialists.

'I was responsible for getting Schumacher invited to England,' he explained. 'It was the first time any German politician had been invited abroad after the war. The anti-German feeling all over Europe at that time was terrifying.'

'Dalton was very much against my inviting Schumacher here – he looked just like Frederick the Great, and was a typical Prussian type of Social Democrat. He was very tough, and really stood up for his country – he had fought against the Nazis. But he was very good, for he gave the German S.P.D. a sense of dignity after the war, and almost anybody with any common sense will have recognized that since the war Germany is the most important country on the Continent. Their problem is the most dangerous in Europe, and encouraging decent Germans, as well as creating good relations with them is absolutely critical.'

His friendship with Willy Brandt blossomed when, in 1947, Healey became the London correspondent (at £3 a week) of the Norwegian Labour paper, *Arbeider bladet*. Brandt was its correspondent in Germany. It was the start of a weekly column for Healey, which he continued until October 1964, by which time he had become a successful journalist, selling the column to a large number of foreign newspapers.

As 'backroom boy' he stood next to the great men of socialist politics in Britain and Europe.

Daniel Norman said that Healey struck him as 'an efficient hard worker with a really quick mind who really knew his dossier'. He added: 'He was also honest and had integrity – one cannot ask more of a politician.'

Ciolcosz was impressed by 'his clear thinking, and his acceptance of ideas, which he sticks to until the weight of the evidence is such that he must change them'. He continued: 'He can also take decisions – and in difficult conditions.'

Others who knew him at the time were also attracted by his lack of pretence and exhibitionism together with his zeal.

Healey was able to observe at close quarters the fighting in the Cabinet among Labour leaders.

'Ernie had a hard fight except that he had the support from Attlee right through. Dalton on the whole supported him, but Laski was unsympathetic to Ernie's policy, and to the Government's policy, all the time. Ernie really had a difficult job getting support in the Cabinet and in the Party.'

There were many others from whom Healey learned. At the Foreign Office, apart from Bevin and McNeil there were Mayhew and Younger. Morgan Phillips encouraged him, and he was very close to miners' leader Sam Watson, who succeeded Dalton as Chairman of the International Sub-committee of the Party. He got to know many who, like himself, were on the way up – such as trade union leader Vic Feather.

He did not always like what he saw. For example, when he prepared the pamphlet *European Unity* for the National Executive – 'Dalton wrote in some of the more savagely anti-European remarks'. Nor did he agree with the Government's handling of the Palestine problem. But that was policy. His main dislike concerned the personalities.

'Cliques almost crippled the Labour Party under Attlee. Almost everyone was in a clique; some were in as many as six. Each Minister seemed to have a private army of supporters numbering from twelve to twenty. I thought it was a terribly bad thing at the time, and I have always been determined never to be a clique man.'

It suited his temperament to walk alone. He was self-sufficient, and knew where he wanted to go. Daniel Norman summed him up when he said, 'His aloofness from cliques is his strength. One cannot have real power if one is not oneself.'

Denis Healey had served his political apprenticeship.

Chapter Four

Trouble at t' Mill

'The selection process was rigged.'
JOHN RAFFERTY, ex-Lord Mayor of Leeds.

'Denis Healey owes his seat to me.'
SOLLY PEARCE, C.B.E.

Chapter Four

COUNCILLOR John Rafferty, the Acting Chairman of Leeds Labour Party, had been in the Party thirty-three years when he stood against the thirty-four-year-old Healey at the conference for selecting the South East Leeds Parliamentary candidate. Rafferty was, at fifty-three, an orator with a real gift of eloquence, and a hold over the Party. He was convinced as he entered the selection conference that it was in the bag. He failed to consider the opposition of Solly Pearce, the veteran behind the scenes of Leeds socialism.

Solly, who, when he finally retired, had been associated with the Labour Party newspaper *Leeds Weekly Citizen* for forty-five years and its editor for twenty-six, got his C.B.E. through Clement Attlee in 1951 for political and public services. As editor of the right-of-centre newspaper, with Jewish and tailoring connections, he was a good example of the moderate and influential forces controlling the Party in Leeds.

When Major James Milner, the M.P. for Leeds South East, and Deputy Speaker of the House of Commons, failed to become Speaker and opted for a peerage, it meant a by-election in the constituency that had been Labour since Jim O'Grady won it in 1906.

'Solly had always wanted Leeds to be the best represented city in the House,' explained the Rt Hon. Charles Pannell, M.P. for West Leeds. 'He didn't want simply anybody to get it. The main contender was Rafferty, a propagandist, a great Tammany figure. And the Establishment didn't want Rafferty.'

Solly Pearce, who knew of Healey's 1945 bid to win Pudsey and Otley, got to know him when he was at Transport House. He had written articles for the newspaper, and had been helpful whenever Solly wanted assistance. Sarah Barker, the Yorkshire Regional Women's Officer for the Labour Party, told him that Healey had been thinking of giving up his Transport House job, and going into Parliament.

As Healey explained: 'After 1950 I became more interested and committed in politics. I realized that if I wanted to influence what went on there was no other satisfactory way of doing it. I decided not to try for a seat until after the 1951 election, and then this fantastic piece of good fortune arose, that a seat where I had contacts and was known became vacant because Milner went to the Lords.'

When Solly saw that Rafferty might win the seat he started to do something about it.

'I found that a candidate, John Rafferty, had already been selected for the vacancy, and it was cut and dried for him. I decided to get in touch with Denis, who was on the Continent at the time. My letter chased him from Strasbourg to Brussels, where I telephoned and asked if he would be willing to let his name go forward as a candidate.'

Healey agreed.

'I was at a conference with Jim Griffiths, and I sent a telegram. Jim knew nothing of this, and when I told him that I had just been asked to go forward in Leeds he was very taken aback. The Executive didn't want me to run. They didn't want anybody from Transport House to run, and they put every obstacle in my path. They were running their own man – Aidan Crawley.'

Aidan Crawley, the junior Minister who had lost his seat in the General Election of 1950, and later returned to the Commons as a Tory M.P., was the least of Solly Pearce's worries.

'Trouble started the moment Denis agreed to stand,' he explained. 'Transport House was a dirty word in those days, so he was taboo. The first real difficulty was to get him the nomination.'

Solly's right-wing Jewish tailoring friends were helpful here. Then there was the struggle to get him on the short list.

In 'safe' seats like Leeds South East the M.P. is not so much elected as chosen – by a handful of men and women. Solly knew this and got to work on the people who mattered.

'Getting Denis on the short list involved me in so much work that visitors were constantly calling on me from all over the division. A number of people didn't want Rafferty, although he was a good street corner orator with a streak of common sense, because they thought he had personal weaknesses. I therefore had to undermine some of his supporters.'

Healey himself explained that the move to get him selected was more an anti-Rafferty brigade than a pro-Healey one:

'The strongest candidate was Rafferty, who had just as many enemies as friends. He thought he had it made, but the people who wanted to keep him out were all working for me. There were some who knew me personally from my campaign in Pudsey in 1945, and others who had friends who knew me. The main thing was that they thought I was the strongest chap to defeat Rafferty.

'I wasn't conscious of the background politicking that was going on. I was very much a figure-head in it because I wasn't able to spend much time in Leeds as I was still working at Transport House. I was close to Solly Pearce, but it was entirely a struggle within the Leeds City Party, and I was in the hands of the anti-Rafferty faction.'

The fight was not entirely a local squabble, however, as the National Executive of the Labour Party had their own candidate, Aidan Crawley, and they wanted to get Crawley back, but they did not have much influence. Hugh Gaitskell, who had been Chancellor and was a Leeds M.P., tried hard, but he had very little personal influence in the city.

Solly Pearce was approached by Gaitskell.

'Hugh rang me and said: "I would like you to use your influence on behalf of Crawley." I had to say, "I'm sorry, but I'm working for Denis Healey." I don't think he was aware that I was trying to get Denis in. Crawley gave the best socialist speech to the selection conference – but it didn't do him any good.'

Solly and Hugh were not the only prominent Socialists canvassing the selectors, however, as the Rt Hon. Alice Bacon, another Leeds M.P., guardedly admitted. 'I did have a lot to do with the conference,' she said. Her explanation that 'Denis got the seat because he was well-known through having fought Pudsey and being a Yorkshire person', is nothing like the whole truth.

The key to the whole struggle probably lies in what Charlie Pannell said about Solly Pearce: 'He doesn't possess the power he thinks he does, but he was the prime mover for Denis. And, he didn't want simply anybody to get it.'

Solly was typical of the Leeds Establishment. As Councillor Jack Pritchard said: 'Leeds constituencies have always taken selection meetings seriously. They will choose a good man rather than a sponsored trade union man who will merely help the funds. They are really more concerned with ability.'

Malcolm Barker, Deputy Editor of the Conservative *Yorkshire Post*, summed up the city's feeling of civic pride: 'A good constituency man from Leeds is sent forth into the world like a son from a village.'

The Leeds constituencies, as Alice Bacon agreed, 'like a high flier'. With Government Ministers like Pannell, Bacon (who was also Party Chairman), Sir Keith Joseph, and Party leader Hugh Gaitskell all serving the area at the same time as Healey, the point is obvious.

But it was not obvious when the selection committee met that Healey should be the 'high flier' to represent them. The forty delegates had to choose between John Rafferty, the local working man who had spoken eloquently at every by-election in Yorkshire since 1926, Aidan Crawley, the ex-Minister from outside the city, Councillor Victor Wiseman, the radical left-wing sociology lecturer who later became a Professor, and Healey, the man with the Yorkshire education, a double First from Oxford – and the stigma of Transport House. Two other faithful servants of the Party stood no chance against such a formidable array of talent.

The Labour Party ruling that the candidate selected must have an overall majority meant that on the first ballot – where Aidan Crawley picked up only three votes – there was no clear leader.

Reduced to a field of three – Rafferty, Wiseman, and Healey – a bizarre note crept into the selection. Rafferty, who still thought he was a winner, polled twenty votes. Wiseman had ten. Healey also had ten. Rafferty did not have the overall majority to clinch it. And his own daughter, Brenda, stopped him from getting it.

Before the conference John Rafferty had said to Brenda: 'Whatever happens, don't vote for anyone but your father.' But, when it came to the vote between Wiseman and Healey to decide which of them should be put against Rafferty, Brenda did vote, and Wiseman and Healey tied with twenty votes each. Had they not tied, one of them would have had to fight it out with Rafferty on the spot.

With twenty committed at the time to Rafferty, who needed only a single vote for victory, it seems probable that but for the double tie he would have left the conference as the next M.P. designate.

The decision of Chairman Ernest Morris to adjourn the meeting for three weeks sealed Rafferty's fate.

Charles Pannell respectfully described the Chairman as 'a significant local figure'. Rafferty bitterly recollected: 'There was a lad in the chair . . . he had not been in the Party a quarter of an hour.'

But Pannell conceded: 'John Anson and Len Williams (Party officials) should have suggested a half-hour adjournment. Rafferty was disadvantaged by the Establishment who didn't want him. During the next three weeks Denis's supporters gained ground. Denis was a dark horse – they didn't know how good or bad a Catholic he was.' (This last was an important point in the politics of East Leeds, where Rafferty was known to be a lapsed R.C.) Healey, however, had never been a Roman Catholic.

At the conference in January Rafferty again topped the poll on the first vote without gaining an absolute majority. Wiseman, who had fallen into third place, then dropped out. In the final vote Healey nudged ahead of Rafferty and the Acting Chairman of Leeds Labour Party was out, beaten by Solly's friends, the intellectuals and the right-wing majority (for example, the four Amalgamated Engineering Union delegates had been persuaded to vote for Healey by an influential ex-Alderman acting on behalf of the Party Office).

Rafferty complained at the time: 'There has been a gang-up against me since the first meeting. These three weeks have been utilized by certain elements working round support against me. Everyone in the city thought I would be the candidate. I feel that my thirty-three years in the movement have been thrown in my face.'

He stated to the *Bradford Observer* that the working-class members of the Party had an inferiority complex, and were 'swept off their feet' by intellectuals like Healey.

Apart from my personal disappointment, this decision is a tragedy for the Division,' he said.

In 1970 he still asserted: 'The selection process was rigged, although Denis was perfectly innocent of it.' But adding: 'I am pleased now. I don't think I could have kept up that kind of pace. Denis has been a credit to Leeds.'

From Dark Horse to Favourite

Healey began the campaign as front runner. The *Leeds Weekly Citizen*, of course, stressed his links with the locality and his distinguished record. But Healey himself showed he lacked the common touch and feel for local politics by contributing an article which began: '1952 will probably mark a turning-point in world affairs. If the Western countries stick to the rearmament programmes which they have now begun, the balance of power should turn during the next twelve months in favour of the democratic world. . .'

Many people were to comment on his seeming lack of interest in ordinary everyday bread-and-butter affairs which the average constituent cares about, talks about, and votes about. As Party worker Dorothy Harrison remembered: 'He didn't seem to know very much about ordinary affairs in the first few years.'

The gulf between him and the rank and file became clear to him at his first Ward meeting. He was introduced as having worked in Transport House, and one of the members said, 'Oh, have you worked on the trams as well?'

But, to Douggie Gabb, constituency secretary and later his agent, 'It was not a question of nursing the constituency at all. It was only a matter of time.'

Because time was short Healey needed money quickly to help finance his campaign. His closest friend in Leeds today, a Jewish warehouse owner, and artistic intellectual, Bernard Gillinson, helped.

'After he had been selected he was sent to me by Solly Pearce for some money to fight his campaign. Denis came into my office wearing a well-worn Anthony Eden hat, which we've never seen him in since. I agreed to give him £50. I supported Denis because he was Labour. I didn't know anything about him but from that time we became, almost immediately, friends.'

Healey needed the money for his campaign literature. Following a man with the common touch – Milner had fought for the unemployed for many years – he seemed, at first, a bit remote. He was opposed by Charles Kirwan, a Leeds schoolmaster. Mindful of the large Roman Catholic vote in the constituency Kirwan posed for a photograph with his wife and family, and a madonna in the background.

Healey concentrated on his Yorkshire background. Alice Bacon introduced him at his opening meeting as Yorkshire born and bred. She justified her description of him being a Yorkshireman through and through by remarking on his ability to sing a song called 'Dahn in t'coil 'oil' at dull international conferences.

Healey – who was born in Kent – emphasized the 'bred' aspect. One of his campaign leaflets smoothly confirmed – 'Our candidate spent his early years at Keighley'.

Healey, quoted by Hugh Dalton in the *Daily Herald* as 'one of our great authorities on international affairs', opened his campaign with a speech on British and American foreign policy; but his personal campaign leaflet showed the influence of his wife, Edna. After talking about national and world crises he made the expected slashing attack on the brief Tory record: partial charges for dental and medical treatment, hire purchase restrictions, and a cut in the meat ration, were all ammunition for the prospective M.P. He was not complacent. As his mother explained: 'He didn't think it was a foregone conclusion because Kirwan, the local man, was a Roman Catholic fighting very hard.'

Douggie Gabb, describing the campaign as 'quite lively', admitted: 'We had a bit of trouble once or twice with the British National Party in York Road.' *The Times*, however, commented on 5 February that the election 'has not aroused any great interest'.

The day of the election, 6 February, was overshadowed by the death of King George VI. The *Daily Herald* observed: 'The South East Leeds by-election will probably go down in history as the quietest Parliamentary election ever known in the city.'

Only 55·7 per cent of the electorate of 48,826 voted, compared to a turn-out of 84 per cent in the General Election the previous October. Healey polled 17,194 votes to Kirwan's 9,995 – a majority of 7,199, and a swing to Labour of 2·7 per cent. Announcing the result, the *Yorkshire Post* remarked: 'The lack of interest which has marked the campaign continued until the end.'

But the result was convincing.

Solly Pearce could justifiably say that Denis Healey owed his seat to him. A fact which Healey acknowledged when he became Secretary of State for Defence in 1964. He wrote to Solly on official Ministry of Defence paper: 'If it had not been for you I should not be writing on this paper today.'

Healey admitted that he was lucky that the Leeds seat came vacant when it did.

'I can't think of a seat which came up in the next two or three years where I would have stood as good a chance.'

Once elected, however, it was expected that he should go out and stamp the name of Leeds on the legislative capital of the land.

'He was so obviously an outstanding chap, even then,' said Solly. 'He had already written a number of speeches for M.P.s, and given the necessary background information to others for their speeches. He was not going to be an ordinary back-bench M.P. . . . I knew he would make his mark.'

Agreement to Disagree

In the Commons Healey quickly became prominent in foreign affairs. In November 1954 he joined Attlee, Morrison, and Gaitskell as official Opposition speaker on the front bench for the two-day debate on European affairs.

The issue of the *Leeds Weekly Citizen* that had announced Healey's selection as Parliamentary candidate, however, also carried an item about something that was to contribute to Healey's problems in the city he represented. It announced that John Archer had been appointed Leeds and District Organizer for the National Council of Labour Colleges. Archer joined a band of left-wingers, Bevanites, Communists, and Trotskyists that gave Healey a very rough time in the years ahead.

On 23 April 1951, Minister of Health Aneurin Bevan, the orator who posed as a workers' champion, resigned from the Labour Cabinet, partly because his ability to influence policy seemed to have lessened and this move gave him scope to organize an opposing force. The occasion was the imposition of charges on teeth and spectacles, but he broadened this into an attack on the growing expenditure of rearmament to fight the Korean War and possibly prepare for a Communist push in Europe. Harold Wilson and John Freeman resigned with him; but Bevan's resignation meant that left-wing M.P.s now had a leader.

The Left, a collection of Christian Socialists, pacifists, Marxists, Communists, fellow travellers, Trotskyists, and syndicalists, had opposed the right-winger Ernest Bevin in his pro-American foreign policy. Bevin, a bitter and determined anti-Communist, had seen the need for alliance with the United States to safeguard Britain's interests and secure the Commonwealth. The violently anti-capitalist Left confused American social domestic policy with their foreign policy, and hated Bevin. In May 1947 they had produced *Keep Left*, an attack on the Government's foreign and defence policies, which Healey then defended in his pro-American *Cards on the Table*. After the Soviet expansion in Eastern Europe in 1947–8, and the Berlin Airlift of 1948–9, the Left produced *Keeping Left* (1950), which reluctantly accepted the alliance with the United States.

Bevan's resignation, however, revitalized the Left, especially in the constituencies, where the demand for 'socialist' policies at home and abroad grew in strength, and threatened to split the Party. There was growing publicity for what Attlee called 'a party within a party'. Douggie Gabb, whom Healey called 'a near Trotskyite at the beginning' confessed that, as Healey's agent, he used to keep the Trots alive – 'the Party is big enough for both'. In Gabb's opinion, 'The Party is on the left of Denis – even today.' He explained: 'He is popular as a person. He could never have been an M.P. in East Leeds if his policies were the most important consideration.'

In foreign policy, the only subject Healey spoke about in his first three years as an M.P., he was consistently opposed by many of his constituents. As Gabb said, 'We have never gone to a Party Conference with a deep resolution he believed in.'

The constituency had been against the United States going into the Korean War in June 1950, and against sending in British troops. But, as Gabb admitted, 'Jim Milner did not really have any strong opinions on foreign affairs.'

Healey argued in the 1952 *New Fabian Essays* that Britain

needed a strong commitment to the United States through NATO, and he rejected the idea of a 'socialist foreign policy' as being irrelevant, given the anarchical nature of international politics.

The issue of German rearmament, which affected Healey locally and nationally, was symptomatic of his battle with the Party. His constituency was against it. Peter O'Grady, the present (1970) left-wing Chairman of the Leeds East Constituency Party, explained:

'The Left were opposed to it, but debated how best to handle it. The Communist Party were opposed to it, and would unite with anybody who agreed with them, on the basis that the end justified the means. Others took a different line, and wanted to oppose German rearmament as well as withdrawing British troops.'

Healey was in favour of German rearmament within the framework of NATO, so he fought both groups.

'When I spoke out on German rearmament my own constituency banged in a resolution to Transport House exactly contradicting what I'd said the same afternoon.'

It was against this troubled background that Healey had to compete for a new seat in East Leeds in 1955. Because of boundary revisions Leeds would have only six seats, instead of seven. There were two possible Labour seats in East Leeds, but none of the three Labour members was willing to stand down.

'After the redrawing of the boundaries in 1955 we had a bit of a fight,' said Solly Pearce. 'One M.P. had to go. I decided that Denis and Alice had to stay. George Porter had to go. He was ready for retiring, but he didn't want to.'

Porter, a representative of the Woodworkers' Union, had little local support. His attachment was to Liverpool. When the Leeds City Bill was debated in the Commons he made one of his rare speeches, referring to 'this great city of Liverpool' – but meaning Leeds. But the Left in Leeds hoped to use the opportunity of the decrease in the number of seats to unseat a right-winger – Gaitskell, Pannell, Bacon, or Healey.

Healey was the most vulnerable. As he explained: 'The Left in Leeds, who were pretty well organized by this time, were gibbering with rage that, with an agreement to get rid of Porter, they would be left with the "prime demons" of left-wing demonology. They were determined to be rid of one of us, and they knew this was most possible in the new East Leeds, which was three of my old wards and two of Alice's. I agreed to let Alice have the easier constituency, and take my chance there.'

Alice Bacon said: 'Some of the left-wingers, who didn't care two hoots for George Porter, were trying to get him in because they could get rid of him quickly, then put a well-known left-winger in. Whereas if they got Denis or me they would be stuck with us for years.'

When Porter, who was in his seventies, eventually succumbed or gave up his seat the Left hoped that Victor Wiseman would be able to move in.

The forces of the Right were marshalling again, however, as they had done for the original selection of Healey.

'We decided Denis should have East Leeds, and Alice South East Leeds,' said Solly Pearce. 'We tipped off Denis's friends in South East Leeds and they helped choose Alice as prospective candidate.'

Then Healey had to face the selectors in East Leeds.

'Everything was against me. The constituency Party was extremely left-wing – there were very few who were moderate at all; it was the middle of the Bevanite row; and John Anson, the Regional Organizer, told the Party they had a free choice, and that they had no need to listen to the sitting candidate before they cast their net wider.'

Healey believed that this was incompetent and a mistake. Peter O'Grady, Chairman of the constituency and left-winger, thought that it was a deliberate ploy of Anson's designed to ensure a second selection conference, which would then be held after Alice Bacon was home and dry in South East Leeds.

Healey didn't give much for his chances. At the second selection conference, held because the Left had followed Anson's hint and suggested another conference with a long short-list, delegates were told by Sarah Barker from Transport House that Anson had been wrong.

'They had at least to listen to me, and *then* they could reject me,' explained Healey.

Just prior to the meeting, as Healey put it, 'Bevan opposed the Party line on SEATO. But it wasn't only that he opposed it – he rushed into the House while Clem Attlee was actually talking, trod on Clem's toes, then immediately got up and made the opposite point.'

At a meeting of the Parliamentary Labour Party on the Wednesday before the week-end selection conference in East Leeds the P.L.P. voted to withdraw the whip from Bevan.

'The first question they asked me at the selection was "How did you vote over withdrawing the whip?" I told them that they had no right to ask me how I had voted at a private meeting of the P.L.P., but "since you have asked me, I'll tell you. I voted for withdrawing the whip" and I added, "if anybody on the city council behaved like that, it wouldn't matter which side of the argument you were on, you would do the same." It was the most ticklish moment of my political life to date.'

Healey was chosen as prospective candidate by a two to one majority. When it came to a call to arms the Left were outnumbered. There was a joke in left-wing circles that the veteran George Murray, a moderate, had gone round the graveyards crying, 'Bring out your dead!' to get the voters. Alice Bacon had asked her friends in the wards that had been transferred to East Leeds from her old division to vote for Healey, and they had done so. On 21 March 1955, Healey was adopted as prospective candidate.

In the quiet campaign leading up to the General Election of 26 May 1955, there were more apparent differences within the Labour Party than between the Tories and Labour. Bevan conducted his own campaign and did not work with Transport House. The Tories exploited the rift in their *Campaign Guide* which contained more entries under Bevan's name than under Attlee or Eden, its own new leader. Attlee was caricatured in the popular right-wing press as being the tool of Bevan.

'The public conviction that we were a divided Party, always quarrelling with one another, did us immense harm, and probably was most responsible for keeping us out of office for so long,' admitted Healey.

The Tory Party also had a much superior organization. This looked like being of crucial significance in Healey's new constituency. As the *Yorkshire Post* commented: 'This new division of East Leeds is in the category of the more-or-less marginal. Mr Donald Chapman, aided by his wife and an efficient local organization is going great guns.'

The result of the local government elections in early May showed that, adding up the votes cast in East Leeds, the Conservatives had a majority over Labour of 760.

Healey worked hard. In speeches he attacked the Tory slogan of 'Peace and Prosperity' as meaning prosperity only for the few. He spoke all over the constituency, working for those few extra votes that might make all the difference. He astonished Barnbow workers at six o'clock one morning by being at the gates handing out leaflets saying he would speak there at lunchtime.

The election result, which gave the Tories a national majority of 55, sent Denis Healey back to Westminster with almost a 5,000 majority. Of a total electorate of 61,944 Healey had received support from 26,083 compared to his opponent's 21,144.

Healey's victory at the polls was again the start of a troubled period, which was to culminate with a Party member taking the Party to court for wrongful expulsion. Alice Bacon noted: 'Most of the Trotskyites in Leeds were in Denis's constituency.' Peter O'Grady said: 'Denis faced a new constituency, and the Bevan expulsion was a signal for all Left groups. There were all sorts opposing him: C.P. members, fellow travellers, Trots, and Bevanites.

'It was easy to lambast the Communists by looking at the U.S.S.R., but the Trotskyites were equally anti-Russian and were a problem,' O'Grady continued. 'There were factions within factions, and they were wholly united only in their opposition to the foreign policy of the Party. But there were really heated debates, concerned with political issues, and the Left would try to broaden the debate. Neither Hugh Gaitskell nor any other M.P. had the problems of East Leeds.'

Healey, however, as many protagonists admitted, was 'a good man for the rough and tumble of constituency fights'. He refused to stand on his dignity, and took every opportunity to mix it with the Left.

'Denis did a lot of debating with the constituency,' said his agent. 'We didn't expect a good M.P. to agree with his constituents all the time.'

The arrangement was an agreement to disagree.

'I've often said to them what Frederick the Great's general said to Frederick when he was ordered into an impossible attack: "Please tell his majesty that after the battle my head's at his disposal, but during the battle I propose to use it in his service." I told them that when the election came along they could chuck me out, but until then I intended to do what I thought best.

'I have always been a representative, never a delegate,' said Healey.

Personally Speaking . . .

Unlike many constituencies that have either removed or tried to remove their M.P.s for holding views contrary to the majority of the leading Party members, East Leeds tolerated Healey. His personal standing with many of the rank and file is largely responsible for this tolerance of Healey's right-wing stance on foreign affairs.

He is regarded as a professional politician who is also a shy man. He joins the Party faithful for a cup of tea, or a supper of fish and chips. In his political conflicts he does not bear grudges, and he aims to maintain good personal relations. Compared to Gaitskell, the Party leader after 1955, he had appeared flexible and open to argument. He has a reputation for helping anyone who approached him with a problem. As Derek Foster, News Editor of the *Yorkshire Post*, admitted, 'He has the common touch.'

One admiring female Party worker succinctly expressed it: 'If he could, he would be at everybody's christening, everybody's wedding.'

In the working men's clubs – and he is honorary president of several – there is no awed hush when Healey enters; he is accepted as just another member.

The feeling of personal goodwill is further strengthened by the work done by Edna Healey. Healey, with his ruthless honesty, once gave little weight to the work done by his wife in the constituency from a vote-getting point of view.

'An M.P.'s wife might make twenty-five votes difference if she's lucky,' admitted Edna.

But to Healey's agent she is 'the kind of wife an M.P. needs if he means to be successful. She is at least as good a speaker, if not better.'

Some constituents even think that Edna should be the M.P.

She is seen as the real public relations officer, with more tact and 'style' than Denis. Edna's work, however, is all for Denis. She is extremely ambitious for him, more than he is for himself. Although he is sometimes personally naïve, Edna is not – she is tougher and more realistic, and not so intellectually detached.

Healey, who is a complex character, however, seems an actor to many of his constituents, as much as in the Commons. He is personally remote, some feel, listening to no-one apart from his wife and his own intellect. He is emotionally 'cold'. Although not aloof, he can be detached. He is arrogant without being conceited. In the constituency, Peter O'Grady noted that 'his smile is the prelude to a tough reply, and he does it afterwards as well. It is both an anaesthetic and post-operational sedative.' Edna says it is a nervous habit.

One local commentator surmised that its automatic nature was caused by his feeling that he was surrounded by morons to whom he had to show attitudes he did not really own. It is perhaps truer to say that Healey rarely feels confident enough to let himself go emotionally. He acts instead. His laughter, for instance, disguises a host of feelings apart from mere amusement – procrastination, embarrassment, self-congratulation as well as being designed to set an opponent at his ease before thrusting a verbal knife in.

Healey's truer feeling for his constituency is shown in his choice of personal friends. Bernard Gillinson, perhaps the closest, is usually host when Healey makes his monthly pilgrimage to Leeds to meet constituents and hear their problems. Gillinson, like Healey, is a radical, and was very left-wing in the 1930s before the Soviet attack on Finland. He was Chairman of the Governors of the College of Art, and his home in a fashionable part of Leeds is crammed with works of art. Detached from Party politics he is interested in history and Zionism.

'When Denis first came to stay there was immediate rapport on an intellectual basis and I can't say that in many ways it has advanced a lot beyond that,' said Gillinson.

'It is difficult to get to know him, because I think that I am like him, too. I am not a man of warm emotions. I like to meet people on a level that I choose. I think he is really a great intellectual, not a politician. In almost any field you like he is much more than just a dilettante.

'One of the most amazing things about Denis is that he has almost complete recall; he has a fantastic memory. Even detective stories, which he will read in half an hour, he knows absolutely. He is a good friend with little sentiment, and certainly no sentimentality. When he buys me a Christmas present he doesn't just send his secretary out to buy it, but he goes out himself to a second-hand bookshop, and finds just *the* book which he knows I want. He always finds something I haven't got – despite my vast library.'

The intellectual Healey delights in the company of Gillinson and his friends. Gillinson arranged parties called 'Off the Record' for postgraduates and lecturers from Leeds University. He was generally sensitive and gentle with the students, but could be brutal and deliberately devastating with lecturers who had too high an opinion of themselves.

Healey also preferred the fine food and wine of the Gillinson household, a place where he could be 'comfortable' in Leeds. It was a sanctuary to which he could retreat after one of his personal appearances in the clubs. The reason-loving and calculating Healey knew that certain formulae had to be adhered to in a marginally Labour constituency. His coarseness and use of four-letter words were out of place with more general refinements of his character. His sincerity, however, pervades his whole personality. As Dorothy Harrison said: 'He is just the same as he was when he was elected. He never gets swollen headed.'

Malcolm Barker, *Yorkshire Post* Deputy Editor, summed up the Leeds feeling when he said, 'Everybody thinks he is most human; you never hear a wrong word about Healey.'

Dr Dilys Hill, an expert on local government, explained that 'Leeds does not seem to demand that people become good constituency M.P.s. They don't want their M.P.s to interfere in local government.' But it was surprising that he should have survived in a constituency with such a left-wing hard core.

As Healey himself said: 'I had awful trouble in my constituency for years. The left wing were Trotskyite and the right were Bevanite.' The secret of his survival lay partly in the personality of himself and his wife, and partly in the local

7

attitude that said – as John Edwards, the *Yorkshire Post* Editor, judged: 'We sent him down there, and he is doing a grand job.'

The row with his constituency Party was summarized by the agent, Douggie Gabb: 'Denis is more of an Atlantic man; the majority of his constituents were, and still are, against alliance with the United States.'

On Germany, NATO and the nuclear deterrent battle raged loud and long. But the result, although wearing for Healey, was greater interest and enthusiasm in the constituency.

'We used to get seventy to eighty people at Sunday meetings,' said Gabb.

'Morale was exceptionally high,' said O'Grady. 'It was never higher than when it was boiling with controversy. Although the Left would attempt to change the policies, they worked extremely hard for the Party.'

The Purge

In 1959 the vast conservative forces of the Leeds Labour Party decided that it was time to settle the issue of the dissident left wing.

The Leeds clothing industry has a considerable influence in local politics, fabric being the main manufacture of the city's half-million population. The solid, Yorkshire doggedness and grit exist in fair measure in the conservative industrial base of Leeds society. The city, which had a broad enough industrial base to withstand the full horrors of the 1930s slump, lacks any tradition of really radical militancy.

The closely-knit Labour Party and trade union bureaucracy fostered important right-wing Labour M.P.s Gaitskell, Pannell, Healey and Bacon. At the end of the fifties the Left could rely on almost one-third of the vote at city Party meetings. The formation of the Socialist Labour League (S.L.L.) provided the Establishment with an opportunity to settle matters.

On 11 April 1959, the Executive Committee of Leeds City Party expelled Councillor Ronald Sedler, Councillor Lance Lake, and seven East Leeds left-wingers because of their 'known association' with the Left's *Newsletter* and the S.L.L., both of which had been proscribed by the National Party. The thirty-four-year-old Sedler, a solicitor, engaged another to write to Leeds Labour Party alleging that the expulsion was legally invalid because: (1) he had not had the charges, nor a chance to defend himself, and (2) only the General Management Committee and not the E.C. could have expelled him. This was the first known allegation of illegal expulsion made against the Party, and the national *Tribune* took up the case to save its left-wing supporters.

The E.C. backed down when Sedler issued a writ against them and held a meeting to 'try' the men and women all of whom had attended a non-Labour Party meeting at the Adelphi hotel which was used as the basis for the allegations. The trial was a farce. Sedler, who, it was alleged on the charge sheet, was an elected member of the S.L.L., walked out because he was given only five minutes in which to defend himself, and not allowed to call witnesses. The G.M.C. then voted 115 in favour of his expulsion, and 42 against.

Lance Lake who stayed to address the meeting was acquitted by 83 votes to 64 with several abstentions. His thirty years work for the Party, including his chairmanship of the local Party branch, were probably taken into account.

He wrote to *Tribune*: 'As to why I escaped I am not clear. On paper my "crimes" were as bad as the others.'

He suggested that his evidence, which was substantially the same as Sedler's – i.e., they had severed their connections with the proscribed bodies as soon at the National Executive had announced their ban – was only accepted because of his service. He was called before the Leeds E.C. to explain his action in writing to *Tribune*.

Because all the charges put to him at the G.M.C. meeting had not been on the charge sheet presented beforehand Sedler threatened further legal action.

A final act of the elaborate drama was called for. The National Executive sent a delegation to hear Sedler. The list of charges presented to him, to be heard before Jim Griffiths and Ray Gunter, had grown. He was accused of being 'dissident and disruptive, supporting resolutions contrary to Party policy or majority decisions already taken, giving interviews and publicity to Tory newspapers, associating with Communists, supporting the extreme left-winger Forbes Burnham (of British Guiana) at meetings, opposing the Party's Conference decision in favour of German rearmament . . . etc.'

In short, for not toeing the line and agreeing with the ruling group of the City Labour Party.

'I had to treat seriously charges with a strong Alice-in-Wonderland flavour about them,' said Sedler.

He was expelled from the Party, said Morgan Phillips in a letter to him, for being 'dissident and disruptive'.

With his expulsion Mr and Mrs Gale, Mr and Mrs Archer, Slaughter, Harding and Walls – all from East Leeds – were also out.

'The rank and file were glad to see them go,' confessed Arthur Harrison. 'They were always troublemakers.'

Healey's role in the affair was described by O'Grady, who had been at the meeting in the Adelphi, but slipped through the net.

'Denis did not want to know. He did not want to be involved. He left the handling of the situation to the local Party. He took the line that it was best left to the experts, and by brute force and ignorance they got results.'

Many of those who were expelled drifted off to other cities like London or Liverpool, where they worked to form new left-wing factions. One or two, like Cliff Slaughter, stayed for a few years lecturing at the university, while his wife ran a coffee bar for Young Socialists whom the moderates still regarded as dangerous left-wing.

Healey fought the Election in October 1959 secure in the knowledge that the main trouble in the constituency had been rooted out. He was becoming a national figure. He had just returned from a visit to Moscow with Gaitskell and Bevan. He had the local problem of getting the many new electors in the great Seacroft housing estate to the polls. Although the electorate had swollen by 4,000, however, Healey secured 28,707 votes to J. A. Fawcett's 23,922 – a majority of 4,785.

The constituency has continued to lean towards the Left. At the time of the Campaign for Nuclear Disarmament's ban-the-bomb controversy, East Leeds Constituency Party not only backed the C.N.D. line while Denis was making one of the most important pro-Gaitskell speeches against them, but it also passed a resolution calling for the withdrawal from NATO as well. Like many in the Labour Party the constituents were split about entry into the Common Market. But while Healey was opposing entry they came out in favour of joining. This has always been the pattern made in a good-humoured fashion by Healey and the militant constituents he represents.

In the early sixties Healey was a member of the Shadow Cabinet, and shared the popularity of the Labour Party as Conservatives dithered and appeared almost incapable of firm leadership in the era of technological change and revolution.

Under Harold Wilson's leadership the Party captured the middle ground of British politics, and in the election of 1964 Healey again defeated Fawcett; this time by 29,840 to 21,434, a majority just over 8,000. Becoming the governing party lessened the scope for criticism and self-analysis which had characterized the Party for more than a dozen years. The constituency continued to criticize the Government and Healey for 'not being socialist enough', but in a quieter fashion. And in February 1966, the Party officially re-admitted the renegade Ronald Sedler to its ranks without fuss.

Mrs Dorothy Harrison summarized the feeling among the rank and file when she said: 'Denis has learnt much more about things like economics and union affairs since he became a Cabinet Minister.'

Her husband, Arthur, summed up the Left's attitude to Healey as Defence Minister: 'We had thought he would become Foreign Secretary, but I think he has done a good job in Defence. He said at a Party meeting in 1964 that his ultimate aim was to do himself out of a job, and he has tried to do that.'

The cuts made in spending on defence, if not the exact nature of them, met with universal approval in East Leeds Labour circles!

The Left opposition is now more in the hands of the Young Liberals. On one occasion Mrs Watson recollected that Healey, on a visit to the constituency, was to be given a lift from Seacroft hospital to the A.E.U. to address a meeting. Her son, Keith, who had just passed his driving test, arrived to pick up Healey in his old Austin.

'I told the porter at the gate that I was calling for Mr Healey, and he let me in. One of the porters came out and put his case in the car. The brakes were faulty, and the car rolled back.'

When Healey came out he asked Keith how much it had cost. When he heard that the car cost £25 he said he thought it was shocking that he had had to pay as much to tax it as to purchase it. The advantages of the old banger as camouflage, however, showed when the car arrived at the A.E.U. building. Students who were expecting Healey to arrive in something a bit plusher did not even have time to raise a banner as Healey leapt out and entered the building.

Every four weeks, on average, Healey performs his duties as a constituency M.P. In the Victorian York Road Library building, stained by the grime and dirt of Leeds, constituents with problems about housing, pensions, sickness benefits and taxes seek his help. In addition 'a certain number of compassionate cases came to me because people tumbled to the fact that I was Defence Minister.'

Apart from small bands of people carrying a petition for this cause or that, there are rarely more than a dozen seeking his aid. As Healey explained: 'In a small town the M.P. is a big figure, and people have more faith that he can do something. The constituency boundaries here change with every redistribution; the M.P. is a much less important figure – the city is the thing which matters.'

Perhaps the last word on how good a representative of that city he is should be expressed by John Rafferty, the man who fought him so bitterly for the selection as prospective candidate for South East Leeds in 1952.

'I think Denis is extremely able,' he said. 'He has an admirable reputation as far as Leeds is concerned.'

Chapter Five

The Road to Power

'He was really worked up [about Budapest and Suez], which is the only time I have ever seen him excited.'

ARTHUR HARRISON

'He constantly says "I am not in politics to be loved", so he never moves an inch from what he wants to do to improve his rating in the polls.'

EDNA HEALEY

Chapter Five

WHEN Denis Healey entered the House of Commons in February 1952 the Labour Party had already begun to tear itself apart publicly over defence and foreign policy issues. Healey played a vital role in shaping Labour policy and in the battles of the fifties and early sixties.

Gaitskell's first Budget, of 10 April 1951, marked the beginning of the rift on foreign and defence policy which was to characterize the public's image of the Party. The imposition of charges on teeth and spectacles to help finance the rearmament programme for the Korean War, which had begun in June 1950, was the excuse for Bevan to resign. Slighted in Attlee's appointment of Morrison to Foreign Secretary, and the young Gaitskell as Chancellor of the Exchequer, Bevan resigned from the Cabinet, along with Harold Wilson and John Freeman. The idealistic left now had a leader of stature.

'The main reason why the Labour Cabinet consciously assumed the political handicap of so daunting an arms programme,' said Healey, 'was not so much the belief in its military necessity, but the feeling that unless Britain gave a dramatic and unequivocal pledge of her readiness to lead Europe in building a serious military force on the continent, the United States might not be prepared to make her indispensable contribution.'

Britain needed the threat of America's nuclear power to deter Russia from any attack in Europe.

When Healey entered Parliament the Labour Party had lost power, and its foreign policy was under fire from the Left who demanded a major modification. They regarded the Party as being too committed to the idea of Cold War, and accused it of siding with the forces of capitalism against the international workers' movement led by the Soviet Union. In 1952, in his New Fabian Essay entitled *Power Politics and the Labour Party*, Healey emerged as the major contributor to the 'power-political' school of thinking on foreign and defence policy in the Party.

Healey argued for a strong American commitment through NATO, rejecting the idea of a 'socialist foreign policy'. The Bevanites had to be tolerated because as 'the Party as a whole lacks any systematic theory of world affairs, it has often fallen victim to the besetting sin of all progressive opposition – Utopianism.' Healey soon became a leader of the 'realists' fighting against 'Utopians' who believed that Britain had to join the side of the workers in the international class war.

'It's very difficult to get everybody to see that, if you want to stop anarchy and get peace, then you have to have some way of making states stick to the rules.'

Healey attacked the Party for its lack of a coherent view of the world. In New Fabian Essays he admitted that the critical influences on the Party's thinking on world affairs came 'from the Liberal-nonconformist wing, with its bias towards pacifism, and the neo-Marxist wing, stemming from continental Social Democracy and Communism.' Characteristically he suggested that Party members seriously interested in foreign policy should read Hobbes's *Leviathan* rather than Fabian or Party literature.

Healey's essays, and articles in the magazine *Socialist Commentary*, established him as the major intellectual force behind collective security. Like other right-wing intellectuals Healey believed that the important thing about international politics was their anarchical nature – as in *Leviathan* only a strong world government could bring peace and order to the state of nature where every country was intent on doing anything that it considered best for it. Other writers in the magazine agreed with Healey that with the lack of world government ideology was almost irrelevant.

Bevin as Foreign Minister had built his policy on alliance with the United States and opposition to Soviet expansion. Healey, together with other intellectuals like Strachey, Younger, Mayhew and Prentice, provided the intellectual backing for such policies. Healey, in particular, besides attacking the Left for being utopian also accused it of tending to 'discount the power element in politics, seeing it as a specific evil of the existing system rather than a generic characteristic of politics as such.' Of utopians, Healey said, the liberal ones thought that left to themselves men would act for the common interest, and the Marxists overestimated economic factors, believing that evil stemmed from bad property relations.

'In both cases,' argued Healey, 'deprecation of the power factor entails an inadequate understanding of the techniques of power.'

The Left did not really understand that foreign policy needed the 'power-political' approach instead of wishful thinking about good intentions of other states.

When Britain rearmed to meet the communist threat posed by the Korean War, the right-wing view that, in the last resort, the nation is defended by its armed forces had triumphed. Bevan and his supporters, while accepting (grudgingly) the aggressive nature of Soviet foreign policy, did not accept that resistance to it needed more arms. Harold Wilson and John Freeman, who also resigned with Bevan, were not so much concerned with the effect on the social services as with whether it was even possible to rearm at the speed which had been suggested.

'I was wrong on that,' Healey admits today, 'and Wilson was absolutely right in saying that an expansion at that speed was impossible.'

Healey's entry into the Palace of Westminster, however, did not bring him into clashes with Wilson, but with Bevan.

'I was very anti-Bevanite indeed,' says Healey. 'I disagreed very strongly with them on the issues, and the way they were rocking the boat and dividing the Party. It was highly personal, not just at the top, but right down to constituency level; people didn't talk to one another.'

The attempt of Bevan and the left to apply socialist principles to foreign policy and defence, however, did not stop with rearmament of Britain for the Korean War but continued throughout the fifties into the early sixties. Healey entered the House in 1952, and the Party waited for him to join the fray as an acknowledged expert on foreign affairs. Leading Labour politicians, including Hugh Dalton, had already spoken of him as a future Foreign Secretary, so much was expected of him.

As Healey rose to make his maiden speech on 14 May 1952, the problem of German rearmament was the knottiest facing the West. The Korean War had made Europeans much keener to put NATO into good military shape. Politicians were attempting to find a formula that would allow the Germans to make a contribution without alarming the peoples of the countries against which they had so recently been fighting. The French had suggested that a European Defence Community (E.D.C.) should be set up. This European army would have French and German soldiers who had been 'Europeanized', owing allegiance to the army rather than the state. It was thought that a supra-national army would prevent the re-emergence of a separate German army.

The E.D.C. proposal, however, was unacceptable even to the German people, never mind to France, where the Left opposed it as it meant rearming Germans, and the Right because it meant the end of the French army and a dilution of sovereignty. Healey saw that in its suggested form it was impractical.

First Impressions

His maiden speech was a personal triumph. He suggested to a packed Commons that E.D.C. was not the way forward, and argued in favour of German membership of NATO.

'I do not suggest that we should now invite the Germans to enter the Atlantic Pact,' he said. 'This is entirely a matter of timing. . . . What I suggest is that we should use that time to strengthen NATO so that it is capable of receiving these favourable new recruits.'

Healey went on to argue for more troops for NATO, particularly from the French.

'I personally would not exclude tightening the military structure of NATO in SHAPE on the technical lines already found practical in E.D.C.,' he argued. 'That is the only way out of the problem.'

He ended this traditionally short speech:

'The problem of keeping a united Germany in the Western camp and out of the Soviet camp is the most crucial and urgent problem facing the whole of the West for many years ahead.'

He called for a new start:

'The Western Powers made a false start; but a pause is now imposed by events. It is our duty to make it creative. I am one of those who believe that the ever closer unity of the Atlantic peoples is one of the most fruitful developments of the post-war era. And I am convinced that it offers to us the one real chance of solving the perennial problem of Germany.'

This was no ordinary maiden speech. *The Times* found it 'particularly impressive'; and the Sunday *Observer* conceded it was 'most remarkable', before adding, 'Denis Healey clearly established himself as a possible Foreign Secretary in a future Labour Government.' The Rt Hon. Charles Pannell, another Leeds M.P., wrote that Healey's speech was 'a Parliamentary occasion'. He said: 'He convinced everyone of his range and power – his knowledge and capacity. There was a threat and a promise: the first to the complacency of the Party opposite, the second to our side of more good things to come, now that, with the maiden over, the brilliant newcomer from Leeds can go next to the wicket in a really offensive mood.'

Healey had made a number of very important points in his speech. He stated a number of his fundamental beliefs, which were to remain at the heart of his thinking: the need to strengthen NATO, the problem of Germany, friendship with the Americans. On the E.D.C. proposal he said: 'Britain cannot join E.D.C.: first, because of its federal structure, and secondly, because it has become a cardinal principle of British policy since the war not to accept additional commitments in Europe that might be treated by America as an excuse for reducing American commitments.'

Healey's statements show him opposed to E.D.C. as impractical, and as a 'little' solution for European powers based on an exaggerated fear of Germany. As he wrote in a letter to the editor of *The Listener* in March 1952:

'We should shed no tears if E.D.C. is stillborn, since its miscarriage will clear the way for a strengthening of NATO, which is the only framework within which a German contribution is either possible or desirable. And we shall at least have learnt from the E.D.C. experiment the techniques by which to build a real international army in NATO.'

Healey was well-informed on the French attitude to E.D.C., and doubted whether the National Assembly would ever ratify the treaty. In a brilliant, long speech on 31 July 1952, he attacked the dishonesty of the British Government over the question of the French attitude.

'Had not the French,' he asked, 'been gravely misled by the

Prime Minister when he was leader of the Opposition? Because the whole concept of the European Army was first presented and put into the minds of the French by the Prime Minister at Strasbourg in August 1949.'

Churchill's Council of Europe resolution had inclined the French to believe that Britain would join in a Continental federal army.

'I shall never forget the appalling despair on the faces of Continental delegates to the Consultative Assembly of the Council of Europe last December,' continued Healey, 'when the Home Secretary told them that this country had no intention whatsoever of contributing troops to a European Army. They were flabbergasted.'

Looking ahead Healey clearly and correctly foresaw that the whole idea of E.D.C. would break down. The process of ratification, which had begun after the Bonn and Paris treaties of May 1952, had fallen flat by June 1954. Four of the six protégé members ratified the E.D.C. proposal, but France rejected it, and Italy withdrew.

The Split Widens

Churchill's purpose in having the debate on E.D.C., however, was not to give the Europeans encouragement, Healey suggested, but to show up the split in the Labour Party. The Bevanites were growing in strength in the constituency parties; and in leftist unions such as the Electrical Trades Union and the Amalgamated Engineers. In *Tribune* and the *New Statesman* Bevanite journalists attacked the right wing. At the 1952 Party Conference at Morecambe they gained six of the seven constituency places on the Executive, with Crossman and Wilson ousting veterans Dalton and Morrison.

At the conference, Mendelson gave a classic statement of the Left's attitude to foreign affairs when he said: 'We can best serve the cause of peace by sticking to our distinctive socialist principles and refusing to subordinate them to American, Russian or any other pressures.'

With its view that socialism was somehow midway between the ideologies of capitalism and communism the Left tended towards neutralism, and were opposed by Healey, who thought British interests lay closer to the Americans, and that neutrality or the creation of a 'third force' would alter the balance of power in the world.

Healey decided to attack Bevan and the left-wing analysis of foreign policy as 'a dream for escapists'. The volatile state of Party policy was matched by the delegates, since most of them had been mandated to oppose German rearmament. Healey had decided to expose the Bevanites as advancing irrelevant and tendentious arguments by mounting a frontal assault on the idol of the Left, the imposing Bevan himself. Healey accused Bevan of reducing debate to the level of 'a diet of candy-floss', urged him to face up to the realities of foreign policy, and called upon delegates to throw away the 'stale mythology of Peter Pans'. Britain must work with America, accept German rearmament, and seek to keep the Commonwealth together, he said.

His speech harmed his own relations with Bevan, although today he asserts: 'Personally at the time I got on nicely with the Left and the Bevanites.'

He criticizes Bevan for being 'almost a total stranger to reason, and a supreme romantic, interested always in the *affect* rather than the *effect*.'

The Party, though deeply split, did not, however, reject the proposal to rearm Western Germany. The real issue became whether the proposal to rearm Germany should be the occasion for a top-level encounter between heads of state. For the next eighteen months, especially after the death of Stalin in 1953, hopes rose that peace could be achieved at a summit conference.

Healey was sceptical. He disliked both ways of looking at summit diplomacy. In the foreign affairs debate of July 1953, he attacked the Churchillian concept that 'sliced up the world into spheres of influence in an orgy of power politics'. The left-wing interpretation that a summit would enable us to talk to the fundamentally reasonable men in the Politburo 'whose attitude to the outside world has been distorted by harsh treatment, but who can be cured of this by a little generosity on our part', Healey dismissed as 'wishful thinking'. Today he says: 'I was very unpopular, because everybody believed in Summitship, and the Labour Party used to attack the Government if it didn't have a summit every other day.'

He adds: 'I don't think Summit Conferences are useful, because you never have time for a proper discussion, and the risk is that you may be taken for a ride.'

Healey further thought that Churchill had become a menace.

'I thought that Winston at that period of his life had really got delusions of grandeur about what he could do through his personality,' said Healey, 'and many things he thought sensible, most people in England, including the whole of the Foreign Office, thought crazy.'

The hope generated by Churchill's suggestion on 11 May 1953, for a summit meeting, dominated the Labour Party's annual conference. One resolution stated: 'Conference welcomes recent indications of an easement of international tension, but deplores the failure of the Western Powers to maintain the initiative in efforts to break the East-West deadlock. Labour pledges itself to make every effort to foster an improvement in international relationships and to end the Cold War. Conference urges renewed efforts to convene at the earliest convenient date a Four Power conference at the highest level in order to seek out any possibility of agreement on outstanding issues.'

On the explosive question of German rearmament the resolution said: 'Conference urges that there should be no German rearmament before further efforts have been made to secure a peaceful reunification of Germany.' This was a classic statement of the left-wing definition of the purpose of summit diplomacy. Healey, however, neither held such a benign picture of the Soviet Union, nor believed in summits.

When the Berlin Conference of Foreign Ministers held in early 1954 produced no worthwhile advances, the left wing were particularly critical of the way Eden had handled the talks. Nothing had been agreed about Germany, and it now looked as if German rearmament would go ahead. East and West had deadlocked over whether reunification should precede security. The Soviet desire for security first seemed to indicate that they were prepared for the Germans to rearm.

The Left were furious at Attlee's tacit support of the Government. They were also annoyed at the way the problem of German reunification – which the Soviets would always oppose, as they feared a united Germany would side with the West – was not being dealt with in the wider context of East-West relations. At the Party Conference in October 1954, at Scarborough, the official policy of rearming Germany received 3,270,000 votes, while the Bevanites got 3,022,000 to vote against it. Only the last minute switch of the Woodworkers' Union had given the Executive a majority.

1954 was to mark the high point of the row which split the Party, and guaranteed it would not get back to power in the coming General Election. Healey himself attributes the blame to something he continually stressed throughout the debate – 'a matter of timing'. As he said: 'In foreign affairs the timing of a decision is very often as important, if not more important, than the decision itself.'

'The argument over German rearmament started too soon. If you have your argument before people are ready for it,' explained Healey, 'you waste energy and temper in fruitless wranglings.' Healey himself had originally been opposed to German rearmament, but by the time he entered the Commons opposed only E.D.C., because he thought it would not work. 'Personally speaking,' he admits, 'I had terrible trouble over my support of German rearmament.' He says of the whole debate: 'German rearmament was really the most explosive and difficult issue we had in the Party in the twenty years after the war.'

Promotion

By July 1954 the French Assembly had debated the E.D.C. proposal and rejected it. When the British House of Commons debated the matter that month, Denis Healey was chosen as one of the four top Labour spokesmen. This rare distinction of speaking from the dispatch box was indeed rapid promotion. From being the House's most junior member he had rocketed to the front bench in just two years. His speech, which was a personal ordeal because of raging toothache, made an enormous impact on the House, and earned him considerable praise from Foreign Secretary Eden.

In a statesmanlike speech Healey ranged over a wide field. The Soviet Union, he said, had hoped that the collapse of E.D.C. would also mean the collapse of Western unity, but both 'Dr Adenauer (the German Chancellor) and M. Mendes-France (the French P.M.) prevented this by settling their outstanding differences over the Saar.' He rejected the idea

advanced by some of the Left, notably Richard Crossman, that
Germany should be neutral and independently armed, as this
'was not acceptable to any of the Western governments, nor
to the Soviet Union, nor the majority of the German people
themselves.' This opinion he modified after the Hungarian
uprising of 1956.

Healey drew attention to two basic problems: NATO, and
Britain's relations with the Commonwealth and America.
NATO needed greater consultation and political unity, he
argued, as the balance within the alliance was as important as
the balance between East and West.

Healey clearly saw that the basic strategic question for
Britain was how best to keep America in Europe.

'I still feel rather uneasy at the fact that we have accepted a
major definitive commitment on the continent of Europe without getting anything very solid out of the United States at the
same time,' he said.

Healey was alluding to the hard lesson of recent history.
Since the hurried staff talks between the British and French
military in 1939, strategists had begun to realize that commitment to Europe must be put on a firm and lasting basis. He had
recognized what some of his colleagues had not: that the 1948
Brussels Treaty provided the framework for a British commitment to a continental strategy on a continuing basis, which
marked a dramatic break with the past.

This was a revolutionary commitment, needing from Britain
a much greater adjustment to the reality of alliance than from
her European allies. In 1954 the commitment was nowhere approaching the open-ended undertaking of the late sixties, but,
as Healey observed, it was contingent on an American resolve
to stay in Europe. He grimly warned: 'There is always a great
danger that America will take a British commitment as an
excuse for reducing her own, and that she will seek to withdraw
from the position of being a partner inside the club to being
an arbiter outside the club.'

The failure of E.D.C., he alleged, was due partly to Britain's
earlier suggestion that she would contribute troops to it, which
she later announced she had no intention of doing. The
strengthening of NATO, however, had probably been crucial
in making the Soviet Union adopt a more moderate line.

8

The speech, which contained a sustained and valid criticism of the Government's commitment to E.D.C., established Healey's reputation as a front bench speaker worthy of election to the Shadow Cabinet, and revealed his flair for analysis and prognostication. Many of his colleagues were delighted, and even Attlee, a reserved man of few words, expressed admiration for the way he had spoken from the dispatch box. 'But,' as Healey admitted, 'it wasn't popular with many of the Party because it was in favour of Germany joining NATO.'

Sir Anthony Eden, the Foreign Secretary, said in reply that Healey's speech had provided 'a brilliant exposition of the international scene'. He added: 'As a technical performance, if I may say so, I thought it was unsurpassed.'

Eden admitted that Healey was one of the few people who could claim to have been right all along about Western Defence. He had always seen that Germany would have to be brought into NATO. Sir Anthony remarked: 'If I congratulate him for one thing above all, it was that throughout the whole of that speech he continued to avoid saying, as he could so well have said, "I told you so". There is no temptation in politics more difficult than that.'

The Foreign Secretary concluded: 'Denis Healey can claim to be one of the few people proved right by events.'

In 1955, another General Election year, the Party was again divided. Fifty-seven Labour M.P.s followed Bevan in abstaining on the Party's amendment in March on the question of the British manufacture and use of the H-bomb. The Parliamentary Committee, or Shadow Cabinet, recommended that the whip should be withdrawn from Bevan. The majority of Labour's M.P.s agreed. When Greenwood died in 1954 Bevan had opposed Gaitskell for the Treasurership of the Party. The solidly conservative unions ensured that it went to Gaitskell with a two-to-one majority. In April 1954 Bevan resigned from the Shadow Cabinet following a disagreement with Attlee over the setting-up of the South East Asia Treaty Organization – one of a string of tougher alliances in the early fifties designed to contain the Communist threat.

With the Labour Party openly split, Eden called a General Election for 26 May 1955. The Conservatives' *Campaign Guide* exploited the rift between Bevan and Attlee. Bevan conducted his own campaign, and did not appear in Labour's radio and television series. Following a period in which pro-Western nations had been establishing strong anti-Communist alliances (NATO to include Western Germany, SEATO established in the Far East [September 1954] and the Baghdad Pact, set up in February 1955 to fill the gap between the other two) there was a growing feeling that negotiation at top level was necessary.

Eden fought the election with the slogan 'United for Peace and Progress'. The prospect of a Summit filled Western leaders with a feeling of euphoria, and foreign affairs were more prominent in an election than usual. The debate crystallized into the issue of whether Attlee or Eden could best represent Britain. In a dull campaign, Healey attacked the image of the Tories as natural custodians of the national interest. The 76.8 per cent of the electorate that voted did not agree enough to reject the Conservatives, and Eden represented Britain at the Summit Conference that began in Geneva on 14 July.

Labour's defeat resulted in criticism of the Party's leadership and outmoded ideas. Hugh Dalton, having decided to go to the Lords, attacked the ages of Shadow Cabinet members – nine were over sixty-five. On 7 December 1955 Attlee resigned as leader of the Party. Morrison, faithful but aging servant, Bevan, left-wing renegade, and Gaitskell, intellectual right-winger, were the contenders for the role of leader. The intellectual Hampstead set, which included Healey, believed that the Party needed a young and vigorous intellectual to bring it back into the political arena with a chance of winning. On 14 October Gaitskell, with 157 votes to Bevan's 70 and Morrison's 40, became the new leader of the Party.

Gaitskell was a close friend, and Healey had a great deal of influence over him; and through him, over the direction of the Party's foreign policy. Although he had tremendous personal influence, however, Healey admits: 'I was never a member of Hugh's personal court, though my friends were – Tony (Crosland) and Roy (Jenkins).' Commenting on his fellow Leeds M.P.s, Charles Pannell agreed: 'Denis was a solid supporter of Hugh, but he was not really *involved* with him.' Jack Pritchard, Leeds Labour Party President explained: 'Gaitskell–Healey links did not show in Leeds. They came to their constituencies separately.'

Healey was a Gaitskellite in views, but not in organization, as fellow M.P.s confirmed. Healey explained: 'I was not exceptionally close to Gaitskell because I had seen too much intrigue earlier on under Attlee, and wanted to avoid becoming linked with a particular faction of the Party.'

Healey believes that Gaitskell achieved tremendous results in helping the Party to break with outmoded ideas – a process that was smoothly continued by Harold Wilson.

Hugh was a man with strong moral and emotional feeling, and like Kennedy in America he changed the whole political climate,' says Healey. His weakness, Healey admits, was that he never became more than the leader of a faction of the Party – the revisionist intellectuals on the right.

'I think Hugh basically failed to understand the Labour Party as a whole. His weakness lay in relying excessively on a tiny band of advisers.'

Healey was an adviser with tremendous influence over the Party's thinking. His opposition to the British Suez adventure, which was ill-conceived and slowly executed, did much to encourage the Labour leadership to adopt a very unpopular stand.

Emotional Issues

In February 1956, at the twentieth Congress of the Communist Party in the Soviet Union, Khrushchev attacked both the legend of Stalin and his policies. By implication Stalin's chosen men ruling Eastern European satellite countries became suspect, as did the validity of Soviet supremacy in the affairs of other communist states. After riots in Poland, Gomulka, Prime Minister and First Secretary of the Communist Party, reassured the Russians, and persuaded them to withdraw their troops in early October.

When Hungary revolted, however, and liberal Prime Minister Imre Nagy declared that he was leading Hungary out of the Warsaw Pact alliance on 1 November 1956, the revolt was brutally suppressed by Soviet troops.

The Anglo-French invasion of Egypt, which began on 31 October 1956, continued while Imre Nagy pleaded in vain for Western help against invading Soviet tanks. The combination of these two events produced the most emotional outbursts of Healey's career.

Following a deterioration in relations between the Western Powers and Egypt in 1955–6 the offer of aid promised by America and Britain to help Nasser build the Aswan High Dam was withdrawn. On 26 July Nasser nationalized the Suez Canal to help raise funds for the project.

In a Commons debate on 2 August Healey attacked the lack of a consistent policy for the Middle East, and called for effective international co-operation to solve problems there. The real problem, he said, was that of transit through the Canal rather than who owned it. If Nasser interfered with the passage of ships, then the use of force against him would be justified.

Gaitskell believed that force could be used in such circumstances, but refused to disbelieve Eden's assurances that no use of force was contemplated. Healey and Douglas Jay, who had heard from Fleet Street friends in daily contact with the Foreign Office that something was being planned, tried to alert Gaitskell, who still refused to doubt Eden's word.

Healey explained: 'Douglas Jay and I were worried at backsliding on Hugh's part, so we wrote to *The Times* putting the issues, and giving the case against the use of force in Egypt. I think Hugh did need a bit of stiffening on this, and I believe I did have some influence over what he thought.'

In the September debate, for which Parliament was specially recalled, Eden again persuaded the House that no use of force was intended. Then on 29 October Israel attacked Egypt. The following day her allies, Britain and France, gave both sides an ultimatum that they would occupy the Canal Zone unless the combatants immediately ceased hostilities, and withdrew their forces ten miles from the Canal.

When news came of the intended British invasion Healey was incensed.

'I felt very strongly about this. When the announcement came I made an extremely strong intervention on the Labour side.'

Healey criticized the Government for taking the law into their own hands, and for acting without consulting Britain's allies. Speaking of the ultimatum, Healey warned: 'We may have the position tomorrow in which British tanks are shooting women and children in the streets of Port Said.

'This after all is the subject we are discussing – the question of peace and war. I think it would be both a crime and a tragedy

if at the moment when freedom and national independence are
being suppressed by Russian tanks in Hungary this Government did anything, without international support, which led to
a similar impression being given to world opinion.'

This speech, which was continuously cheered by Labour
M.P.s, was the most effective one from the Labour benches.

Gaitskell, whose Jewish wife may have made him more sympathetic to the Israeli case, had first made a fairly non-committal
speech. After hearing Healey, followed by another strong anti-
invasion speech by Bob Mellish, Gaitskell came back and made
a strong attack on the Government. He later confided to a
senior Lobby correspondent: 'Denis led from the back that day.
It was a remarkable speech. He set the pace for Labour's unpopular decision on the policy over Suez.' To Healey it had been a
matter of principle, and he took a firm stand that was unpopular
in a Britain which longed for a demonstration of power from
British leaders. As Gaitskell admitted to a prominent American
diplomat: 'All our chaps, the beer-drinking working men, think
we are wild on this – they think we are way out of touch.'

A Blow to Idealism

It was a traumatic time for Healey. His mother said: 'It's the
one time Denis has been really emotional.' The key to his attitude, both she and his wife said, lay in the Soviet invasion of
Hungary.

Healey himself agreed: 'I will never forget driving to address
a meeting in York and hearing on the radio of the collapse of
Budapest and the invasion of Suez. I was violently anti-Suez,
especially when some of my Tory acquaintances suggested that
we ought to make a deal with the Russians to give us a free hand
in Egypt if we would give them a free hand in Budapest.'

Edna Healey admits that he lost his usual good spirits at the
time of the two invasions. 'There was no buoyancy or song in
his heart, and he was very angry – which very rarely happens.
He was morally affronted. There are some areas of life when
the logical politician reveals a power of moral feeling. Suez
aroused this in Denis.'

Arthur Harrison, who attended the 600-strong meeting which
Healey addressed after he had heard the news about Budapest
and Suez, described Healey's performance:

'He was really worked up, which is the only time I have ever seen him excited. He gave a really good speech, comparing what we were doing with what the Russians were doing in Hungary. He is normally a chap who can control himself, but he got carried away that night. He was very excited, shouting, and passionate. He rose to the occasion, and got a great reception. It was inspiring.'

Behind the violence of his speeches, however, Healey was thinking in rational terms of the ill-effects of invasion. Of the reasons for his opposition he explains: 'Firstly, it was totally immoral – inconsistent with any attempt to get order in world affairs; second, totally dishonest, because it was based on deceiving all our friends and allies except the French; third, it was bound to fail because we wouldn't get away with it; and fourth, it coincided with Hungary, which made it shaming beyond belief.'

And, almost as an afterthought: 'On top of everything, it undermined the rest of our foreign policy, based on the Anglo-American alliance.'

There is a coolly-reasoned strategist's argument here, which one Tory Minister believes was the real reason behind Healey's thinking:

'He had a tremendous, deeply-felt attachment to Anglo-American solidarity. In public he used a lot of respectable arguments against the Suez policy, but in private he said we must not lose touch with the Americans.'

This is perhaps the key to Healey's thinking on foreign affairs, during his period in Opposition, and for a time after he became Secretary of State for Defence in the Labour Government.

In the 1952 Labour Party pamphlet *Problems of Foreign Policy* Healey wrote: 'The security of Europe against Russian attack and German domination depends on America being permanently involved on the Continent.'

This remained the core of his policy throughout the fifties.

Healey fought continually with the extreme Left of his Party, whose antipathy to the American social system led it to react against Labour's foreign policy. In *Britain and Europe* he had argued that there was an organic unity between all non-Communist forces against the U.S.S.R. and her allies. In *The De-*

fence of Western Europe he argued for an expenditure of ten per cent of the gross national product by Britain on the defence of Europe against Russian expansion. And at a Fabian Conference in 1951 he argued that an anti-American posture by Britain would either make America isolationist or would encourage her to ally with even more right-wing governments in Europe as the basis of her foreign policy.

The other reasons why Britain needed an alliance with the Americans, he said, were to help solve the Russian problem, to find answers to the problems of German rearmament and demilitarization, to hold the Commonwealth together, and to help Britain and under-developed countries on economic issues.

In a November 1953 debate in the Commons he clearly showed he had come to terms with the declining power of Britain: 'I am very proud to be an unrepentant Bevinite,' he said, referring to the man who had done most to get NATO established. He spoke of the two basic principles of British foreign policy; the first being the alliance 'to build up a new community of like-minded nations' and the second 'to reorganize the whole basis of Britain's international position so that it rests not on force, but on consent.'

In a nutshell: 'Interdependence replaces an independent foreign policy'.

In July 1955, in an article in the *News Chronicle*, he defended NATO as the means whereby peace was guaranteed, and emphasized that it was a political as well as military alliance.

Neutralism

In his book, *Neutralism*, published in the same year, 1955, he attacked the left-wing dislike of alliance: 'Neutralism,' he wrote, 'based upon the belief that Socialists should stand midway between Communist Russia and Capitalist America, is faulty, not only in its vision of the Soviet System as in some way Socialist . . . Indeed this type of Neutralism depends essentially on the argument that there is nothing to choose between a little of a bad thing, and a great deal of a bad thing.' He stressed the need for a definite stand against Soviet expansion as being necessary in any step towards an international society.

This was typical of his attacks on the Left, and more precisely, the Communists. In the *Daily Herald*, in October 1952, he had emphasized clearly just how anti-Communist he had become, when he wrote: 'It thrives on betrayal', and listed Communist spies recently captured, including Klaus Fuchs and Allan Nunn May.

'A good Communist cannot be a good patriot', wrote the fresh-thinking Healey. 'Every Communist is a potential traitor – though, of course, a great many do not realize the sinister implications of the movement they have joined, and would undoubtedly leave it if they did so.'

In 1955 he warned that a summit meeting might bring about a weakening of NATO and the Anglo-American alliance that was essential to British interests. When in January 1956 he wrote *When Shrimps learn to Whistle: Thoughts after Geneva*, he summed up the Communist threat: 'The main aims of Soviet foreign policy, as defined by Soviet leaders themselves, remain unchanged – to get Germany out of NATO, to get NATO out of Europe, and to persuade the West to abolish all nuclear weapons while leaving conventional forces in being.'

He remained firmly anti-Communist, and on the Right of his Party on foreign and defence policy throughout the fifties and sixties. He also developed a strong interest in defence – discussed in the next chapter.

Disengagement

But his anti-Communism and pro-NATO position did not prevent him from producing the Party's most novel foreign policy suggestion of the fifties – disengagement.

The idea of 'disengagement' in central Europe was not entirely new. It had been discussed in 1952, and M. Paul Van Zeeland, a former Belgian Foreign Minister, advocated it in 1953. German strategists like Colonel von Bonin, Dr Pfleiderer, and Weinstein had also suggested some kind of militarily neutral and politically independent area as the only way in which Germany might be reunited. Even Sir Anthony Eden had suggested the possibility of a demilitarized zone at the 1955 Geneva Conference – but his insistence that this would be conditional on free elections and unfettered government in Germany made this a non-starter.

The Gaitskell/Healey Plan, however (which Healey devised) was better thought-out. It had its origins in the brutal Soviet invasion of Hungary. This event perhaps made Healey more interested in the political freedom of Eastern Europe than in the military security of Europe as a whole.

Out of his belief that the *status quo* was intolerable came his pamphlet *A Neutral Belt in Europe*, which was published in January 1958. The *Daily Telegraph* grudgingly admitted that this reduced a 'hitherto vague and nebulous concept to fairly precise and manageable terms'.

With the Soviet invasion of Hungary, and the first Soviet sputnik launched in 1957, the West was becoming increasingly alarmed that another possible Soviet move could be followed, for example, by West German retaliation that might lead to global war. Healey therefore devised a plan that he hoped would lead to a neutral belt in central Europe, with the NATO and Warsaw Pact armies no longer facing each other across a border.

Healey had high hopes for the plan. M. Rapacki, the Polish Foreign Minister, proposed a nuclear-free zone for central Europe at the end of 1957. Professor George Kennan, former State Department specialist in Russian affairs and U.S. Ambassador to Moscow, supported the broad idea of disengagement in the B.B.C.'s Reith Lectures. At the Labour Party Conference in October 1958 a resolution was passed urging the peaceful reunification of Germany within the framework of a European Security Pact.

Five Points for Peace

Labour's plan was in five parts: (1) The gradual withdrawal of foreign troops from Poland, Hungary, Czechoslovakia, East and West Germany. (2) The establishment of controls over these countries' national forces – if possible, as part of a wider disarmament plan. (3) The reunification of Germany, with free elections. (4) A European Mutual Security Pact endorsed by the U.S.S.R., U.S.A., France, and Britain to guarantee the territory of the new neutral states. (5) If desired by Russia, the simultaneous renunciation of NATO by Germany, and of the Warsaw Pact by Poland, Hungary, and Czechoslovakia. The Rapacki Plan would be included under the first two points.

The plan aroused great interest and debate. The idea of a security pact to replace military alliances was novel and risky.

There were three major criticisms. First, that the Russians

would not look at it because they would be frightened to weaken their hold on Eastern Europe. Second, that removing Germany from NATO would weaken the West more than the withdrawal of forces from the Warsaw Pact would strengthen it. And third, that it would be impossible to guarantee the security of Europe: the confrontation of the major powers across the border in Germany is, in fact, a guarantee of peace in itself.

Healey has decided why the plan did not work: 'The Russians wanted the Americans right out of Europe, and weren't prepared to discuss anything less than that. When I visited Eastern Europe in early 1959 the Poles and other Eastern Europeans were very keen on mutual force reductions, but the Russians never showed the slightest interest. They wanted to control Eastern Europe, and not to start a process they couldn't control.'

The plan shows evidence of Healey's interest in the wider Europe – one not divided into camps, either militarily or economically. It also shows his preoccupation with Germany as the key to European problems. He accepted the Rapacki proposal because he thought that Poland perhaps held the key. By the end of 1958 he was beginning to have doubts about the viability of the plan. In an American lecture, later published in *NATO and American Security*, edited by Klaus Knorr, he said: 'The most the Labour Party hopes for as a first step in this direction is an agreement on the limitation and control of armaments on both sides of the Iron Curtain.' This, he added, would leave alliances untouched, and smaller numbers of troops facing each other.

He now admits that his disengagement proposal was not a credible policy.

'The thing which made me keen on it was the invasion of Hungary. I don't now think it was feasible, but even soon after producing the pamphlet I began to talk about force reduction and arms control instead of total disengagement.'

Rather tellingly, he concedes that 'the case for it was political, and the problem was to find a strategic concept with which it was compatible.' He agrees also that the denuclearization of central Europe, proposed by Rapacki, was a non-starter, as it could benefit only the Russians, who had more conventional forces. It also became increasingly irrelevant as the means of delivering nuclear weapons over a long range were improved.

The weakness of the plan lay in the consequences of what would happen if the Soviet Union violated neutral territory in the 'disengaged' area. The West would need to use tactical nuclear weapons, but might hesitate to do so because of the danger of the conflict escalating to the use of thermonuclear weapons. As Secretary of State for Defence after 1964, Healey made it a priority to get NATO to adopt a really credible policy for the use of nuclear weapons.

In July 1959 Healey visited Moscow with Gaitskell, Bevan, and Ennals. He had been clearly accepted as Labour's chief 'technician' on foreign affairs.

'Our discussions with Khrushchev about arms control were useful. We got a clear idea of what the Soviets were thinking.'

On his return Healey told the American magazine *Newsweek*: 'The Russians are seriously concerned about the colossus on their eastern frontiers.' He went on to forecast increasing Sino-Soviet tension and dispute. This was long before other observers of Communist affairs noticed that anything was wrong between the two giants.

The Non-nuclear Club

On his return Healey was plunged into the 'Never-had-it-so-good' Election, which the Conservatives won, gaining 365 seats to Labour's 258 and the Liberals' 6. On foreign affairs the Party manifesto had argued that Labour's loyalty to the United Nations and International Law made them more able to speak at any summit than the Tories who had carried out 'the Suez gamble'. Labour would stop nuclear tests, it said, and advocated a comprehensive disarmament treaty, disengagement in central Europe, and the formation of a 'non-nuclear club' of nations which Britain would join, in order to prevent the spread of nuclear weapons.

The idea of the non-nuclear club was Healey's.

'I sold the idea to Strachey who was the Party defence spokesman. It was never much of a starter in real life because the chance of other people joining it was very small by that time – the French especially were already well on the way to a nuclear programme.'

The result of the election, however, condemned the Party

to another five years in Opposition. The intellectuals criticized what they saw as a preoccupation with working-class interest, which, in an affluent age, lost vital middle-class votes. They demanded that the Party's objects should be revised. Gaitskell took up the case of Clause Four (that vague phrase about common ownership of the means of production, distribution, and exchange) and demanded that the Party revise it.

Healey did not agree with Gaitskell over this.

'It was an argument about nothing. Until Hugh picked on Clause Four nobody in the Party knew it was in the constitution – no one had read the constitution up to then. He was asking the Party to rewrite its ten commandments at a moment when it was feeling humiliated by defeat. That is the worst possible moment to ask them to do it.'

Gaitskell's desire to educate, rather than persuade, his concern for academic argument rather than political decision, led him to demand that followers should both understand and acquiesce.

Healey, even though he thought Gaitskell was wrong and making a political mistake, weighed in loyally on the side of the leader once the battle began. At the annual conference of 28–29 November, Healey was blunt about the growing gap between the Party and the voters, and spoke of the need to regain power in order to implement a socialist programme. Such jabs and his tough approach have made him many enemies both at conferences and in the House.

Party Man

A fortnight after the 1959 election Healey was chosen to lead for the Opposition in the foreign affairs debate. This marked his promotion as Bevan's successor as foreign affairs spokesman – which was confirmed at the end of January 1960, when he was chosen during Bevan's illness to lead at Question Time. In November 1959 his fellow M.P.s had elected him in twelfth position, with ninety votes, to the Parliamentary Committee, or Shadow Cabinet. At forty-two he was the youngest member of the front bench team, and the only one to have been elected to the House since Labour had gone out of office in 1951.

He succeeded because of his ability, rather than his personality. He had at his command a vast store of knowledge, based on extensive rapid reading. As his wife and friends admit, he is continually showing competence in fields they did not know he was interested in. He believes intensely in logical argument and reasoning: 'In a marginal situation,' he says, 'I would let instinct decide, but I would very rarely let it overrule argument.'

He collects information early because he searches for it, and then prognosticates by intuitively selecting issues he thinks important, and which will develop in importance. His memory rarely lets him down. In the Commons he showed a capacity for retaining obscure and detailed information when answering questions off-the-cuff. His wife says that he remembers remarks she made about books twenty years earlier.

Because he reads and absorbs the written word so quickly, he is impatient of the spoken word. He is reluctant to listen and isn't a great talker himself. He pays little attention to the way he delivers a speech, although he works hard on content. What he writes is what he thinks. His best speeches are off-the-cuff, which stimulates him, as do hecklers, whom he handles well. His set speeches tend to be lectures, packed with facts and analysis. A supporter, Alice Bacon, has admitted that 'in the House of Commons there have been times when he has had a marvellous speech which has perhaps not been as well-delivered as it could have been'. More bluntly, his speeches have on occasion evoked comments such as 'Aye, very good for a lecture room', and chants of 'Reading, reading' – which is not permitted, except from notes.

A former Conservative Minister and friend said: 'His style is a bit heavy, especially for the Commons, where you need a light touch.' He added: 'I defended him over the years to people in both Parties who complained that he lectured them all the time. I said "That's just his style; he can't help it" – but they were right. It probably held him back, and I think it would militate against him ever being leader of his Party.'

The Personality

Although he is reserved, and rarely commits himself, he has immense energy and conveys the impression of a buoyant and fun-loving man. He is a perfectionist who concentrates on what he thinks important.

Edna Healey describes him as 'arrogant, but not conceited'. Lord Glendevon calls him 'arrogant intellectually, but never offensive'. Intellectually, Healey can be an intolerant bully, contemptuous of lesser brains. His comments are often rude and tactless, although he rarely realizes it. His wife concedes: 'He isn't aware that he hurts – it is tactless, it is a lack of sensitivity.' With his three children, Tim, Jenny, and Cressy, as with colleagues and opponents, he makes a point, then goes on to rub it in. He does this because such an attitude would never hurt him.

He is remarkably self-sufficient – if 'self' includes his family – and lacks personal vanity. He is not self-important, and dislikes it in others. For this reason he is not vulnerable to criticism, believing that he is right, and is impervious to personal attacks.

Politics, to Healey, is about getting things done. For him, as with Bismarck, it is the art of the possible. It is about deciding how to do things in the most efficient manner so that the things Healey considers *really* important in life – the arts – have a chance to grow. He has a passionate interest in films and music. He has his own darkroom in which he processes his photographs. He plays the piano, and relaxes to the music of his favourite composers pouring from his stereo speakers. Poetry, opera, philosophy, literature, art – these affect him deeply, and greater efficiency in politics is the means to allow more people to do these things.

Within the Party, Healey, because he was becoming politically aware at the time of the Spanish Civil War and Munich, is internationally-minded. When he has taken a stand he has not really thought whether it would do him some good in the Party. As Edna puts it, 'He constantly says "I am not in politics to be loved", so he never moves an inch from what he wants to do, or feels he can do, to improve his rating in the polls.'

Healey believes, as Gaitskell did, that 'often people want the love of the world when they're not getting the love of one person', and adds: 'I am very much a family man.' A fellow politician who remembers talking to Healey about his life in 1954 recollects that he said he preferred not to work in the mornings, but to stay with his wife and children. 'He didn't seem to be wanting to be a full-time politician.' A former friend commented: 'When he was first in the House he was shockingly cavalier. He would not know whether to go to the debate or see a French film. His reputation initially declined.'

Charles Pannell complained: 'Denis has been an absentee of the House over the years. He has failed to court it or give it his due. He is with us, but not of us. I think his neglect of the smoke room and tea room springs partly from his authoritarian attitude, and partly from being a multilinguist who spends his time writing pamphlets, articles, and attending international gatherings.'

Healey's claim that 'I was going to the House all day and every day', although probably substantially true, is not borne out by the impression others have of him. One important secretary of a Commons Select Committee summed up the feeling voiced by many: 'He doesn't go to the House often. Some do it naturally, some do it deliberately, he doesn't do it at all. He is a lone wolf in politics.'

Healey, in fact, is not a warm man, having little time for others. He wins respect and admiration, rather than love and devotion.

His behaviour stems from two things. First, his reading ability, which enables him to read the Parliamentary happenings of the day in Hansard much faster than he could listen to them. Second, his preference for going it alone and his dislike of cliques.

His wife says: 'He isn't by nature a joiner.' And his former secretary, Pat Evans, succinctly observes: 'He is not a man for chewing the fat in the tea room. He has not got a taste for intrigue – probably because he has no need to compensate for any personal inadequacy.'

Healey himself comments: 'I have never had clique support – nobody is ever identified with me, personally or politically. I was elected on to the Shadow Cabinet by the P.L.P. largely because of my ability, rather than my supporters.'

So, like Harold Wilson, Healey advanced in the Party because of his ability rather than clique support. This lack of a power base, however, could be Healey's strength in time of crisis. Although he has few political friends, he also has few political enemies. He is concerned with getting things done in an efficient and often novel manner; intensely practical, his colleagues recognize that he does not use his intellectual power in speculative and unrealistic pronouncements but in trying to change the real world.

His feeling of natural superiority, fostered by his double First from Balliol College, Oxford, has made him an intellectual tough. He rose within the Party despite his personality: politically he is not the most likeable of men, as he does not suffer fools gladly, and is contemptuous of the less intelligent; he dismisses his critics as being ill-informed.

Dr Rita Hinden, editor of *Socialist Commentary*, summed up the feeling of a large section of the Party when she said: 'Denis over-specializes on international affairs – he can't deal with domestic issues. He will have to broaden out a bit to take a bigger place in the Party.'

Healey's indifference to domestic matters was probably the main reason why he failed to capture a seat on the National Executive of the Labour Party as a constituency representative until 1970, being runner-up for five years, before getting on in bottom place after the 1970 General Election defeat of the Party.

Among Labour M.P.s, however, Healey advanced because of his expertise. He always did his homework, and knew his facts. A colleague said: 'Whatever aspect of foreign affairs you thought of, if you wanted to find out what the situation was, then the answer always came – "the man who really knows is Denis Healey".' In the voting for the Shadow Cabinet, Healey had seventy-one supporters in 1958 and was twentieth, ninety in 1959 – and just in. After the ban-the-bomb rows of 1960 his support of Gaitskell was rewarded with 136 votes in the same year, and in March 1961 he was unanimously selected to be Chairman of the Labour Party's foreign affairs group.

Ban-the-Bomb

Healey was a front bench supporter of Gaitskell when the ban-the-bomb debate split the Party. In March 1960 Healey's New Fabian pamphlet *The Race Against the H-bomb* was published one day after forty-four Labour left-wingers, including Crossman and Wigg, had abstained in the defence debate because of Gaitskell's support of nuclear weapons. Healey emphasized that the anxiety of NATO members to get their own nuclear weapons was undermining the alliance, as well as draw-

9

ing America into isolation. It was a typical example of the statesman Healey looking beyond the frontiers of Britain to see the wider implications of British policy.

The debate about nuclear weapons had been going on inside the Party from about 1955, when a resolution to oppose the manufacture of the H-bomb was defeated at the annual conference by some five votes to one.

By 1957 it regretted 'the undue dependence on the ultimate deterrent', although there was still a 5,000,000 majority at the Brighton Conference in favour of continued manufacture of the bomb. The right-wing trade union support for the Executive ensured that three similar resolutions at the 1958 Conference met the same fate. Gaitskell's attack on Clause Four after the 1959 election, however, lost him this support; the unions were determined to show who was boss.

Gaitskell, unwilling to diminish the power of his possible future job, defended Britain's independent nuclear capability because of 'excessive dependence on the United States'. Britain might wish to act independently of America against the Soviet Union, he argued. This gave Britain influence in world affairs, and bargaining power. Unilateral disarmament, argued the 'realist' right-wingers, was only a moral gesture which would have no effect on other powers.

George Wigg, who became obsessed with the excessive reliance on nuclear weapons that he thought had been imposed on Britain by the Sandys White Paper on Defence of 1957, and left-winger Richard Crossman drew attention to the difference of opinion between Gaitskell and Healey. They demanded that conventional forces should be strengthened at the expense of the nuclear deterrent.

They were joined by the Campaign for Nuclear Disarmament, an organization supported by Christian pacifists, left-wingers, Communists, and large numbers of the idealistic youth of the country. Healey himself had been at the meeting of a small group of friends – Kingsley Martin, John Collins, J. B. Priestley and his wife, and George Kennan – who had got together to discuss nuclear problems. Out of this C.N.D. had started. Healey and Kennan did not join.

Healey criticized the C.N.D. movement 'because they tended to argue that we mustn't think rationally about force, which is the beginning of evil'. He adds: 'It was the precursor of the hippy movement, and the anti-political movement among the young.'

The right-wing of the Party regarded it as a truism to talk of nuclear weapons as being 'evil'. Fred Mulley in *The Politics of Western Defence* and John Strachey in *On the Prevention of War* argued that the moral force of the argument against nuclear war hindered people from looking properly at the problems; problems that Healey emphasized could not be ignored in the real world where power is the major factor governing the relationship between states.

With the cancellation of the British Blue Streak missile in April 1960 the case for having an 'independent' deterrent collapsed by default – although the Conservative Party continued to talk of Britain's ability to use nuclear weapons independent of America if necessary. In July 1960 the Labour Executive and the Trades Union Congress accepted the Healey line as official policy. They opposed an independent nuclear weapon for Britain, and called for arms control in central Europe as a step towards disengagement. They demanded less dependence on nuclear weapons in NATO strategy, and called for an agreement to end nuclear tests.

At the Scarborough Conference, where Gaitskell presented the policy, he accused the Left and C.N.D. of being neutralist. Knowing that the big unions were mandated to vote against the policy, he declared that he would not accept the defeat: 'There are some of us who will fight and fight and fight again to save the Party we love.'

Healey spoke out in support, urging Boilermakers' Union leader Ted Hill to be realistic about Khrushchev, who was unlikely to be impressed by fine gestures. 'I would like to see Ted Hill going into industrial negotiations armed with nothing except the purity of his intentions,' he said.

Gaitskell, who saw clearly that 'the issue ... is not really defence at all, but the leadership of this Party' was narrowly defeated by 3,339,000 votes to 3,042,000. When Parliament reassembled he was re-elected to the leadership with 166 votes to Wilson's 81. It was necessary, however, for Gaitskell and his supporters to regain the confidence of the Party.

Gaitskell received the support of the Campaign for Democratic Socialism (C.D.S.), which was active in the constituencies, unions, and Parliament. Its leaders, through their magazine *Campaign*, supported Gaitskell over almost everything. Healey, and other Shadow Ministers, did not belong to it, but used it as a platform and a flag under which they could congregate. The unorganized 'right-wing' sector of the Party backed the official line on defence under C.D.S. leadership, and the unions swung back to Gaitskell.

In 1961 the National Executive had set up a 'Committee of Twelve' to draft a policy document on defence. Of the major drafts, the Healey draft was most committed to the NATO alliance. 'Britain must remain a member of NATO, and seek to reform it from the inside', it said. It added that the Party should 'cease to attempt to remain an independent nuclear power, since this neither strengthens the alliance nor is it a sensible use of our limited resources'. The Healey draft was accepted while Crossman's was rejected, and became the official *Policy for Peace*.

At the Blackpool Conference in October 1961 the Party rejected unilateralism by 4,526,000 votes to 1,756,000, and overwhelmed a resolution in favour of neutralism by nearly 5,000,000 votes. The debate on the British bomb had been defused.

Looking Ahead

In December 1961, Healey, at the age of forty-four, became a front bench spokesman in his own right, with a brief for Commonwealth affairs, instead of being second string to Gaitskell on foreign affairs. He immediately went to West Africa.

'I got a wonderful idea of what the whole of West Africa was like.'

On his return he criticized the Government's 'flabby pandering to the illusions of the tiny white minorities in Angola, Katanga, and Rhodesia', and forecast that the white minority in Rhodesia could go the same way as the South Africans if correct measures were not taken. Soon afterwards he warned of the dangers of guerrilla warfare breaking out in Central and Southern Africa. Here, again, was his flair for gathering the facts and analysing them correctly.

In 1961, in articles and speeches (mainly on Laos) he criticized the Americans for being slow to learn 'that armed force is not the answer to the problem the West now faces in Asia'. He spoke of the Indo-China terrain as being 'better suited to Communist guerrilla tactics than to the American way of fighting' – a lesson learned the hard way by Americans in Vietnam in the late sixties.

Premier Macmillan had decided to apply to join the Common Market, following the advice he received as a result of a general review of Britain's place in the world which he had asked for after winning the election of 1959. Healey once again showed his acute analysis and influence over Gaitskell in the debate which followed the decision to apply to join the European Economic Community (E.E.C.) in August 1961.

'I think Gaitskell would have made me Foreign Secretary if he'd lived,' explains Healey. 'But he couldn't make me spokesman in Opposition when Bevan died because my status in the Party wasn't high enough, which really determines your role in the Shadow Cabinet.'

His influence over Gaitskell on the issue of entry into the Common Market was substantial. Gaitskell first hesitated about the line he should take, and then adopted the anti-Market line advocated by Healey, Douglas Jay, Barbara Castle, and others.

At International Socialist Conferences in Frankfurt (1951), Milan (1952), and Stockholm (1953), Healey clashed with the European federalists led by M. Spaak. Vilem Bernard, who represented the Czechoslovak Social Democrats, summed up the feeling of the other delegates: 'Many European socialists were disappointed, believing that the aim should be socialist internationalism, and they expected leadership from the British Socialist Party. Denis was unwilling to push Britain into a lasting federal solution.'

Healey rationalized his opposition to Common Market entry in 1961–2 with complex arguments, including his dislike of a world dominated by a few super-states. He favoured the existing links with the Commonwealth and the United States. 'The fact that you believe in marriage does not mean that you have got to hitch up with the girl next door,' he argued. But the crux of the problem, he said, was this:

'I was certain that de Gaulle would veto entry because he wanted to be cock of the dunghill. You only had to read the books and you could see that our entry was incompatible with his whole vision – he was as predictable as Hitler.'

Charles Pannell says of the Healey position: 'He never believed that we would get in. He does not clutter his mind up with things he does not think will happen, so he did not bother about it.'

Healey was also opposed to entry because he is suspicious of intellectuals who quickly shift their position without good reason.

'The support for entry came from many people who had opposed it only a year or two earlier, then lost confidence in Britain's abilities to solve its problems under any government. They felt the problems were too big for us, but if we joined the Common Market we would be compelled by market forces to do the right thing. I believe that the weaker we were, the worse the immediate consequences of joining would be. I was disgusted intellectually with the cant talked by Marketeers.'

Four days after de Gaulle vetoed the British request to join, on 14 January 1963, Hugh Gaitskell died. Healey perhaps showed a lack of political judgement in supporting Callaghan against Wilson and Brown. In October 1960, at the height of the C.N.D. row, Healey had called Wilson 'a man who is not fit to lead the Labour Party because he thinks the split over disarmament is not an important issue'. Healey, as a confidant admitted, 'didn't trust Wilson because he had done everything possible to knife Gaitskell'. At the time of the leadership debate, Healey told his mother that he felt Callaghan would hold the Party together, and would build up into a good Prime Minister. On the first ballot Brown got 88 votes, Wilson 115, and Callaghan 41.

Today, Healey admits that he underestimated Wilson's capabilities. Wilson, who defeated Brown by 144 votes to 103 on a second ballot, 'got the Party to take a Gaitskellite line on everything within three years without ever admitting it', says Healey admiringly.

On 22 February 1963, Wilson promoted Healey to be Shadow Defence Secretary. When Wilson led the Labour Party to electoral victory in October 1964, Healey had the necessary ability and experience to make him one of the best-informed and most important Defence Ministers of the twentieth century.

Chapter Six

The Defence Intellectual

'The rise of Hitler, the Spanish Civil War, actually being involved as a soldier for six years, and then the major problem of the fastening of the Soviet empire on Eastern Europe – it's been very difficult not to take an interest in foreign affairs in my lifetime.'

DENIS HEALEY

'I slowly realized the essential role of power in politics; Marx was wrong in believing that people are more interested in money than power in a political world.'

DENIS HEALEY

Chapter Six

HEALEY'S education, social background, and experience moulded his thinking on defence policy. He rose to the top as a defence intellectual of original distinction. His interest centred on strategic questions (once regarded as geo-political issues), and this training fundamentally affected the policies followed by the Labour Government after October 1964.

Healey acquired his interest in defence and foreign policy through his early Marxism, his Oxford politics and war experiences, and then the Communist take-over of Eastern Europe in the late 1940s. As Healey has said on television: 'The rise of Hitler, the Spanish Civil War, actually being involved as a soldier for six years, and then the major problem of the fastening of the Soviet empire on Eastern Europe – it's been very difficult not to take an interest in foreign affairs in my lifetime.'

His interest in Marx at Oxford provided a methodology that helped him gain a coherent, if complex, picture of reality arising from the clash of historic forces that Marx rather naively described. Marx's approach to politics brutally emphasized the role of institutions whose existence arose from the economic structure of society. Class conflict, spurred on by the industrial revolution, he maintained, led to the modern bureaucratic state. The state itself was an instrument of coercion, and a parasitic growth on society.

The young Healey accepted the theory of class conflict, and the basic Marxian description of the capitalist state. His Marxism taught him that politics was about power: how to get it, and how to use it. In international affairs, conflict was endemic. Without a superpower to dominate the stage each state will act for its own self-interest, and where interests clash, war results. Unlike the liberal-democratic left-wing of the Labour Party, Healey did *not* believe that international peace was the natural state of world politics, interrupted only by greed and mischance that could be banished by collective action.

Healey saw full well that peace between the social classes at home was underpinned by the legal sanction of coercion; and its acceptability rested on the consent of the majority. The totalitarian state was prepared to use force more readily in both internal affairs and external affairs. Healey saw that international peace could be maintained only if other states were prepared to threaten or to use force. Coercion might be necessary to force anarchistic states to keep the peace.

The frequency with which totalitarian states like Hitler's would resort to the use of force seemed in direct proportion to the unwillingness of other states, such as the liberal democratic Britain and France, to use force in their own defence if an alternative course existed. The insistence on legally valid but unenforceable or ineffective measures got nowhere; and Healey turned initially to the Communists as an alternative to the rising Fascist menace in Europe.

His wife explains this impact of the thirties: 'Denis grew into Defence. His passionate interest in foreign affairs sprang out of the idealism engendered through the Spanish Civil War. Being internationally-minded is part of his socialism.'

Healey himself thinks that what he learned from Marx was how to understand the world as a whole – the synoptic view. His flirtation with Communism – which ended with the Nazi–Soviet Pact and the Russo–Finnish War – left him with a philosophical appreciation of the logical niceties of the doctrine of dialectical materialism, and an international outlook. His first real appreciation of the role of power in politics came to him during his period as International Secretary of the Party at Transport House in the late 1940s.

'Through having to deal with problems at Transport House I slowly realized the essential role of power in politics,' said Healey. 'Marx was wrong in believing that people are more interested in money than power in a political world. They are not. The desire for power as an end in itself is very important.'

At Transport House, Healey realized that his Party needed a more realistic approach to international relations. This period, and the influence of Bevin, Labour's Foreign Secretary, is the first phase in his development as a defence intellectual (defined here as someone who thinks about strategy in the nuclear-missile age).

His second formative period in active politics can be seen as his time as a back-bencher. Until about 1960 he was an influential M.P. talking in a somewhat academic manner about such questions as German rearmament, NATO, defence, and disengagement.

Then, as a front bench spokesman in the 1960s he emerged as a power in his own right, putting forth ideas on foreign and defence policy. At Transport House Healey drafted foreign policy documents for the International Affairs Committee chaired by Hugh Dalton, and interpreted Bevin's policy for Party rank and file. He also had the job of fostering relations between the British Labour Party and Social Democratic Parties elsewhere. This had a profound effect on his thinking. Bevin's ideology was a bitter and determined anti-communism, which had its seeds in his Transport and General Workers' Union days, and strengthened as Eastern Europe fell into the hands of Communists.

Healey entered Transport House in 1946 speaking in unsophisticated terms of 'the United States' desire to control the world by the dollar and the atom bomb', and stressing the need for friendly relations between Britain and the Soviet Union. His experiences with Eastern European regimes, however, together with the influence of Bevin, soon made him shift his position to the right-wing. In May 1947, left-wing M.P.s produced *Keep Left*, a critical analysis of the Government's foreign and defence policy. Healey drafted the National Executive's official reply, *Cards on the Table*.

Cards on the Table set the tone of the militant anti-Soviet right wing. *Feet on the Ground*, a further pamphlet published in September 1948, put the idea of Western European union firmly on the map. In a bitter anti-Soviet analysis, Healey wrote: 'Western traditions are incompatible with the leaden uniformity which Russia imposes wherever her influence extends. The example of Czechoslovakia and Yugoslavia shows that it is not enough to agree with the Soviet Union on all matters of foreign policy, it is not enough even to adopt a wholly Communist regime; Russia is satisfied with nothing less than total surrender.'

Singling out the threats of 'armed aggression by the Soviet Union', and 'the growth of Communism through economic misery', Healey talked of the need for Western Europeans to get together in 'a Common Defence Policy', which was 'both possible and necessary'. This would allow the formation of a 'Third World Power', which 'could be a bridge between the U.S.A. and the U.S.S.R.'

He continued by suggesting that if the nations adopted a single armaments industry and 'specialized in the functions for which they are best suited', creating 'a single common defence force', then they would have a 'powerful vested interest in a permanent union'. Healey was here asserting one of the fundamental tenets of his philosophy: the belief in common interests and union being achieved through functional integration, rather than through a federal political union imposed from above.

Economic independence of America and political security from Soviet expansion were advocated in *Feet on the Ground*, which was a positive assertion of a faith in democracy and liberty. They were the principal pillars of Bevin's 'Grand Design'. At a time when the American commitment to Europe was still in doubt – before the creation of NATO – the reasoning of this pamphlet was novel, and strategically important.

The strategic thinking is further demonstrated by the reservations Healey had about a federalist European union solution. In articles and speeches in 1948 and 1949 he talked of a 'third power' under British leadership 'that will stretch from Iceland to New Zealand', and stressed the importance and value of the Commonwealth. Healey quoted with approval Bevin's contention that an association of Western European states with Britain and the Commonwealth 'can establish a force for peace and equality and equilibrium, which ought to make for peace for generations to come'.

As he wrote in an important article entitled 'Can there be a Socialist Foreign Policy?', published in the *Spectator* in June 1953: 'It was Bevin's major aim in world affairs to transcend crude power politics by constructing new international communities in which the habit of co-operation and increasing interdependence of function would produce lasting unity.' This was to be achieved by 'persuading states to concentrate on the interest that they had in common', so advancing from consultation via co-operation to integration, and thus achieve collective control of national power. Bevin's trade union background, Healey contended, was relevant to this kind of analysis.

Because of Bevin's background and strategic analysis he was interested in the Atlantic Community, Healey argued, and reluctant to commit Britain more deeply to European union because it might weaken American ties with Europe and justify withdrawal. Healey saw clearly that it was the guarantee of superpower America that really backed up the credibility of independence for Britain and Western European states.

Bevin's influence on Healey's thinking should not be underestimated. As his wife put it: 'Bevin influenced Denis for years after his death. For a long time, whenever he made a speech in the House, there was a slight tip of the hat to Ernie.'

Bevin encouraged Healey to think of wider foreign policy implications in all that Britain did or proposed. Healey did not shrink from saying, therefore, that Western European union existed only because of the close association with the economic, political and military strength of the United States. Strategically, the economic recovery of Europe depended on American readiness to defend Europe against the Soviet Union. He wrote: 'Europe's most valuable military protection against aggression from the East is the few thousand American troops in Germany and Austria, because their presence would involve the U.S.A. immediately in any European War.' He crisply added: 'The Europeans themselves do not possess the forces needed to resist aggression by a world power.'

This hard-headed approach was brought to other foreign policy analyses, and then to defence and questions of strategy. Typically, he did not reject European federation outright, but contended that 'the main argument against approaching Western union through federation – rather than by completing Western union by federation – is that in itself, federation would not solve the immediate problems of Western Europe; while the attempt to achieve it would exaggerate the differences between the West European states instead of exploiting common interest.' He added that 'even in the U.S.A., Australia, and Canada the adequacy of federalism for a modern industrial society is increasingly questioned'.

In *Feet on the Ground* Healey showed he preferred a practical approach in reconciling difficult political problems. With the vexed question of state sovereignty, territorial division and legal powers he reflected a stolid Anglo-Saxon view of politics. This was a plan for Britain to lead Europe and to act as 'honest broker' between the superpowers. It was a nebulous concept, which inspired *ad-hoc* agreements and a readiness to co-operate on specific problems and in certain well-defined areas.

The growth of economic prosperity in Europe, and the continuing British desire to play a world role, backed up by the Anglo-American alliance, however, pushed aside ideas advanced by Healey at Transport House.

The Back-bencher

As an M.P. after 1951, however, he soon came into his own. He consistently argued the case for NATO, and German re-armament within it. He spoke and wrote freely on foreign and defence topics.

As an M.P. he gained importance through his influence on Gaitskell and others, because the Labour Party chose to debate foreign and defence policy, which aroused the emotions of British socialists. It became especially important in the context of the struggle over who should lead the Party. The endless wrangling put Healey in a position where the debating society was arguing about the subjects on which he was the authority.

Healey had learned from Bevin the need for solidarity and the sparing use of the threat to wield the big stick. Like Bevin, he believed in NATO and the policy of giving Britain a diplomatic role worthy of her traditions and industrial/technological strength. As a back-bench M.P. he consistently argued that Europe could achieve healthy unity only within the framework of a strong NATO alliance. In November 1954, during the debate on the ending of the abortive E.D.C. proposal, he stated his position on the need for close links with America quite clearly.

He argued that with American backing Britain was now able to make a contribution to the defence of Europe on a lasting basis. This was a new 'Continental' strategy, and he urged the Government to think about the more complex issues involved of economic co-operation with European states – the wider implications of 'strategy'.

In his lecture on 'Britain and NATO', given at a seminar in America in 1958 (which led to the production of Klaus Knorr's book *NATO and American Security*) Healey showed a clear understanding of strategic problems.

He talked of NATO as being of first importance, but added that 'the primary deterrent remains the atomic bomb, and the ability of the highly-organized and trained U.S. strategic air power to use it', with a British nuclear force in reserve to pick out selected targets. It was necessary also, he argued, to have ground troops in Europe capable of holding any fighting that might break out following the Soviet suppression of an Eastern European state – as in Hungary in 1956. 'It is vital to have military forces that are capable of smothering the outbreak without risk of total war', he said. If Soviet troops over-stepped the Iron Curtain, or Western European citizens spon-taneously rose to help their Eastern brethren, then NATO must have forces capable of holding the vast numbers of Soviet divisions.

Healey accused the Conservative Government of spending insufficient on conventional weapons at the expense of giving the air force 'weapons it could not afford to use except in the most unlikely contingency of all – a direct nuclear attack on Britain herself'.

Showing a sound grasp of modern strategy, Healey continued: 'If ever Britain finds herself engaged in fighting, she should use the minimum force required to bring the fighting to a halt – but not to "win the war".' He added that 'the essential condi-tion for limited war is limited war aims, and that the old slogan "There is no substitute for victory" must be replaced by the slogan "There is no substitute for survival"'.

Dealing with various academic strategic points, such as doubts about the use and distinction between various types of nuclear weapons, and different strategies, Healey revealed a good grasp of the major problems. Stating the dangers of the spread of nuclear weapons to other countries, he spoke of the need for a nuclear test ban, and correctly estimated that in practice only France, among European powers, was likely to produce nuclear weapons unless a technological breakthrough reduced costs of production and development of systems to deliver the weapon.

In an article written for *The Observer* in June 1959 Healey lamented that only a small minority of the public cared about NATO's tenth anniversary. Like many Healey speeches and writings it was packed with ideas. The level of its analysis ranged from accurate prediction and acute perception to wrong guesses and poorly-argued hypotheses.

On the credit side, for example, his emphasis on such questions as the need for a NATO-inspired initiative to deal with the problem of world poverty and thus help Afro-Asian countries deal with their problems, and the need for – 'a new strategy which does not depend on America's readiness to commit suicide . . . or on her allies' ability to make her commit suicide against her will' was of wide-ranging strategic importance.

The 1950s and 1960s showed a marked increase in outbreaks of violence in the poor countries of the world: a problem which threatened to drag the superpowers into war, as with the Americans in Vietnam. The question of replacing 'massive retaliation' (where a big country, such as America, might theoretically use H-bombs in response to a small ground attack) was still under review in the West. Until the strategy of 'flexible response' was announced by American Defence Secretary McNamara in 1962 NATO's strategy was still largely 'incredible'. Its further refinement by Healey after he became Defence Minister was a major contribution to what Healey defined as NATO's main function – 'to give its members security'.

Parts of the *Observer* article, were, however, questionable. Healey's description of the Afro-Asian peoples as 'an independent and perhaps decisive factor in world affairs' was a typically optimistic liberal interpretation of the rise of a cohesive new force. In reality the poverty and general disunity of the 'Third World' of underdeveloped nations led to a reappraisal of its power and importance. This was shown in the late sixties by the decline in aid given by industrialized countries to poor nations.

In writing of the dangers of the atomic arms race Healey embraced the old-fashioned idea that it was responsible for the Cold War, and implied that it was likely to lead to war. This argument is widely regarded as false, because arms races are usually the effect rather than the cause of international tension.

Disengagement

If Bevin and the East European refugees were the most important influences on Healey in the 1940s, Suez and Hungary were dominant in affecting Healey in the following decade. Out of his anger and frustration over these incidents Healey devised disengagement – a neutral area guaranteed by a security pact – which he hoped would achieve two things at once: 'the freedom of the peoples in the satellite countries, and the security of that part of Europe'. As has been seen, however, the plan was political, and largely failed because it did not match with strategic reality.

Disengagement moulded Healey's thinking in two important ways. First, it made him more aware of the need to reconcile political analysis with strategic necessity. Second, it made him more concerned with a stable security system in Western Europe, which could help influence events in Eastern Europe by stabilizing the great power relationships.

A third major influence on Healey's thinking began to emerge as his reading and international contacts widened. He was one of the few British politicians to familiarize himself with the work of American academic strategists during the fifties and early sixties.

After leaving Transport House he maintained his international contacts. He was a regular attender at international conferences, such as those at Königswinter, in Germany, devoted to improving Anglo-German relations, where he met many prominent German politicians and writers, and the wider Bilderberg conferences (chaired by Prince Bernhard of the Netherlands) for opinion-leaders in Europe, North America, Canada and the United States. Healey's role in the organization, and active part in discussion and writing, kept him in close touch with important political and strategic developments throughout the world.

Following a Commons speech, suggesting that the superpowers might engage in a war where they dropped atomic weapons only in European countries – a comical thought to M.P.s – Healey was approached by a number of defence analysts who agreed with him. He then collaborated with three of them to produce *On Limiting Atomic War*. This work on graduated deterrence, designed to prevent a total nuclear holocaust, coincided with work being done by the British Council of Churches on the implications of massive retaliation.

Informal discussion between the writers and church leaders led to a meeting at Brighton in January 1957, where bishops confronted hard-headed military men, leading journalists and politicians. The eighty-strong meeting was organized by Sir Kenneth Grubb and the Rev. Alan Booth, chairman and secretary of the Church's Commission on International Affairs.

Lord Salter summed up feelings about the meeting when he said that it was too valuable to be allowed to stop there. So the Brighton Conference Association was formed whereby articles on nuclear strategy that appeared in various parts of the world were circulated by newsletter. Leading members of the Association, however, decided that something more permanent and comprehensive was needed. To set up a British centre for strategic studies, however, needed money. Healey's international contacts were decisive in getting it.

Setting up the I.S.S.

'I met Shep Stone, head of the social and political studies part of the Ford Foundation, at a meeting of the Bilderberg Group in Fiuggi, Italy, the day the Russians launched their first sputnik,' remembered Healey. 'I took him out for a walk in a heavy mist under the wet plane trees, and said we were starting this thing and we would like about $10,000 to keep it afloat. He told me they never looked at anything under $100,000, but he was very interested in the idea, so if we revamped it and put in a formal request it would stand a good chance.'

When Healey returned to London he and his colleagues realized that something more ambitious than they had thought about could be established. He played an active part in setting up the Institute for Strategic Studies, as it was called, signing the Articles of Association with Christopher Woodhouse, Anthony Buzzard, Kenneth Grubb, Alan Booth, Michael Howard, and Donald Tyerman. He suggested the appointment of a journalist who specialized in strategic questions, Alastair Buchan, who became its highly-successful first Director. By the end of 1958 the I.S.S. had begun its work, with the Ford Foundation giving $150,000 over three years, as a strategic think-tank; with study

10

groups, journal, specialist library, conferences, and research
into strategic questions.

Healey's catalytic role is summarized by Alastair Buchan:
'His part was crucial. Without Denis and his contacts we might
never have got the money, and the I.S.S. might never have been
born.'

Healey was keenly interested in the strategic debate going on
in America at this time. As Buchan said: 'He was very much
in touch with the American debate, and helped me a lot with
Survival – the I.S.S. journal – pointing out key articles in
American publications.'

The influence of the I.S.S. should not be underrated. Although
little known outside a specialist circle it has had an important
impact on such strategic questions as the structure and nuclear
planning of NATO, arms control and nonproliferation of
nuclear weapons.

Healey, who had become really concerned about nuclear
weapons around 1954, and wrote on them for *Encounter* in
1955, was a leader in the British field. As an American analyst
said: 'There were not many people who paid much attention
to this sort of thing in the mid-fifties, but Denis was not only
reading about it, he was writing about it as well. With the
formation of the I.S.S. he began making Britain a forerunner in
Europe in understanding nuclear strategy, and with Alastair
Buchan he began making defence thinking respectable in
Europe.'

Healey's main interest, however, lay in the ideas being discussed by American strategic thinkers. He was keen to examine
and debate the little-publicized thinking which had such a
tremendous impact on the foreign and defence policies of the
great powers.

From the Americans Healey acquired a specialist vocabulary
which helped in discussing complex problems meaningfully.
His criticisms of American specialists concerned their 'isolating
of strategic factors from all other factors in inter-state relations,
which is a degree of artificiality that distorts reality'. He also
accused them of thinking exclusively of a world of only two
powers, where a gain for one meant a loss for the other.

American strategic analysis, however, directed his attention
to four important areas of policy he was later to be concerned

with as Secretary of State for Defence. First, making NATO's defensive strategy credible. Second, the need for more cohesion, planning and consultation for NATO's tactical and strategic nuclear weapons. Third, setting up a European defence group to offset a possible Russo-American deal which might sacrifice European interests. And fourth, the problem of arms control to underpin a strategic nuclear balance that could change with a rapidly-advancing technology.

New Thinking

Healey's clear appreciation of these problems is shown by an analysis of a lecture he gave at the University of California in February 1961. This contained the essence of his thinking on the alliance, deterrence, nuclear planning and arms control. His high-powered academic audience was astonished at the clarity and vigour of his thinking, which represented a marked improvement upon the strategic thinking of other British analysts, whose work was often regarded in America as complacent and bland. Conservative politicians who had lectured in America had seemed condescending and ill-informed about American policy, and complacent about their own.

Healey's lecture, however, was forthright and honest. It was both critical, and far-seeing in its proposals for changes in NATO defence thinking.

Healey attacked American policy for encouraging General Norstadt, NATO Supreme Commander, in his absurd and ill-considered proposal to make NATO a nuclear power in its own right. The dangers of any NATO general having to decide on the employment of nuclear weapons (with obviously political as well as military implications) in a crisis, and seemingly without reference to any higher political authority should be apparent to all, argued Healey.

Healey defended the policy of the flexible response – which President Kennedy was about to introduce to the NATO Council. He said that there was a basic need for the alliance 'to develop a strategy that will give time for a collective decision on the use of atomic weapons', and to this end 'it is vital to train and equip NATO's forces so that they can force a pause at any level at which they have to fight, not only at the conventional level ... but also at the level of battlefield atomic war'.

He identified the major problem of the alliance as being one of confidence, and advanced the Healey theorem: 'Nearly all the strategic problems of the alliance are due to the fact that it takes five per cent probability of massive retaliation to deter the Soviet attack; but none of America's allies would ever be happy in a situation in which there is a 95 per cent possibility that the Americans won't respond.' The main difficulty was to bridge the gap between 'what is required to deter Soviet aggression and what is required to reassure the allies who do not themselves have the power of thermonuclear response'.

The first requirement in resolving NATO's difficulties, he said, was to restore 'general confidence in American leadership', which had diminished during the Eisenhower administration. It was necessary, also, to have consultation about the deployment and use of nuclear weapons to restore European confidence in the alliance and America's role in it. Planning and consultation had both to be improved, argued Healey, if NATO was to be made workable.

Emphasizing European doubts and fears, he told his American audience that a conventional war in Europe was just as unacceptable as an atomic one; but that there was a special need 'to produce a conventional shield force, which can suppress a local conflict without recourse to atomic weapons'. He warned: 'The real problem NATO has to face is that of a local conflict arising in an ambiguous situation', and discussed the dangers arising from an uprising in Eastern Europe, which might drag in the superpowers. To reduce the perils, Healey said, 'What NATO needs is mobile, well-equipped, conventional forces that can contain this sort of conflict without resort to atomic weapons at all.'

This lecture contained every major argument that determined his own policy when he became Minister of Defence.

In the early sixties Healey acted as the Labour Party's strategic conscience over the question of entry into the Common Market. His writings and speeches of the period show a wide-ranging analysis opposing Britain's application to join. He no longer supported the idea of Europe being a 'third world power', which he had proposed in the 1940s. The world had changed, as he clearly saw.

He raised various points encompassing agriculture, EFTA, foreign trade and the constitution, and said that 'discrimination against the outside world was the essence of the Common Market's original conception'. He emphasized that Britain often had different ideas to her European neighbours about such strategic issues as deterrence and disarmament.

His reluctance to embrace the narrow European market showed his wider conception of where Britain's natural interest lay. He spoke of her 'broader international aims' being given first priority. The great dreams of Ernest Bevin still lingered.

Healey is not a petty nationalist. His dream is based on a larger vision, and a sound grasp of strategic reality. The crux of his opposition was, as he wrote: 'Our links with the Commonwealth and our influence with America are too valuable to throw away today simply because of something that might happen at least ten years ahead, if it ever does.' It was an ideal he carried into the Ministry of Defence when he became Secretary of State in October 1964.

Chapter Seven

Defence, 1945–64

'The major problem for the next Labour Government is to decide whether there are any real British interests overseas which it is going to be both politically and militarily possible to protect by force.'

DENIS HEALEY, addressing a meeting in Durham,
22 February 1963

Polaris – 'Britain's phoney deterrent'
DENIS HEALEY, quoted in *Daily Herald,* 5 March 1963

Chapter Seven

BRITISH defence policy has traditionally meant the protection of the British Isles, its far-flung Empire, and the great sea routes, whose vulnerability was diminished by the existence of permanent bases abroad. In the post-war period the direct defence of the U.K. has been regarded as irrelevant or unnecessary. A seaborne invasion is unlikely. So is one by air. Bomber attacks are also a greatly diminished prospect, and provision for fighter and missile defence now plays no significant part in defence planning. Although considerable provision is made for the protection of shipping against submarine and air attack, the notion of a third battle of the Atlantic is also now unsupportable.

British defence policy is largely ruled by the need to influence American policy. This aspect may change as the need to play a European role increases in importance for Britain and diminishes for America. Clearly defence policy has been influenced by the need to have a major say in any European diplomatic negotiations or crisis, and by the need to be in a position to influence the conduct of any general war. But general war has become increasingly regarded as disastrous and unacceptable as an instrument of policy. As Macmillan quipped after the Geneva Summit Conference of 1955: 'There ain't gonna be no war.'

The British commitment to NATO since 1949 has been through a desire to influence American policy in either the prevention or waging of war in Europe.

By standing with the U.S.A. in most situations Britain could depend on its support against the Soviet Union in Europe. Britain had to contribute forces to NATO to ensure a credible American military power and technology.

In the early post-war period the Anglo-American alliance

also meant a British readiness to participate in the Korean War, or any war in which America was involved. Yet fear of American reluctance to play a major role in Europe persuaded Britain to manufacture an independent atomic strike force.

The British Deterrent

Clement Attlee, Labour's immediate post-war Prime Minister, became in 1946 the architect of the British deterrent. His attitude was explicit: America could not always be relied on to honour her commitments to Europe. Britain's bomb would give insurance cover in case America defaulted or the premium she demanded for her European role became unacceptably high.

Churchill saw this as well and argued in favour of joint British and American targetting in the event of war, so that strategic targets important to the U.K. would be attacked.

The British atomic weapons programme became public knowledge on 3 October 1952, but its origins go back to the Second World War. Since the Quebec agreement in 1943, and despite the American McMahon Act of 1946, Britain and America shared an atomic weapons connection. Because it was put in doubt by the McMahon Act – which left Britain without its own nuclear weapons, and with no right to the results of research carried on – Britain decided to become an atomic power in her own right. It was the natural decision for Britain, who still regarded herself as a great power.

Inevitably Britain then decided to manufacture the H-bomb – built and tested (at Christmas Island in May 1957) under a Conservative government.

The Sandys White Paper on Defence, published in February 1957, committed Britain to a deterrent strategy based on massive retaliation – the threat to use nuclear weapons on the whole of Russia.

But Britain embraced 'deterrence' as a central doctrine of her policy well before America committed itself to massive retaliation. Marshal of the Royal Air Force Sir John Slessor, Chairman of the Chiefs of Staff in 1952, later admitted: 'The aim of Western policy is not primarily to be ready to win a war with the world in ruins – though we must be as ready as possible to do that if it is forced upon us by accident or miscalculation: it is the prevention of war. The bomber holds out to us the greatest, perhaps the only hope of that. It is the great deterrent.'

Churchill in the 1955 Defence debate argued in favour of a nuclear deterrent that enabled Britain to attack, independently, strategic targets which the U.S.A. might consider less important. Britain wished both to deter aggression by the threat to use nuclear weapons, and, should threats fail, to use these weapons against selected targets.

This was made possible by the V-bombers – Vulcans, Victors, and Valiants – whose all-round performance gave the R.A.F. a credible deterrent. But not for long. Already in 1957 plans were being laid for the development of a liquid-fuelled Inter-Continental Ballistic Missile, Blue Streak, which was to replace the manned bomber.

Dependence on the U.S.

Blue Streak proved a non-starter because it was a 'first strike' weapon of a type already being abandoned in the U.S.A.; and in 1960 the British Government faced facts and cancelled the project. With a four minute warning system Britain was building a rocket with a twenty minute fuse. The 200 V-bombers were equipped with the Blue Steel stand-off bomb until something more satisfactory could be developed or purchased abroad.

A fully autonomous British nuclear force came to an end in 1960. But in the same year, when the slow-reacting Blue Streak rocket was abandoned, Macmillan was able to obtain from President Eisenhower a promise of the air-to-surface missile Skybolt, then being developed in the U.S.A. In late 1962, however, President Kennedy cancelled the Skybolt programme.

The Conservatives were beside themselves with anger and frustration. The Labour Opposition had been sceptical about Skybolt from the outset. It appeared to them that President Kennedy was merely being logical about the implications of the McNamara graduated deterrence strategy, which clearly implied an end to Britain's independent deterrent system. America was now committed to the strategy of the flexible response, which McNamara had spelt out in an important speech at the University of Michigan in the summer of 1962. This speech had important implications for British policy.

McNamara had emphasized the invulnerable nature of a 'second strike deterrent' based on the I.C.B.M. Minuteman and the nuclear-powered submarine carrying Polaris missiles. Both these second strike weapons could survive nuclear attack. He also advanced the idea of 'graduated deterrence', to try to counter local Russian aggression first with conventional weapons – i.e. without an automatic use of nuclear weapons.

This new doctrine caused some disquiet in London; and with the cancellation of Skybolt the Conservative administration took fright. Yet the Government negotiated its way out of the awkward situation at Nassau in December 1962 with the agreement that Britain should buy Polaris missiles in nuclear-powered submarines, with four or five in service by 1970. This agreement, hailed as a success for the British, showed America's reluctance to see British power too drastically reduced, on her contribution to the alliance crippled by a sudden loss of confidence.

Nassau was a logical continuation of the policy of extending technological knowledge to Britain, covering the means of delivery and development of nuclear warheads. So, the history of the British nuclear deterrent became one of increasing technological dependence on the U.S.A., accompanied on the political level by the plan to assign the British force to the American projected mixed-manned NATO Multilateral Force (M.L.F.).

This increasing British dependence on America came just as Europe as a whole was growing restive about its dependence on the American deterrent. A number of factors in the late fifties affected the relationship of the U.S.A. to its European allies, and also affected British defence perspectives.

The surprise launching of the first Soviet sputnik in autumn 1957 indicated an American vulnerability to Soviet attack, and alarmed Western opinion. The resultant American interest in a more flexible strategy, in an effort to avoid an all-out retaliation, alarmed Western Europe and raised doubts about American interest in helping Britain maintain its independent deterrent.

British defence planners noted the 1963 hot-line agreement between Moscow and Washington, American attempts to get its allies to increase their conventional forces, and the decision to withdraw the vulnerable medium-range 'soft' missiles – the Thor and Jupiter – from Britain, Italy and Turkey in spring 1963.

Those developments showed a growing American readiness to pursue a strategic doctrine that prevented automatic escalation of a conflict irrespective of the issues at stake. The automatic American guarantee of help began to look less credible, and the differences of opinion over the graduated response doctrine emphasized the growing strategic divergence between some European members of the alliance, such as France, and the U.S. The American resolve to stand by West Berlin, symbolic outpost of Western freedom, appeared less than staunch. This encouraged the Franco-German alliance, which did so much to complicate American and British policy in Europe.

The McNamara doctrine and the rise of Gaullism combined to produce a crisis in NATO. This forced Britain to choose between continuing to back American strategy, or attempting to lead an attack on a policy that might show that the deterrent strategy upon which NATO relied was 'incredible'. Britain backed America. Though she was always strongly influenced by American policy it was frequently resisted. Britain resisted, for example, American pressure to reinforce B.A.O.R. during the Berlin crisis in 1961. The quarrel with America over the M.L.F. is another striking example of British truculence. Yet the interlinking of Anglo-American policy remained throughout the fifties and sixties as a factor of enormous importance.

Two important examples relate to the British part in the Skybolt programme (which enabled the American Air Force to prolong the project for an additional six months) and the pressure brought on the Royal Navy by the U.S. Navy to take part in the Atlantic striking fleet. Yet difficult though relations were with America, it was the European end of NATO that caused Britain most difficulty and concern. This problem was not new, and was to receive considerable attention from Denis Healey as Secretary of State for Defence later on.

British Objectives

Britain's schizophrenic attitude to Europe is mirrored by the twin strategies she has pursued in the past: the maritime and Continental strategies which so uneasily co-exist. Geography dictates this problem. Since the seventeenth century Britain has had considerable overseas security problems, requiring a world-wide military presence and capability. Yet the security of the British Isles has rested on a European balance of power which needed an occasional military contribution in Europe. Skilful diplomacy in peacetime, and reliable allies when combat became necessary, were the essential prerequisites of survival. In the twentieth century two massive interventions as a Continental power (assisted by Commonwealth countries) and a continuing presence within NATO for more than twenty years became necessary.

British defence policy had to give her a major place in any European conflict or settlement. She joined NATO, however, to keep her freedom hoping for American backing for an independent British role; but later saw it as a means of establishing a new relationship based on 'interdependence' both with her Continental allies and the United States.

Problems arose when membership of NATO involved Britain in a direct clash between military and political objectives which needed to be brought into line. This was not achieved until Healey's Defence White Paper in February 1968, which made Europe the main military commitment

Britain has had three objectives in Europe.

First: To help secure Western Europe against war or invasion – which since the late forties, in the British view, could best be assured by the maximum commitment of American forces.

Second: The attempt to play a big role in any crisis, which needed military forces that could sustain her as a loyal NATO ally, and as a European power of a certain rank. Both Labour and Conservative administrations have consistently regarded Britain as a major NATO power, with political influence far greater than, say, Italy or Canada. This policy created an irreducible minimum, independent of strategic assessments. For example, the empty threats of Macmillan and Lord Chalfont that Britain would cut back her military presence in Europe if the Six persisted in trade discrimination against non-members could be comfortably ignored by Europeans. Everybody knew that Britain dared not reduce her military forces significantly in Europe without undermining her own diplomacy.

Third: Britain had tried to uphold an Anglo-American

system for Western Europe. This consisted of Britain maintaining good relations with the U.S.A., a capacity and will to deal privately with the Soviet Union (Eden in 1954, Macmillan in 1959) and, until the late sixties, consistently mistrustful relations with West Germany. France eventually rejected this image of the NATO alliance.

Britain's political objectives committed her to a strategic doctrine that caused increasing public disquiet. Basically, Britain was in favour of the lightest possible military contribution to NATO. The ending of conscription made this desirable, if not inevitable. This forced her to embrace the doctrine of nuclear retaliation. She set her face against a NATO conventional and nuclear superiority in every category. This was beyond her economically, because it needed a bigger army in Europe – which was too big a burden on top of her role as world policeman.

'Overstretch' and Empire

Britain's reliance on the atomic deterrent helped her to meet her considerable global responsibilities. It was argued that the atomic striking force, and the improved means of using military power overseas through the Strategic Reserve and the naval task force, could be a cheap and efficient way of safeguarding British interests. But this did not work out as intended.

It was soon discovered that a strategic nuclear capability was irrelevant for internal security operations which were the major challenge to Britain's interests outside Europe. Moreover, Britain found herself wanting the very troops needed for overseas security to bolster the defence of Europe. With her large conscript army she could meet the competing commitments, but only just. Yet the 1957 White Paper announced the end of conscription by 1960. It was obvious, therefore, that both the overseas commitment and the British Army of the Rhine faced further reductions. The era of 'overstretch' had begun.

Between 1950 and 1966 Britain was involved in eighty-five military operations. Twenty-two were major ones. Those military/civil operations can be divided into four basic types: (1) Counter-insurgency; (2) Intervention; (3) Specific deterrent; and (4) U.N. operations.

Counter-insurgency was the biggest job, and amounted to ten

operations, such as in Cyprus, Malaya, and Kenya. These insurgencies involved terrorism, subversion, and armed insurrection, as well as the more methodical Chinese-inspired insurgencies – of protracted struggle conducted according to Mao's principles.

Intervention operations (such as that in Kuwait, in 1961) have numbered five. These depended on the mobility of naval forces built around the essential aircraft carrier.

Deterrent deployments became increasingly urgent as a means of dissuasion. The Anglo-Malaysian resistance to Indonesian Confrontation, for example, was kept to platoon level as far as actual fighting was concerned by 'dissuasion techniques' such as V-bomber flights. Dissuasions like this were numerous: patrols in the Persian Gulf, off Abadan, in the Bahamas, off Beira and around the West Malaysian coast. These examples represented diverse but substantial force deployments. Some were more modest: for example, the Iceland or Arctic patrols.

The West Malaysian patrol, and the naval and air strike force that faced Indonesia, represented in turn a greater preparedness to threaten the use of considerable power. Like the tip of an iceberg the deterrent deployment of naval and air forces in the West Malaysian patrol represented a readiness to activate the nuclear strike force stationed on Malaysian airfields if necessary, along with the tactical nuclear power deployed in Malaysian waters. The risks for Indonesia appeared to outweigh the gains.

United Nations operations involving Britain in the period 1950–66 were in Korea, Cyprus, and the Congo. Britain wanted to take part in U.N. operations for diplomatic reasons, as well as make a contribution to international security.

The transfer of power in 1948 removed the Indian army from Whitehall's control, but left the main overseas deployment of British power on the routes to India via Suez, and in Singapore – originally the base for a defence of the eastern approaches to India.

De-colonization quickly undermined this base structure, especially in Cyprus and South Arabia, and played a part in the independence negotiations in Malaysia and Kenya.

The post-colonial states were often quick, however, to request military assistance; and were encouraged to think that London would always respond. The British effort to defeat communist insurgency in Malaya (1948–60) was a major campaign. Later full support was offered to Malaysia in the face of Indonesian demands which resulted in Confrontation, in 1964–6.

The economic cost of such operations was beginning to be a major factor by 1962, and the growing European school of opinion – now increasingly influential in both major parties – pressed for membership of the European Economic Community, together with a frankly 'Eurocentric' defence policy. In contrast, professional military men favoured an East of Suez strategy, and asked for a costly military infrastructure to see it through.

The Royal Air Force virtually demanded a new air force. Between February and March 1964 the Conservative Government agreed to place orders for the P-1154 vertical take-off aircraft, and the Hawker Siddeley 681 short take-off transport. In addition to this £500 million order, the British Aircraft Corporation was authorized to spend what was needed to get TSR-2 into production. Thirty models were ordered and, on 27 September 1964, only four weeks before the Government's election defeat, the aircraft climbed into the air.

The Royal Navy was planning an expensive refit, with the aircraft carrier playing a major role in keeping Britain as a credible military power East of Suez. The Chiefs of Staff favoured a global policy; and Lord Mountbatten persuaded the Navy to abandon its attachment to a broken-backed war (that phase of the struggle which follows the use of nuclear weapons) in favour of limited wars overseas.

The Army, which had been saddled with a Continental role, often equipped with weapons from other European powers – Belgian rifles, Italian howitzers – was still essentially colonial and imperial in its outlook. It much preferred service in the tropics to prolonged inactivity in Rhine-Westphalia. Even the City of London looked favourably on military operations overseas that were thought to protect essential raw materials, maintain access to markets and sustain the position of trading partners. But although this applied to Malaysia and Australia, the British military effort in Malaysia was in fact quite disproportionate to the actual economic value of Malaysia to Britain.

Defence policy by the late fifties and early sixties presented a confused and complex picture. The contradiction between a maritime and continental role was underlined by the growing belief in a Eurocentric role for Britain. The Treasury lined up behind this view, and urged defence cuts. Logically, Macmillan's attempt to negotiate entry to the Market in 1961–3 implied a shift of British defence efforts from overseas to Europe. Strategists concluded that the Hong Kong–Borneo–Malaysia–Singapore–Australia complex of interest would fall outside Britain's – indeed outside Europe's – sphere of influence.

But it was thought the Mediterranean, the Middle East, the Persian Gulf, and Africa might still continue to concern the British and Europe for some time to come; with Malta, Cyprus, Aden, and East Africa increasing in importance, and India and Indian Ocean islands diminishing.

As the Foreign Office and the Ministry of Defence fixed their forward-planner's eyes on a Eurocentric policy, politicians and the tax-paying public looked critically at the growing cost of military equipment.

Between 1952 and 1962 thirty major projects were cancelled, at a total cost of nearly £250 million – a prodigious waste of manpower and resources. Expensive projects such as Thunderbird, a tactical missile for which there was little need, and the long delays in cancelling controversial programmes such as Blue Streak, Blue Water and later TSR-2, caused grave public disquiet – especially since delays in cancellation often compounded the economic problem and worsened industrial relations.

Defence reform was needed. But it was not merely a question of better management or rising defence costs for small output. The real defence problem concerned foreign exchange costs, which were accelerating. The end of support costs made the British position in West Germany expensive in foreign exchange. In the last fifteen years Britain has probably contributed more than £300 million to the West German surplus in this way. The exchange costs of the role East of Suez were extremely high at a time when the country had a deficit on its balance of payments.

Need for Reforms

The need to reform the Ministry itself, and model it on the centralized U.S. Pentagon, was vital. Peter Thorneycroft's

11

Defence White Paper of February 1963 began the job. Already *The Times* (9 January) had urged the need for reform with an article entitled 'Bases for a Logical Policy'. This declared that – 'until the Admiralty, the War Office, and the Air Ministry are reduced to the size and scope of administrative head-quarters, defence policy in Britain will continue to be be-devilled by inter-service politics and prejudice.'

But Britain's basic defence problem was whether she could afford to belong to every major military alliance: NATO in Europe, CENTO in the Middle East, SEATO in Southern Asia, and the very considerable obligations in the Persian Gulf, as well as commitments to Asian Commonwealth countries.

Could these commitments amount to a logical policy for Britain in the seventies if achieved at the cost of economic growth and prosperity? At what cost could Britain get more security, with less risk? Such questions had become the dominant theme in strategic analysis both inside and outside the Ministry of Defence. But would the Labour Party provide an answer to these vexed strategic questions? Labour had chosen its best informed defence intellectual for precisely this task.

The Labour Alternative

On a cold winter's day towards the end of February 1963, Denis Healey became the Loyal Opposition's spokesman on Defence, succeeding Patrick Gordon-Walker as the next pos-sible Labour Secretary of State for Defence. That evening, 22 February, Healey spoke at a public meeting in Durham and categorically stated that – 'The major problem for the next Labour Government is going to be to decide whether there are any real British interests overseas which it is going to be both politically and militarily possible to protect by force. That is going to entail a total revision of our defence policy.'

But the Opposition's policy did not offer a total revision of British defence policy at this time. No doubt such a drastic revision of policy could emerge, given time, but in the period of the run-up to the 1964 General Election, the Opposition, under Harold Wilson's shrewd influence, seemed more intent on acquiring a credible defence posture. A new policy could come later.

Labour gradually acquired a defence policy closely linked to America. Looking to America for leadership and inspiration under Kennedy was not so depressing or politically unattractive as it had been during the Eisenhower era. The anti-American stance of the Campaign for Nuclear Disarmament, once so popular among Labour's rank and file, quickly changed with Kennedy's successful handling of the Cuban missile crisis in October 1962, and the signing of the partial nuclear test ban treaty in August 1963.

Healey was pleased that the Party had now adopted a policy broadly in line with the views that he had advanced during the great defence debate which had split the official leadership from the rank and file of the Party. The impact of the Mc-Namara doctrine, and de Gaulle's isolationism encouraged this.

Four-point Attitude

This new policy was in line with American strategic analysis: the merging of the British deterrent in NATO, and the build-up of conventional forces in an attempt to delay the use of nuclear weapons in a European conflict.

Labour quickly agreed on a general defence policy, which by 1963 had committed it to four specific points.

First, re-negotiation of the 1962 Nassau agreement. The V-bomber force would be allotted to NATO and the purchase of Polaris missiles abandoned if it were discovered to add nothing to the deterrent power of the alliance. The nuclear submarines would be converted into 'hunter-killers' which, according to Labour, made greater sense than giving them a second strike nuclear retaliatory role.

Healey had been reported by the *Daily Herald* on 5 March 1963 as saying that 'the Government's decision to have a fleet of Polaris submarines was like something out of the satirical TV programme "That Was The Week That Was"'. But in the summer of 1970 he admitted that the Nassau Agreement was a brilliant achievement, and gave Britain an effective, as well as cheap, deterrent. It was certainly that, since the cost of the five-boat force did not exceed £400 million overall – less than four per cent of the Defence budget per year for seven years.

In the Commons defence debate of March 1963, however, Healey was very critical of the deterrent's growing cost. He complained of the financial commitment of £400 million on Polaris, £400 million on the TSR-2, £200 million on keeping the V-bombers going, and an additional £200 million committed to establishing 'a multinational deterrent without any political or strategic explanation being given'. He therefore costed the deterrent at more than £1,200 million, which he later admitted was greatly exaggerated.

He also asserted that Polaris – 'Britain's phoney deterrent' – would be obsolescent by the time it came into service in five years' time, because the Soviets by then might well have acquired the ability to destroy it. The Soviets, he declared, had set up their first Polaris interceptor bases near Leningrad, which would increasingly threaten the British force.

The second feature of Labour's defence policy related to the mixed-manned multilateral force (M.L.F.). Though it was of doubtful military efficiency, Labour committed itself to joining if it seemed the only way to prevent the spread of nuclear weapons. Healey, however, had no doubt about his attitude, and that of his Party.

'In our view the mixed-manned surface fleet now under discussion would be economically wasteful, and militarily inefficient. This might not be enough to condemn it if it nevertheless fulfilled its political purpose; but in fact it is more likely to exaggerate than to moderate the psychological strains inside the alliance over nuclear sharing – it will stimulate rather than satisfy national nuclear aspirations.'

He concluded, in an article published in NATO's *Fifteen Nations* (July 1964) that 'by offering to renounce national control of its own nuclear forces in favour of a new system of NATO control, a Labour Government in Britain might succeed in shifting the focus of discussion away from the M.L.F. towards a more relevant alternative proposal for collective control of all the alliance's existing weapons'.

The third policy point related to British commitments overseas, which required strong and flexible mobile forces capable of fulfilling her obligations to Commonwealth countries as well as for peace-keeping duties with the U.N.

Healey regarded Britain's contribution to stability in South East Asia as a major factor in helping to keep the peace. He had written in *The Listener* of 2 August 1962 that 'the real threat to world peace at present lies less in the insanity of the great powers than in the instability of little ones'. He concluded that though it would be dangerous for the superpowers to intervene in the Afro-Asian world – the Congo crisis had revealed this – there was a place for Britain in assisting Commonwealth countries to surmount both internal and external threats by a combination of economic, technical and, if need be, military assistance. Moreover, in an earlier article in the *Observer* of 22 April 1962, he stressed, in opposition to British membership of the Common Market, that, in his view, Britain was not wholly, or even primarily, a European power. He therefore accepted the logic of a British world role.

The fourth point of Labour's defence attitude related to Britain's conventional forces, which needed to be better armed and equipped. In the Commons Defence debate in March 1963 Healey roundly declared that 'the British Army of the Rhine is undermanned and underequipped'. Labour pledged itself to spend more on conventional forces for use at home and abroad.

This, then, was Labour's policy on the eve of its accession to power. Increasingly Labour's anxieties centred on the cost of the deterrent, which, with the abandonment of Blue Streak in April 1960, meant that Britain could no longer remain a genuinely independent nuclear power. According to the Opposition the major reason for the Government's failure to produce a rocket delivery system was its cost. Research and development costs of delivery systems as with other complex military weapons were rising fast. The United States defence budget listed $6,943 million for research alone in the year ending June 1964. This was considerably more than the entire British defence budget for the same period. Moreover, as Healey frequently argued, the U.S.A. recognized the need to diversify its deterrent to achieve credibility: hence Minuteman, Polaris, Atlas, and Titan missiles, as well as bombers and 'tactical' short-range missiles. Therefore, according to Healey, Britain's argument that credibility could be achieved solely with a small number of one type of missile, Polaris, was both dangerous and irresponsible.

Healey was also anxious about the future of the V-bombers. Their recent conversion for low-level flight raised some sus-

picion, because the whole point behind earlier hopes of Skybolt
was that by 1964 or so actual bomber penetration would be extremely hazardous.

Specific criticism of the V-bomber force raised five doubts
about their credibility. First: the sub-sonic V-bomber would
be slower at low-level. Second: low-level flight inevitably sub-
jected the aircraft to enormous stresses, and must considerably
shorten the airframe life, as well as using more fuel. Third: the
Blue Steel was designed for launching 150 miles from the target,
and at 40,000 feet. Low-level launching, however, would make
it highly unlikely that it would reach its designated target from
150 miles. Fourth: the approach to the target, through the thick-
est local guided weapon defence system, was an even more formidable task for the V-bomber than for the projected TSR-2.
Finally: Labour regarded the V-bomber conversion as a jerry-
built affair because the R.A.F. itself – and not the aircraft industry – was actually responsible for the work being done. And
whereas the U.S.A. was spending £4,000,000 each on conversion
of B-52s for low-level approach, the R.A.F. had earmarked a
ludicrously inadequate amount for this purpose.

The Stand-off Bomb

Healey was even more disturbed by the deliberate vagueness
of official claims about the R.A.F.'s short-range complement to
Blue Steel, the stand-off bomb – first mentioned in the February
1963 White Paper. This weapon was heavily emphasized,
Labour concluded, to help offset the Skybolt disaster. At that
time it was particularly linked with the hastily erected strategic
nuclear 'bonus' role of the Buccaneer and TSR-2 aircraft. The
idea behind this 'new weapon' was that the supersonic low-level
approach by such aircraft lobbing the stand-off bomb on to
target from five to seven miles out by means of a sharp climb
(which also facilitated a getaway) could still make strategic
strike by conventional aircraft a credible threat.

A reference to the weapon appeared in *The Times* of 30
November 1963, which stated that 'a low-level air-launched
missile has been effectively tested, and R.A.F. officers believe it
can be brought into service within two years'. The report
linked the weapon with extending the life of the V-bombers.

In the event, however, the R.A.F. Wittering briefing, and

the attendant newsreel publicity for low-level V-bombers, put all the emphasis on Blue Steel as the stand-off weapon, and the complementary 'wonder bomb' quickly disappeared from the 1964 Defence Paper. It appeared to Healey at the time that if the wonder bomb was ever to be played up again it would be in conjunction with TSR-2. It was.

Healey said at the Electrical Trades Union College at Esher on 5 November 1963 that the TSR-2 affair showed every sign of becoming the biggest scandal in British politics since the South Sea Bubble. The Government should, he claimed, set up an independent inquiry. 'In fact,' he said, 'it is an unsound insurance policy for a programme of nuclear isolationism that does not make sense in the first place.'

Estimates of research and development, plus forty aircraft delivered, put the cost at £500 million. But Healey realized that far more than forty were needed if this expensive aircraft was to fulfil a 'strategic' role, as well as replace the Canberra as a tactical/strike reconnaissance aircraft. The probable number actually expected in service was a minimum of 150, at an estimated further cost of £340 million.

The confusion over the intended role of the TSR-2, which the Air Staff in the original operational requirement for this aircraft (O.R.343) had said they wanted as a tactical/strike reconnaissance aircraft only, was made worse by the statements of Harold Watkinson when he was Defence Minister and by Julian Amery, as Secretary of State for Air, who agreed that the aircraft had a 'strategic bonus'.

An element of farce crept into the affair when Peter Thorneycroft, as Defence Minister, proposed to the NATO Council in mid-December 1963, that NATO should set up a mixed-manned air squadron of TSR-2s. *The Times* on 21 December, in a leading article on the proposal, referred to Thorneycroft as having presented 'an idea with a seasonable air of pantomime'. The *Daily Telegraph* on 19 December said the plan had a cold reception in Washington. It quoted the *Washington Post*, which said that an American source in Paris had described the proposal as 'the stupidest damned thing I ever heard of'. Labour grew concerned at the growing frivolity of Conservative defence policy which the Profumo affair had so dramatically highlighted the previous summer.

The political atmosphere got hotter as the General Election approached. Healey's growing disquiet about defence was taken up by George Brown, Deputy Leader of the Labour Party, speaking to a mass meeting of trade unionists at Barking Town Hall on Thursday, 19 March. He said: 'One of the more serious charges against the Prime Minister is that he is deliberately subordinating the defence requirements of our nation to the political interests, as he conceives them, of the Conservative Party.'

A fortnight earlier Healey had said at Widnes that Sir Alec Douglas-Home would harm Britain's influence in the world by basing his campaign on crude appeal to ignorance and chauvinism.

'We all know the Prime Minister has to spend most of his time and energy nowadays learning off the slick phrases his ad-men work out for him. But he really must try to find a few minutes a day to read what his own Ministers are saying.'

This was an echo of George Brown's charge in his Barking speech that on defence 'senior Ministers talk publicly like a bunch of crazy, mixed-up kids'.

Election Battle

The Tories decided to attack Labour's defence position for its lack of patriotism and started to spread the charge that the defence policy of the next Labour Government would result in widespread unemployment.

Sir Alec Douglas-Home, Macmillan's successor, attacked Labour's plans to re-negotiate the Nassau Agreement. He also attacked the intended run-down of the British deterrent, the projected ban on the sale of arms to South Africa, and Labour's opposition to the sale of blueprints of naval vessels to Spain because, he alleged, it would result in thousands being thrown out of work, and a massive contraction of those industries dependent upon defence contracts. Labour, however, could point to the major contractions in defence industries that had already taken place under the Conservatives – particularly in shipbuilding and aircraft manufacturing.

Massive contraction had occurred both in the Royal Ordnance factories and in Naval dockyards. The Royal Ordnance factories had been particularly hard hit by successive Conservative Governments, and with the run-down in conventional forces under the Sandys *diktat* between 1958 and 1963 the number of workers employed dropped from 26,000 to 18,000 – more than a quarter in five years. In the Royal Navy dockyards from 1958 to 1963 the work force had been reduced by a third – from 68,345 industrial civil servants to 47,944 in 1963.

Labour spokesmen began to suggest that under Labour the evident mismanagement of the defence industries that had so weakened Britain's conventional capabilities would end. Instead, a Labour Government would concentrate on building up conventional forces and weapons, so that Britain could play a much more effective role than under the Tories. Healey now felt he was ready to assume the mantle of Defence Secretary, and that his Party had a rational and consistent policy as set out in the Transport House publication *Policy for Peace*.

In *Policy for Peace* three crucial paragraphs stood out:

'7. We seek the banning of all nuclear weapons everywhere. But the West cannot renounce nuclear weapons so long as the Communist bloc possesses them.

'8. Britain, however, should cease the attempt to remain an independent nuclear power, since this neither strengthens the alliance nor is it now a sensible use of our limited resources.

'9. The West must never be the first to use the H-bomb. The NATO armies, however, are at present perilously dependent on nuclear weapons of any kind, which would turn a conventional conflict into nuclear war. With this end in view Britain should press urgently for the following objectives: To make it possible for NATO to halt a local conflict with conventional weapons alone. To stop the spread of nuclear weapons to individual countries inside the alliance. To establish satisfactory collective political control of Western nuclear weapons and military strategy.'

This was coherent policy, even if it was not a radical policy involving a fundamental change in Britain's basic defence posture. To prepare himself for his forthcoming job Healey undertook two important visits abroad. From Washington he returned on 3 March, convinced that the U.S.A. would not pursue the idea of M.L.F. without British support. His own attitude to M.L.F. also hardened: 'M.L.F. was a non-starter and nuclear consultation and planning with NATO was a much better way forward,' he said.

On 26 May he started a Far Eastern tour that convinced him that Britain could still count for something, provided she pursued a more rational defence policy. In Tokyo he said it was 'politically, militarily, and economically undesirable' for Britain to maintain an independent nuclear capacity.

He reiterated this theme in his Cheltenham speech on 13 July by declaring: 'If Britain and France kept independent weapons Germany would have her own within five years.' He later admitted that he had exaggerated the danger of the spread of nuclear weapons, which the partial nuclear test ban treaty greatly inhibited. But he believed that the N.T.B. treaty did not go far enough, and the next step must be an attempt to stop the spread of nuclear weapons, and to provide arms control. In *A Labour Britain and the World* he wrote: 'For this next step Britain's possession of independent nuclear power and, even more, the extravagant claims made by the present Government for the importance of her nuclear power, are a very serious obstacle indeed.'

It would not be possible, Healey contended, to persuade the other European powers to accept arms control that froze Britain in a position of permanent superiority to them in the nuclear field.

Sir Alec Douglas-Home called the General Election for 15 October, 1964. In a lively campaign the P.M. concentrated on Labour's threat to phase-out the nuclear deterrent. But despite his attempts to make defence a major election issue the electorate concentrated its interest on the cost of living and material comforts.

Labour won by a narrow majority and on 16 October Denis Healey became Britain's Defence Secretary.

Chapter Eight

Value for Money

'Within a month I had discovered we could save £1,200 million.'

DENIS HEALEY

'In 1964 our foreign policy was much more ambitious than we could afford. The Defence Review compelled the Foreign Office, for the first time, to make decisions. Previously it had avoided them.'

DENIS HEALEY

Chapter Eight

ON Friday, 16 October 1964, the Russians had deposed Khrushchev, the Chinese had exploded their first atom bomb, and Harold Wilson had led the Labour Party to victory in the General Election. His majority of five showed he had the confidence of the nation, but only just. In the year and a half before he called another election Wilson showed that his administration was not one of radical reform, but as sound and conservative as its opponents.

Wilson was determined to run things. He appointed Patrick Gordon-Walker (who had lost his seat at Smethwick) as Foreign Secretary, because he needed a weak figure in the Foreign Office if he was to get his own way. Healey, whose training had equipped him ideally for the job, lacked standing in the Party, and had no administrative experience. He settled down to tackle the problems of defence as the first Labour Minister of Defence since Shinwell first held the post in 1950–1. Both policy and administration had changed a lot. He found the forces were overstretched, and under considerable strain because of Confrontation – the war against the Indonesians to protect Sabah and Sarawak.

Healey recognized the enormity of his task, but characteristically faced the challenge with robust confidence. He declared to *The Times* on 17 October that his general aim was 'to get the best value for every £ spent on Defence'. He had already decided to initiate a complete review of policy before deciding the future role, shape, and size of British armed forces in the seventies.

It was clear, however, that a number of more immediate issues had to be faced, and required speedy resolution. An early meeting in Washington was essential because of the hiatus over the mixed-manned multilateral force, which the Conservatives had largely caused by their ambivalent approach, and also because of Labour's own commitment to 're-negotiate' the Nassau Agree-

ment of December 1962, which gave Britain the means to build
a five boat Polaris submarine force, based on American missile
technology. The incoming administration wished now to re-
examine this agreement in the light of its own policy of winding-
up Britain's independent deterrent. But Denis Healey's immediate concern was over the R.A.F.'s expensive re-equipment
programme. Until and unless this was drastically pruned the
task of reducing defence expenditure would become impossible.

The Treasury decided that defence spending should be
pegged at £2,000 million at 1964 prices.

'I had no incentive to push further,' said Healey. 'It was really
arbitrary. We were obsessed by the fact that there was this automatic increase in defence costs if one didn't do something. We
were faced with a programme that went up from £2,000 million
to £2,400 million in five years, so we decided that we would
make sure that in five years time it didn't go up at all.'

'On the assumption that our Gross National Product went up
three per cent a year this would have meant that we would have
reduced the amount spent on defence by one per cent of the
G.N.P.,' he explained. 'But the Treasury had totally miscalcu-
lated its ability to run the economy.'

His immediate aim, in line with Labour's election pledge 'to
put our defences on a sound basis and ensure that the nation gets
value for money', was clear enough: to establish a more rational
relationship between the size and cost of Britain's armed forces,
the commitments they were expected to fulfil, and to reduce
the overall burden to the nation.

As he put it, 'during the first year we were looking for economies', and with the decision on whether to have an aircraft
carrier or not finally taken at the end of 1965, as well as the
cancellation of three of the R.A.F.'s aircraft announced earlier,
the process of retrenchment was well under way even before
the publication of the major Defence Review in February 1966.

Healey, it appeared, had few intellectual surprises waiting for
him. Sir Henry Hardman, former Permanent Under-Secretary
of Defence, later said: 'When Denis came to the Ministry, he
was surprised how little he didn't already know from what he had
been able to gather outside in his reading and conversation.'

What did surprise Healey was 'the extremely low cost of the
deterrent'.

But the first few weeks had a marked impression on him, as he admitted to the House of Commons: 'One thing I have already learned from my first five weeks in office . . . is that Britain is spending more on defence than any other country of her size and wealth. We are still trying to sustain three major military roles – to maintain an independent strategic nuclear striking power, to make a major contribution towards the allied defence of Western Europe, and to deploy a significant military capacity overseas, from British Guiana through the Mediterranean, Africa, and the Middle East to Hong Kong.'

Big changes appeared certain in the effort to reduce the 'overstretch' of Britain's military capabilities. The Defence Review would report on that in due course; meanwhile, urgent consideration was being given to the projected talks with the Americans over nuclear strategy and strategic interests.

Interest inevitably centred on the pledge to re-negotiate the Nassau Agreement of 1962, and the problem of finding a more acceptable substitute for the mixed-manned multilateral force. These issues were related because of the nature of the Nassau Agreement. As Healey observed: 'The interesting thing about Nassau was that the Americans agreed to give us Polaris submarines instead of Skybolt [missiles] on condition that we agreed to participate in a Multi-National Force.'

The M.N.F., as it became known, was a scheme to enable the European nuclear powers to pool all or some of their nuclear capabilities, but was quickly superseded by the proposal for a mixed-manned force. M.L.F. was the American proposal to make NATO's nuclear spearhead from twenty-five surface ships carrying Polaris missiles, and manned by mixed crews drawn from the navies of NATO member countries. Labour had now to take up this issue, and was even less keen on it than the Tories, because it appeared to add to the problem of how to stop the spread of nuclear weapons. Even Conservative opposition to it after the 1964 election hardened because, as Sir Alec Douglas-Home feared, M.L.F. would 'split the alliance wide open'.

'Weekend of the Crunch'

The Cabinet's attitude to this, and the related question of talks with the Americans emerged during the 'weekend of the crunch', as the press dubbed it, held at Chequers on 21–22 November 1964. This was a vital meeting for Healey, and became something of a personal triumph. His ruthlessly logical attitude and lethal candour demolished the views of George Wigg and Lord Chalfont, who feebly tried to destroy the British nuclear force, which was committed to NATO. He carried the support, however, of the Prime Minister, Chancellor of the Exchequer Jim Callaghan, and Roy Jenkins, the Minister of Aviation.

The decision to keep Britain nuclear was taken on the Sunday morning. The 'antis' had presented their case the previous day, but were overwhelmed by Healey and the professional advisers. 'There was a tremendous argument about it,' one adviser said, 'but in their heart of hearts I think the Government wanted to keep Polaris.' The strategic reason, as Healey later explained, was that 'if you are inside an alliance you increase the deterrent to the other side enormously if there is more than one centre of decision for first use of nuclear weapons'.

The Polaris programme was getting into its stride, and the decision to build the fifth boat had just been taken. 'The second one was nearly finished, the third was laid down, and we'd already ordered long-lead items for the fourth, so it would have been very wasteful to stop that,' said Healey. The fifth vessel was cancelled. Once built, running costs were negligible. But the admirals were worried about the drain on technological manpower. 'It sucks up a tremendous number of men,' Admiral Sir David Luce said. It was not even certain that Britain had enough qualified men to maintain their submarines; when one boat's centre section had to be repaired five years later, it took American help and nine months' work.

Although it is not really cost-effective each submarine also has a hunter-killer capacity. It was thought to be wasteful for them to sit doing nothing after unleashing sixteen rockets, each with a punch nearly fifty times more powerful than the bomb that destroyed Hiroshima in 1945.

One side effect of Britain's nuclear weapons, however, as some strategists believed, was that they gave her an extended and mistaken belief in a global role. Being nuclear gave us delusions of grandeur.

Of the four Polaris submarines, however, only one may be at sea at any given time. The others could be changing crews in base, or undergoing refit. Given the extensive Soviet submarine fleet, and advances being made in submarine detection, there is a question mark over how long they may remain a deterrent. But having only one at sea was enough for Healey. As a defence aide said: 'He was concerned at the outset to demonstrate where he thought we were getting value for money. He took the view that he couldn't justify the fifth submarine on these terms, although he thought the Polaris force was tremendous value for money *in political terms.*'

Polaris had enough power to worry the Russians, he argued, and gave Britain an important position in NATO, and in non-proliferation and disarmament talks. The cut in the number impressed his colleagues. 'He had immense power at Chequers,' a top adviser admitted. 'This came partly from his skill in mobilizing a case and handling opponents. He crushed people like Wigg and Chalfont.'

A junior minister agreed that 'with the Prime Minister, Healey, Jenkins, and Callaghan were the most influential'.

Lord Longford, Lord Privy Seal, and Leader of the Lords in the Wilson Government, said: 'He was very effective. He was not courting favour, or playing to the gallery – he simply gave an honest opinion.'

In the key sub-committee of the Cabinet – termed the Defence and Overseas Policy Committee, a nucleus of all the senior Ministers – Longford thought him 'the best-equipped person I have seen'.

Healey's technique was explained by a member of the Committee: 'He did not consult his Service Chiefs very much; he took up a lot of time explaining and answering points – always replying immediately to any point raised, and at considerable length; he was rational, and overwhelmed them with science; and he could not bear criticism.'

He exerted his powerful personality at the November 1964 Chequers meeting, where the discussion covered a wide range of issues, including nuclear arms, the multilateral force, the future of the TSR-2 and P-1154 aircraft, overseas bases, the problem of conventional forces, the local strategy of NATO, and even the war in Vietnam. Lord Mountbatten, Sir Solly Zuckerman, Sir Henry Hardman, and other Defence chiefs, together with their new political masters, hammered out a common policy for the forthcoming talks with President Johnson.

First: Renewed British emphasis on NATO in an attempt to forestall a French withdrawal or to reduce the harm caused to alliance unity should the French attempt to disrupt the alliance by a unilateral withdrawal.

Second: A British initiative in establishing conditions in NATO Europe for a phased mutual East–West reduction of arms.

Third: Continued British presence East of Suez, especially in the light of the military assistance to Malaysia. Britain would not abandon her world role.

Fourth: Some strengthening of the effectiveness of the United Nations' capacity to carry out its peace-keeping role in conjunction with America and Canada.

Some recognition of the dominant feeling of the numerous 'Third World' members of the United Nations, as well as the implementation of a pre-election pledge in line with left-wing desires, was fulfilled on 17 November 1964 with the announcement of a ban on arms sales to South Africa. After existing contracts to supply sixteen Buccaneer aircraft and spare parts had been met, there would be no more arms to aid Verwoerd's apartheid policy.

This announcement followed soon after the Autumn Budget of 11 November in which Chancellor Callaghan announced that National Health prescription charges would end on 31 January. International financiers – the 'gnomes of Zurich' – were amazed at seemingly irresponsible measures which did little to strengthen the British economy, suffering from an acknowledged record deficit in the balance of payments.

On 26 October a White Paper had been produced (dubbed the Brown Paper, after its principal architect, George Brown) which pledged the Government to carry out 'a strict review of all Government expenditure', with the aim of improving the economy by cutting 'expenditure on items of low economic priority, such as prestige projects'.

Sir Eric Roll, the Permanent Under-Secretary at the Department of Economic Affairs, took the draft of this to Washington for American approval and comment. It contained the reference to cancelling prestige projects. By Friday this had been amended to include a reference to cancelling Concorde, in line with American wishes. On Saturday the British Ambassador

12

was recalled from France, returning on Sunday to tell M. Couve de Murville, French Foreign Minister, that Britain was cancelling Concorde. But the wily Julian Amery, former Aviation Minister, had deliberately omitted any 'break clause'. If Britain cancelled during the development stage she had to pay the total cost, unless the French also wanted to cancel.

As the pound came under heavy pressure in the second half of November the Government took crisis measures to prop it up. On Monday, 23 November, the bank rate was raised dramatically, from five per cent to an unprecedented seven per cent. With America working hard for Britain, a loan of $3,000 million (more than £1,000 million) was announced on 25 November, and another $1,000 million followed from the International Monetary Fund on 1 December.

When the British delegation flew to Washington on 6 December to acquaint President Johnson with the new Government's foreign and defence policy they were told that more money would be forthcoming if unnecessarily expensive projects, such as the TSR-2, were rigorously examined.

Fleet Manoeuvres

The main problem to be sorted out, however, after Britain's desire to stay East of Suez had been established, concerned the future of Britain's nuclear weapons.

It had been decided that no specific re-negotiation of the Nassau Agreement was necessary. On 23 November Healey had told the Commons: 'We must use this opportunity presented to us in the alliance by the crisis over the multilateral force to produce ... an arrangement which will make national nuclear forces unwanted and unnecessary.'

The British proposed a modified suggestion, named the Atlantic Nuclear Force (A.N.F.). This suggestion combined mixed-manned and nationally-manned nuclear delivery systems (not just Polaris, but other weapons, including V-bombers) under a comprehensive allied nuclear command. It was a scheme which, it was hoped, would satisfy the anti-nuclear left-wing of the Labour Party as well as reassert Britain's important position in the alliance. Like Bevin, Wilson and Healey were trying to establish an economic, military, and diplomatic special relationship with America as the corner-stone for their foreign policy. Dick Taverne, then Healey's Parliamentary Private Secretary, said: 'I think Denis would have accepted the A.N.F. proposal if it had come off as a way of shifting out of the Party's anti-nuclear deterrent commitment.'

It was hoped, also, that A.N.F. would keep in check the Germans, who had signed an agreement with the Americans in June 1964 to set up M.L.F. by the end of the year. Healey continually fought to keep Britain as America's foremost European ally. Franz-Josef Strauss, a former German Defence Minister, recognized the true nature of the A.N.F. proposal, however, when he described it to Taverne as 'the only fleet that had not been created that torpedoed another fleet that hadn't sailed (M.L.F.)'.

'We devised the A.N.F. as a means of scuppering the M.L.F.,' admitted Healey. 'The Ministry of Defence was totally opposed to M.L.F., and the Foreign Office wasn't terribly keen on it, but felt that our relationship with the Americans required that we should put it to sleep quietly, rather than directly oppose it.'

'President Johnson had become quite sceptical about the M.L.F. and was ready to be pushed off it; the A.N.F. proposal gave him a very good excuse for abandoning it. This was always my point, that it is madness to build a new force with a lot of expensive hardware without the slightest idea of how you are going to control its use, so that it was just so much junk so far as solving political problems was concerned.'

An American commentator said: 'Johnson agreed to drop the M.L.F. idea and go for the A.N.F. on the understanding that Britain would give up the nuclear deterrent, and sell the A.N.F. to Germany, and become the nuclear equal of Germany.'

Taverne explained the advantages and problems of A.N.F. in an article entitled 'The Future of the Atlantic Alliance' which appeared in the German *Wehr Kunde* (Defence News). This was a transcription of a speech, cleared first by Healey, and completely in line with his thinking.

After stating that the firm involvement of America was necessary for a strong NATO alliance, Taverne stated: 'Political solidarity is the core of the NATO problem,' and added that both M.L.F. and A.N.F. were schemes designed to help achieve this. They were of doubtful military necessity, however, as

America would probably use her own nuclear weapons at the same time. A.N.F. or M.L.F. would only be two per cent of the nuclear deterrent of NATO. 'Without the American deterrent they would therefore be pointless. Together with it they would be unnecessary.'

The arguments in favour of such a force, however, concerned the need to get closer consultation on the use of nuclear weapons in the alliance, and a system of comprehensive control. 'The problem of control,' Taverne argued, 'should be solved first, before a definitive resolution can be made concerning a collective force.'

M.L.F. and A.N.F. dropped out of sight, while the real problem of what should be done with existing nuclear weapons in the event of war was tackled by the NATO allies. Nuclear planning, rather than nuclear sharing, was the primary task, and here Healey was to make perhaps his most important contribution as Defence Minister.

A.N.F. was only part of what the British wanted to discuss with Johnson and McNamara, for both Wilson and Healey believed that the major threat to peace lay East of Suez. Britain's defence priority, Johnson was told, was to ensure that commitments in the Far and Near East would be maintained. American policy in South East Asia would be backed by Britain.

This policy carried two short-term implications: that there was a need for a rapid provision of force on request, which could prevent small local conflict from deteriorating into a general war or anarchy; and that Britain should be prepared for limited war on at least the scale of the Malaysian Confrontation operation. There was no fear at this time, with America strongly backing Britain, of being isolated in a major war. That fear grew as the war in Vietnam escalated.

Healey's view of the situation in NATO Europe also carried the day. It was that the existing nuclear arsenal constituted a more than adequate deterrent to possible Russian aggression. The real problem in Europe, he felt, was to reorganize the nuclear control arrangements if necessary along the lines of the proposed A.N.F. The military task would be to provide a well-equipped mobile force capable of responding to a local conflict before it grew into a full-scale war.

The visit was a great success: M.L.F. was abandoned and

A.N.F. adopted. When it was out of the way the path would be clear for genuine consultation and planning. The Americans were delighted that Britain was to continue to shoulder some of the burden in the Far East.

The policy was confirmed a year later when, after another visit to Washington, Wilson told the Commons that there was 'complete agreement in Washington with the British Government's decision to continue to maintain a world-wide defence role, particularly to fulfil those commitments which, for reasons of history, geography, Commonwealth association and the like, we, and virtually we alone, are best fitted to undertake'.

In 1964 Labour's Prime Minister, Defence Minister, and Foreign Minister were all pro-Commonwealth and anti-Common Market. Paul Foot in his book on Harold Wilson neatly analysed Wilson's preoccupation with the Commonwealth, which he saw as a new power bloc that could challenge the superpowers. Gordon-Walker in his book, *The Commonwealth*, described it as 'a real force in the world', adding, 'the Commonwealth will grow greatly in power'.

Healey was such a strong believer in the idea of a wider European grouping (suggested in his pamphlets of the 1940s) that he led the rearguard action in the Cabinet when it later considered the question of whether or not Britain should apply for entry into the Common Market which was solely for Western Europeans. Enoch Powell, who as shadow Defence Minister courageously fought the Conservative mania for seeing any rock as part of a world-wide empire, trenchantly observed that – 'The Commonwealth goes round the world, and if you believe in the brotherhood of man you must believe in international policies.' Powell, who tried to persuade both his own Party and the Labour Government to concentrate on the essentials of defence as he saw it – forces for the defence of Europe only – thought that the Labour Party emphasized the Commonwealth's importance because it was the best group of states through which they could exert any influence.

The early months of the Labour administration reflected this preoccupation, with much talking and collaboration between Commonwealth countries. Only the gradual realization that the Commonwealth was declining as a major force, and moving towards a talking shop in which developing nations could air their views, pushed Britain towards a more European-orientated policy. Initially, however, Healey worked to make Britain's commitments round the world viable, by streamlining defence and getting that value for money.

P-1154, HS-681, and TSR-2

Healey had to make some critical decisions in the vast R.A.F. re-equipment programme. In his first few months, he decided the fate of the Hawker Siddeley 681, the P-1154 and the TSR-2. But to cancel British military aircraft affected the aircraft industry; and Healey's department therefore had to agree on a common strategy with Roy Jenkins at the Ministry of Aviation, and Frank Cousins at the Ministry of Technology.

Four factors were involved: the impact of the cancellations on the aircraft industry which, according to press reports, could drop to merely one and a half times the size of the French industry; the need to reassess the urgency of the operational requirements set down for the aircraft ordered; the availability and operational capabilities of any U.S. aircraft which might be ordered as replacement aircraft; and, of course, the major problem of increasing defence costs arising from the fulfilment of the demands of the air staff for the R.A.F. in the seventies.

The Ministry of Aviation opposed the immediate wholesale cancellation of military aircraft – although it was willing to consider axeing some; and the Ministry of Technology was worried about the impact of the cuts on the aircraft industry, especially on Britain's capacity to sell aero engines abroad.

The three Ministers involved were on a collision course. Yet the initial confrontation was between Healey and Aviation Minister Roy Jenkins – especially over the TSR-2 which Healey wanted to cancel much sooner than Jenkins would allow.

Jenkins had his problems because the aircraft industry had become too dependent on the Government's financial backing. In 1965 alone the Ministry of Aviation was paying out about £210 million on its own account in research and development contracts on top of the £325 million being spent by the Ministry of Defence, largely for production contracts. More critically, one project – the TSR-2 deep strike and reconnais-

sance – in that year would, according to Jenkins (speaking in
the aerospace industry debate in the House on 9 February
1965) 'require an average contribution of £15 from every man,
woman and child in the country, £50 or so from the average
family'.

Sir Henry Hardman explained the difficulty of estimating
the final cost of the aircraft: 'When someone told me that TSR-2
was going to cost £105 million I added £45,000,000, which in
the light of experience, I did not think unreasonable.' Before
the axe fell, an estimated £750 million was thought to be
needed for the research, design and production of 150 aircraft.
It was even feared that this figure could be doubled.

Healey later thought that Mountbatten's advice, to develop
the Buccaneer instead, should have been taken.

'One of the tragedies of the aerospace industry,' he said, 'is
that the R.A.F. didn't buy the Buccaneer and develop it when
it first came out; but they were determined to have their own
aircraft. By the time I came in the cost of development and the
"life" of the aircraft meant that it would scarcely have been
worth the money.'

The export performance of the industry since 1958 had also
deteriorated. It had fallen from more than thirty per cent of
the total output to about twenty per cent. The only probable
improvement was on the civil side, with the sale of the
BAC-111. Export prospects on the military side – seventy per
cent of the industry at this time – were for all practical purposes
non-existent. Healey could thus consider the military side of
the cancellation of the TSR-2, the P-1154 and the HS-681 without having to consider the potential harm done to exports,
since no substantial orders had yet been placed.

'Almost the first instruction I gave on my first day as Secretary
of State was to the man concerned with our aircraft programme
to tell me if there was any way of getting a capability equivalent
to that provided by the TSR-2, P-1154, and HS-681, at less cost,
by buying abroad. Within a month I'd discovered we could
save £1,200 million.'

If the three projects had gone through, not only would they
have been expensive, but, in the case of the supersonic tactical-
strike interceptor, the P-1154, and the short take-off and landing transport, HC-681, they would have been delivered well

after the R.A.F.'s need for them; and they lacked export potential. 'When we looked at the map we found that runways were multiplying like rabbits all over the world, and there was really no case for short take-off planes like the HS-681,' said Healey. 'Furthermore we could buy three Hercules transports for the price of a single HS-681.'

His immediate problem was with Roy Jenkins, who favoured axeing the P-1154 and the HS-681 but not the TSR-2, which, with its programme for about 150 aircraft, might cost £750 million.

Heally recalled that 'I wanted to cancel TSR-2 in February, but my colleagues didn't agree. It was always on my conscience that on TSR-2 we were spending in every two or three days as much as the whole of the Arts Council got in one year – money down the drain!'

But he expected Jenkins to fight for TSR-2 as a good departmental Minister should – just as, three years later, when he became Chancellor, Jenkins pressed for the cancellation of the U.S. F-111 purchase – the replacement agreed for the TSR-2 – much to Healey's own chagrin.

The case for cancelling the P-1154 and HS-681 Healey regarded as unanswerable. On the question of availability alone neither aircraft could meet requirements. The P-1154 was intended as a replacement for the Hawker Hunter fighter that was due out of service by 1968–9. The P-1154 itself would not be available before 1970–1 at the earliest. The HS-681 transport, intended to replace the Beverley and the Hastings, would not be ready until 1968–9, and unlikely to be in full service before 1972 or even 1973.

Healey had decided by the early part of 1965 to order the P-1127 (the Harrier jump-jet) because of its military characteristics and export potential. His big problem was the TSR-2, where Roy Jenkins would be the final arbiter in the decision-making chain.

Hawker Siddeley's last minute proposal for the HS-802 with a Comet wing and HS-681 fuselage was not suitable because, once again, even the early models would not be available for two years. The purchase of the American C-130 was therefore inevitable. Britain would also purchase the U.S. Phantom, but it was to have a British engine and reconnaissance pods – and possibly some British airframe work, employing about 7,800 people by the end of 1967. This was an important consideration.

Healey's decision that the R.A.F. could do without the P-1154 and the HS-681 was related to a potentially serious situation arising from the fact that the MIG-21 fighters operated, for example, by Egypt, Iraq and Indonesia, were superior in performance to fighters in service with the R.A.F. The R.A.F.'s Hunter, which was used in a ground attack role, could not be replaced before the end of 1970, when it would have been in service for fourteen or fifteen years. This was also true of the Canberra. By the time the TSR-2 replaced it it would have been in service fifteen years.

Both the Hunter and Canberra were overstretched and overused. This was also critically true of the Valiant bomber and the Beverley freighter. As Healey alleged in the Commons on 9 February 1965: 'If we had stuck to the previous Government's aircraft programme, we faced a real danger that the R.A.F. would literally have no aircraft at all for some of its basic tasks.'

Six years' Dither

But that was not all. Healey felt bitter because his own freedom of action had been curtailed by the six years' dither over aircraft replacement between 1959 (two years after the Sandys White Paper rejected supersonic manned bombers) and 1965.

Healey had opened the books, and found that a firm contract for TSR-2 had not been placed until 1959. Contracts placed for the aircraft to succeed the Hastings and Beverleys of Transport Command (as it then was) came even later, together with replacement decisions over the Hunter and Sea Vixen aircraft of the R.A.F. and the R.N. On the Hastings/Beverley replacement Healey complained in the Commons: 'It took them (the Conservatives) two more years to issue a firm operational requirement; another two years passed before even an order for a project study was placed with Hawker Siddeley for the aircraft now known as the HS-681.'

The case of the Hunter/Sea Vixen replacement was even worse, according to Healey, because 'another three years were spent in the attempt to get the R.A.F. and R.N. to agree on a common aircraft'. That was announced on 26 February 1964 when the Conservatives had to admit that it was impossible for both branches of the Services to share a common aircraft. So, a short time before Labour came into office, it was announced that the R.A.F. would get the P-1154 as a Hunter replacement, and the Royal Navy would have the U.S. Phantom to replace Sea Vixen. The R.A.F. would not have the P-1154 in service before 1970 – well after the Hunter should have been permanently grounded.

Healey said in the House that his immediate predecessor, Peter Thorneycroft, had 'left office knowing that continuing failures of decision by himself and his predecessors faced the R.A.F. with a gap in its light aircraft that could be fatal to the nation's security and the lives of its airmen. He must have welcomed the events of October 15 last [the election] as a happy release.'

Healey decided that both P-1154 and HS-681 had to go. His decision was made inevitable by escalation of costs. And, as he solemnly warned the Commons on 9 February 1965: 'If we look at the three projects now under discussion, we find that the estimated cost of the HS-681 has doubled since the operational requirement was first issued nearly four years ago. In the case of the P-1154, the estimated cost has trebled in under three years.'

But costs apart, the case against the two aircraft was simple and irresistible. They would not be ready before existing aircraft fell to pieces, or became obsolete. So, he ordered the British P-1127 Harrier jump-jet and the American Phantom. Taken together, these two aircraft met the R.A.F.'s requirements. This was a good, determined and clear-headed start to his task.

He also announced the purchase of the C-130 giant transport as a Hastings/Beverley replacement which would come into service at the end of 1966.

With the TSR-2 Healey showed some initial hesitation and uncertainty. A sharp backstairs inter-departmental struggle over this aircraft was under way, although as far as Healey was concerned his mind was made up by February 1965. Yet owing to the Cabinet's indecisiveness he failed to cancel it immediately, even though he thought it was a mistake to demand the ultimate in technical sophistication irrespective of cost, delivery dates or the possibility of foreign markets; and that the air staff

tended to define operational requirements in terms of the technological optimum, rather than specific and operational needs.

The R.A.F., which knew that the end of TSR-2 might not
mean the end of a sophisticated strike and reconnaissance role,
was optimistic about its future. As one senior officer remarked:
'At least under Healey we are going to get what we want today
– instead of the promise that we have to wait until tomorrow.'

The 1965 White Paper

The publication of the White Paper therefore brought few
surprises. And the Commons Defence Debate, though devoid
of drama, produced the anatomy of the Defence Review itself
which was still in preparation. Defence was to 'serve the objectives of our foreign policy' and prove 'compatible with the
needs of our economy'. Healey confessed that 'this year's Defence
White Paper is simply the first engagement in a long campaign
to re-establish control of the nation's defence, and to take a
firm grip both on policy and on expenditure'.

The problem facing NATO was 'to reach agreement on a
strategy for the defence of Western Europe that makes sense
in terms of the political and economic realities of 1965'. That
involved the need to 'concentrate on using forces we have for
the danger which we think is likely ... to reduce our reliance
on nuclear warfare by using these forces in a conventional role'.

Britain's contributions to stability overseas could not be
open-ended. 'We cannot do it indefinitely on our own. We cannot be the permanent policeman for the whole of Africa and
Asia. Whatever might have been possible in the nineteenth
century, the days of Pax Britannica are over. We must share
our responsibilities with our friends and allies.' This was all in
line with Healey's thinking as expressed when in Opposition.

On the vexed question of the provision of tactical/reconnais-
sance capability Healey declared – 'The case for a TSR-2 or the
F-111, a Canberra replacement, rests primarily on its potential
role in conventional warfare and also on its role in warfare
outside the European theatre.'

The End of TSR-2

TSR-2 was finally cancelled on 5 April 1965 – Budget Day.
A storm of protest broke out. Violence had been done to the

beautiful daughter of the British Aircraft Corporation and the Conservative front bench.

Conservative anger was genuine, though misplaced. Cancellation was inevitable. A very senior defence planner of impeccable political neutrality said of this decision: 'It would be an illusion to say that a number of the issues that were taken up by the Labour Government couldn't have arisen with Thorneycroft. . . . The TSR-2 would have come up with Thorneycroft and the advice to him would have been the same – cancel.' Even a British Aircraft Corporation executive (who held the *Economist*'s Mary Goldring personally responsible for the bad public image of TSR-2) conceded: 'The Tories would have cancelled it just the same – politicians don't understand the first thing about aerodynamics.'

It is a curious fact that the TSR-2 cut-back decision was mostly a political row among politicians; and between some of them and the aircraft industry. There was no serious split within the Ministry of. Defence over this issue. All the top officials favoured cancellation. Lord Mountbatten, Chief of the Defence Staff, Sir Solly Zuckerman, the Government's chief scientific adviser, and finally the Air Staff themselves all realized the inevitability of Healey's decision.

An influential Air Vice-Marshal agreed that 'the TSR-2 cancellation was an inevitable decision which made perfect sense from whatever angle you approached it'. He was proud of the fact that when his opinion was canvassed on the question he had bluntly replied: 'It must be cancelled – the loss of one of those machines would be a national disaster, and no pilot wants that responsibility. The damn thing was never intended to be a strategic-strike aircraft anyway.'

According to a civil servant involved in the project, controlling it 'had got very complicated, and procedures were inadequate – but you must remember this was a very sophisticated aircraft, ahead of its time. . . . Once the aircraft became overloaded, costs shot up alarmingly – the trouble was the airmen crammed the thing full of expensive kit.' Healey himself said, 'Cost in military aircraft is a direct function of weight', and that the cost of TSR-2 'didn't make sense'.

This aircraft, which had been credited with a 'strategic bonus', was essentially a tactical strike reconnaissance aircraft, and really useful only in that role. The idea spread by some Conservatives – in particular Stephen Hastings in his book *The Murder of the TSR-2* – that the aircraft was cancelled because of left-wing pressure backed by a hostile press is a grotesque oversimplification. This was confirmed by a top Ministry of Technology official who played a big part in the planning of TSR-2: 'Denis Healey cancelled a project that had more financial thrust than Blue Streak. The nation's financial watchdogs sitting in the Treasury had more influence in this than the nuclear pacifists on Labour's back-benches.'

But was the cancellation of TSR-2 completely justified? A number of doubts persist, mostly related to some of the official explanations advanced to justify its cancellation. The decision to cancel was justified, given the increase in costs and the Government's argument that Operational Requirement 343, governing the specifications and role of TSR-2, was still valid for the 1970s. Yet at the time of cancellation Healey was at great pains to avoid giving the impression of having prejudiced the outcome of the Defence Review. He argued in the Budget Debate on the day of cancellation that 'the review may show that the number of aircraft required with TSR-2 performance characteristics is essentially below the existing TSR-2 programme. On certain hypotheses and long commitments it might even be possible to reshape our defence in such a way as to dispense with this type of aircraft altogether.'

But the conclusion that TSR-2 was expendable was made possible because a low-cost substitute existed in the high performance multi-mission F-111, which the American Government was prepared to sell to Britain. Had this aircraft not been available then TSR-2 might have been saved. One of Healey's top planners admitted that 'the F-111 made cancellation of TSR-2 possible, and prevented us from either having to withdraw O.R. 343 or rewrite it, or even cancel it. This avoided the possibility of a major revolt on the part of the Air Staff, whose attachment to O.R. 343 was very strong indeed.'

The two arguments advanced by Healey and James Callaghan in the Budget Debate – that the cancellation of TSR-2 made possible a restructuring of the aircraft industry, with a redeployment of part of its labour force, and that the future of the industry lay in joint co-operative production in Europe (financed by the funds released by cancellation) – were not as critical, or as relevant, as they appeared.

This impression is strengthened by the observation of a member of the Air Staff who recalled that 'the cancellation of TSR-2 was a close run thing – two factors weighed very heavily with us. Firstly the F-111 was immediately available – which was an enormously important point in its favour – but, secondly, we had to consider the TSR-2 weapons system, which we reckoned was superior to the American versions. When we did cancel, we had to be certain that the F-111 was a better aircraft. It was.'

So cancellation of TSR-2 cannot be justified simply in terms of the cost escalation factor: nor indeed as a decision that made European collaborative projects more attractive and feasible.

Healey felt that he had done the right thing. A Ministerial friend commented that 'the TSR-2 decision strengthened Healey's position in Cabinet because he had shown resolve, courage and skill in insisting that this aircraft, though scrapped, did not automatically scrap the need for a replacement. And that that replacement must be American. This naturally didn't please everyone.' Indeed not.

Healey on the Continent

Healey was busy with visits abroad explaining to allies and Commonwealth partners his unfolding defence policy. His initial difficulties lay with the West German Government who were very suspicious of Britain's A.N.F. proposals. His trip to Bonn at the height of the TSR-2 controversy was, however, satisfactory, and may be said to be the beginning of the real Anglo-German defence collaboration in NATO over nuclear planning. A West German diplomat said that 'Denis Healey was the first British Defence Minister to have the complete confidence of Bonn'; and this was undoubtedly because of his consistent attitude to defence in Europe. He had always, in his thinking, taken account of the German attitude to nuclear deterrence which naturally stressed the consequences to West Germany of any kind of conventional or tactical nuclear war. His reiterated belief that the job of NATO was to prevent war not win one, found an echo in the West German demand that NATO strategy should strongly emphasize inevitable nuclear escalation. A German journalist, Hans Werbke, explained why Healey was such a success: 'The Germans like experts. After all the Tory Ministers of Defence he stood out as the first person who knew and understood what it was all about.'

Healey's emphasis on the London-Bonn axis, rather than the London-Paris axis, paid dividends later. It arose from his evaluation that Germany was the most important of the European states, and was going to become more important still – de Gaulle notwithstanding. His relations with the French were poor for other reasons also. They found his analysis of defence problems very different from their own.

At the February discussion in Paris military collaboration was high on the agenda, and did produce a number of projects including the Jaguar, an Anglo-French fighter/trainer aircraft, the Martel, an advanced airborne missile, and eventually, the Anglo-French variable geometry aircraft, but the first two of these projects were already in the pipeline. Only the A.F.V.G. showed that Britain 'and France could push collaboration further. And that project was doomed.

But it was on the question of NATO strategy that Healey collided with the French. An adviser close to President de Gaulle confided that 'even the mention of Healey's name pained de Gaulle because of his blunt and oversimplistic arguments in favour of American-orientated NATO strategy'. But a French general who knows Healey well said: 'It is wrong to blame Healey for pointing out the weaknesses of French nuclear thinking, since his real offence was to say things that the French military secretly shared. They knew the real consequences for France of withdrawal from NATO and so did Healey. He merely said so, whereas they couldn't.'

Healey undoubtedly upset President de Gaulle, who was sensitive about the loyalty of his generals. A French security chief observed that 'some of de Gaulle's personal aides even thought that should France withdraw from NATO – as she eventually did in 1966 – the General Staff would stage a C.I.A.-backed coup to oust the President'. That was nonsense, but it did appear to the French military adviser that 'Healey had displaced McNamara as the villain of the piece in Charles de Gaulle's demonology' because of his determined bid to keep France in NATO 'virtually on American terms'. Yet when it came to it, according to a source close to the President, 'De Gaulle's dislike of President Johnson', whom he regarded as a coarse, insensitive intriguer unworthy of high office, 'cannot be compared to his view of Healey whom de Gaulle regards as clever but not yet politically important'. According to the same source, de Gaulle personally liked Healey but distrusted Harold Wilson who 'represented the archetypal politician he had fought so hard to displace in the Fourth Republic'.

According to Sir Henry Hardman, Permanent Under-Secretary to the Minister, Healey's stock was highest among French military and defence chiefs. He was regarded as a professional military expert 'and not a politician, since his attitudes were apolitical'.

His contact with the French left a lasting impression of 'a tough man in the tradition of Churchill', but inevitably 'a bit remote and unpopular since in untroubled times defence is as fashionable as short hair'. These words, by one of de Gaulle's prominent Cabinet Ministers, sum up Healey's image among the French defence intelligentsia: 'Had he been French he would still have ended up as Minister of Defence – he's born to it.'

Healey regarded de Gaulle's attitude to defence as completely irresponsible, and at a *Socialist Commentary* meeting in London he said that de Gaulle was 'a bad ally in NATO, and a bad partner in the Common Market' – an indiscretion for which he had to apologize publicly. Yet many sympathized with Healey's remarks. An American diplomat observed – 'What Healey said was correct. De Gaulle was a bad ally and had offended Healey's fine understanding of defence. You don't split alliances over theological issues and base national security on unusable weapons-systems.'

Economic Problems

The economic situation in Britain continued to deteriorate, and, policy apart, the question of how much could be spared for defence remained unanswered. Healey had committed his Ministry to saving £400 million by reducing defence expenditure to £2,000 million at 1964 prices by 1970.

The Government's overall economic strategy depended on demonstrable cuts in public expenditure to keep the confidence of people holding sterling abroad.

International confidence in sterling fell as deficits in its balance of payments rose under the Conservatives. In 1964 the deficit had been £747 million. The advent of the Labour Government caused near panic among foreign investors, and the Government could restore confidence only by publicly declaring a marked deflationary policy.

In July 1965, however, the run on the pound became once again a question of great concern to the Chancellor of the Exchequer. James Callaghan turned to Denis Healey for an assurance that cuts would be effectively and quickly achieved. Healey responded by announcing at a press conference on 4 August that he was halfway to his target of £400 million in cuts, having so far achieved a total of £220 million.

Public opinion was generally behind him. Most people were interested only in spending less on defence – provided the country did not become defenceless. Healey explained also, that 'in the early years everybody saw defence cuts as the answer to the economic problem. The tragedy was that the money I saved on defence was squandered on increases in consumption and civil expenditure.' (There was little real attempt to control civil expenditure until 1969, when Jenkins was Chancellor.)

At his press conference Healey said that 'the only real hope of savings lies in the possibility that commitments can be revised'. On 5 August he told the Commons: 'I readily confess that to bridge the remaining gap to the target will require redeployment of our forces and a smaller total of manpower in the services.'

The difficulty, as Healey admitted, was that 'the Foreign Office wouldn't agree to look at commitments until we saw how far we could go by cutting expenditure on equipment'.

'Our defence has always served our foreign policy, but the difficulty in 1964 was that the policy was much more ambitious than we could afford. We were very overstretched, but unfortunately the Foreign Office hadn't established any priorities itself in relation to the costs of policies. The Defence Review compelled the Foreign Office for the first time to make decisions. Previously it had avoided them.'

Before the Defence Review was complete or his policy could be made public Healey needed to sound out Commonwealth opinion. He had always been close to Commonwealth leaders

13

and in sympathy with their security demands, if a little impatient of their lack of consistency and understanding of British problems. He carefully explained Britain's attitude to the Commonwealth statesmen (and was warmly received in Canberra on his visit early in 1966). But he emphasized that the economic situation was the real determinant of policy. Sir Henry Hardman stated Healey's position: 'Denis was the servant of events. There were few resources, and there were going to be fewer still.'

In July 1965 Healey had announced that £20,000,000 would also be saved by disbanding the Territorial Army – a decision which outraged traditionalists like the Duke of Norfolk, Chairman of the T.A. Angry television interviews with T.A. worthies lamenting the passing of the old force soon followed. But the T.A. was better suited to the conditions of 1914 and 1939 than the 1970s, and Healey was ruthlessly logical about it. In its new role the T.A. would reinforce the regular army only in specific situations.

Yet Healey did not get his own way entirely, and in February the following year the Minister of Defence for the Army announced in the Commons that a new volunteer reserve force would 'act generally in support of the civil authorities in the event of a general war'. This force was not, however, related to the Army Volunteer Reserve, and was to cope with the consequences of war on British society. One general remarked that 'Healey could see no place for the Territorial Army in his concept of war in Europe'. This was so. He took the view that there was no place for the amateur in the fully professional army of today, apart from a few well-trained specialists. *The Times* became his most trenchant critic over the issue of the reserves, and its anti-Healey campaign quickly followed.

On 16 September the Government published its five-year National Plan, which aimed at increasing Britain's production by twenty-five per cent. This meant increasing the Gross National Product by four per cent a year, and George Brown, whose plan it was, expected the Gross National Product to be £8,000 million larger by 1970. 'The Plan shows that, big as this sounds, we can do it,' he said.

But the Plan failed dismally. The Labour Party philosophy had ensured that social services should benefit most under the

Plan, with a commitment to spend money early in education, health, and welfare. When the Plan failed defence had to be further cut, instead of being gently reduced.

This contributed significantly to the weaknesses which subsequently appeared in defence policy.

Rhodesia and U.D.I.

The next crisis was not to be financial or economic, however, but political and diplomatic; and it was to bring Commonwealth unity almost to breaking-point. With the Rhodesian declaration of independence Britain faced a challenge to its power and authority that came on a day of symbolic significance – 11 November, Armistice Day. The prospect of a war, or even an exchange of a few rounds, with the Royal Rhodesian military forces utterly dismayed Her Majesty's forces.

Healey admits that after a brief look at the military side of intervention in Rhodesia, however, the overwhelming conclusion was 'that it was just not on'. He recalled that on a previous occasion, under the Central African Federation, Sir Roy Welensky had shown how easy military resistance to the Crown could be. 'He had them roll drums on to the tarmac of Rhodesia's main civil airport to show that our military transports would be unable to land.'

Healey's view that there was no easy military solution was strongly backed by his professional military advisers. They were unanimously of the opinion, as one senior officer put it, 'that military force could have been successful only if we had sent in an extremely large intervention force prepared to fight every bloody inch of the way against both soldiers and civilians'.

The practical difficulties of mounting an invasion were enormous. Britain's closest base was Aden, which was as far from Salisbury as London is from Cairo. 'It would have taken us three months to build up a mounting base in a neighbouring country, and it would have been continually vulnerable to attack,' said Healey.

'Even if we ignore the very important argument that had we invaded we would have made the problems of Central Africa even more difficult, the British people would not have stood for it,' he added. 'And if we had somehow managed to carry out a successful coup, there was practically no African administration at all. This would have meant the imposition of colonial rule over a long period.' With the evidence of the United Nations' attitude in the General Assembly, and Trusteeship Council, Britain would have been condemned by countries anxious to divert attention from their own shortcomings and inequalities.

The Rhodesian declaration of independence (U.D.I.) raised problems, however, of a philosophical character that could have had an impact on strategic thinking. As a senior ex-Cabinet colleague of Healey's put it: 'The trouble with Denis's global role was that having shown that Rhodesia could not be unilaterally defeated at an acceptable cost, he might have convinced others wishing to challenge us that Britain would back down again – especially in an economic crisis.'

Certainly there was something odd about Britain's readiness to start counting the political cost of a military operation, which on the face of it appeared more modest than operations then proceeding in Borneo. Did Britain's military overstretch prevent her intervening in Rhodesia? A senior defence planner said he was sceptical of this because 'there was always the possibility that part of Rhine Army could have been deployed there'. Obviously, in 1965 no leading politician really wanted to think about a military shooting match with Smith's illegal regime.

There was also a danger, if Britain did attack the Smith regime, that the Government might fall. Since the defeat of Gordon-Walker in a by-election in January 1965, Wilson was pushing Labour's policies through with a Commons majority of only three. If right-wing renegades such as Woodrow Wyatt and Desmond Donnelly defied the Party Whip the Government could have been defeated and an election called at a time when the majority of the electorate would want to show they were not in favour of military action against Smith.

Healey later convincingly argued (at a public meeting in Bradford) that the use of force over Rhodesia 'would have been a prolonged and difficult military operation, and as the Rhodesian armed forces were roughly the equivalent of those of Norway, logistic problems would have been immense'. The Defence and Overseas Policy Committee (D.O.P.C.) considered the matter in that light, and the Cabinet took the same view. Even the bombing of strategic points was dismissed as unlikely to produce worthwhile results. But this is not to say that no plans exist or have ever existed to intervene in Rhodesia.

Almost certainly the Prime Minister, Harold Wilson, told Ian Smith as early as his visit to Rhodesia in 1965, and at subsequent meetings on H.M.S. *Tiger* in 1966, that British military assistance was available if there was an attempted right-wing coup to throw out Smith and the 1961 Constitution, or an African attempt to rebel which might lead to a Congo-type situation.

For Healey, however, the Rhodesian crisis had only fleeting military significance, and his department was not involved in the political aspects of the crisis. He himself drew a number of conclusions about the episode which he thought reflected on the competence of some African states because 'the only countries which today seem prepared to use force as an instrument of policy (over Rhodesia and elsewhere) are those which are non-aligned'. He condemned their recklessness, which could imperil world peace, and drew the conclusion that 'the main threat of war at the moment lies not in the countries of NATO or the Warsaw Pact, but in the third world such as Nigeria, the U.A.R. and in the Far East'. That turned out to be profoundly true.

When the Defence and Overseas Policy Committee decided (with Healey dissenting) to send troops to deal with a little unrest in Anguilla in 1969, however, it appeared to the 'Third World' nations that Britain was prepared to 'bash the blacks' – but not the whites.

This venture, undertaken on the flimsiest of evidence, probably arose from the Colonial Office's absorption by the Commonwealth Office in August 1966. This nostalgic attempt to revive gun boat diplomacy was seen, philosophically, by the Ministry of Defence as 'a good training exercise'.

Chapter Nine

The Defence Review

'No bloody fear. I'm the boss.'
> DENIS HEALEY to Navy Minister Christopher Mayhew's
> request to address the Cabinet.

'"Confrontation" was not an imperial war. It was just an inconvenient war.'
> DENIS HEALEY

Chapter Nine

THE aircraft cancellation decisions had now been taken but critical defence decisions remained as the Government's Defence Review went through the motions of exhausting every possibility, using 'scenario studies' and 'cost-benefit analysis'. A new defence policy was called for, more perfectly expressing national aims in military terms and in the wider context of foreign, defence, social and economic policies.

The Review was a Government attempt to set broad objectives with depleted resources. The ultimate responsibility lay with the Prime Minister and the Cabinet; but below them the resolution of critical issues was taken in the Defence and Overseas Policy Committee – D.O.P.C. as the Ministry of Defence preferred to call it. This had all the 'heavyweights' – the Prime Minister as Chairman, the Foreign and Commonwealth Secretaries, the Chancellor of the Exchequer, Home and Defence Secretaries, and other senior ministers; in addition the Chiefs of Staff attended from time to time. They in turn were supported by a committee of senior officials serving on the Defence and Overseas Policy (Official) Committee, chaired by the Secretary to the Cabinet, with a number of Permanent Secretaries and the Chief of the Defence Staff as members. Its job was to see that defence policy kept in line with existing commitments and resources and that necessary adjustments were made in time, and without exposing the country to military danger.

Healey's presence and performance in the D.O.P.C., before his Cabinet colleagues, was probably decisive in determining the Government's overall defence policy.

But policy making did not simply start with the Government and Cabinet, and flow through Secretaries down through Departments of State. The whole process was, in fact, a two-way affair, with proposals and alternatives going up and down the line. The Defence Review was a good example of this interaction, and Healey dominated the Cabinet and D.O.P.C. A colleague recalled that throughout the sixteen-month Review, 'Healey simply overwhelmed his critics on the D.O.P.C. – and in Cabinet – with science, and reeled off fact after fact that bemused those who were half inclined to doubt his judgement.' It was essential for Healey to carry conviction before the D.O.P.C., because the inter-service conflict in the Defence Ministry might otherwise be raised in committee.

Healey firmly put his foot down when Mayhew, the Navy Minister, asked to be allowed to address the Cabinet about the need for CVA-01 – the new aircraft-carrier. Healey told him he couldn't: 'I said "No bloody fear. I'm the boss." I didn't *forbid* other Ministers going before Cabinet – they had no *right*. People like to feel that the Minister is in charge.'

Healey was in charge. During the Defence Review he was working twelve to fourteen hours a day to stay on top of his job. It was a task few Labour M.P.s envied, but it suited his tough, insular character. In January 1970 he told a meeting of Labour supporters in Pudsey: 'As Defence Minister it is very easy to forget within a week or two that there are any human beings outside – or inside either.'

During the Review, however, as Taverne said, 'Denis became regarded as the top administrator in Whitehall. He could out-argue anybody on their own subject.'

His senior advisers thought he was a decision-taker, using a quick brain to aid his intellectual bullying. His confidence in himself grew, but he made no attempt, as did other more ambitious politicians, to gather support within the Party. 'He doesn't seem to get on confidential terms with anybody, which people expect if he is to make a bid for the leadership,' said a colleague. Healey, however, established a reputation as a tech-nocrat with real ability.

But he was not simply a talker, as two battling encounters with the extreme right showed. In January 1965, while he was speaking for Gordon-Walker in the Leyton by-election, burly right-wing leader Colin Jordan, who had been hiding on the platform, burst out – and, in full view of the television cameras, Healey knocked him off the platform.

In March 1969, while he was addressing a meeting for Dr Colin Phipps in Walthamstow, there was a twenty-five minute demonstration by National Front members. A man hit

Arthur Bottomley, the sixty-two-year-old Commonwealth Relations Secretary, and Healey chased after him. He told a reporter:
'I saw Arthur holding his stomach, and I wanted to identify
the man so that the police could deal with him.'

The Carrier Issue

The battle inside the Ministry of Defence over the fate of the
Navy's virility symbol, the aircraft-carrier, never came to blows,
but it was an intense conflict between the Navy and the Air
Force, which both of them believed to be a battle for survival.
Healey's domination of the discussion in the D.O.P.C. was
reflected in his control of the Ministry as he presided over the
bitter inter-service struggle. It was complicated by the fact that
the Navy had conceded the importance of long-range tactical
air power – and hence the need for the F-111 swing-wing aircraft
as a replacement for TSR-2 – but the Air Force would not concede that the aircraft-carrier programme was vital for operations in the sophisticated environment of the seventies.

By early 1966 this inter-service wrangle had slowed down the
Defence Review, because Healey insisted that the carrier issue
be exhaustively examined and tested before taking a final decision.

The East of Suez strategy could stand or fall with the carrier.
Healey says that the problem was exhaustively examined: 'We
looked at dozens of scenarios which had been agreed between
the services, and were heavily weighted in favour of the Navy.'
But Healey thought the Navy made out rather a weak case
('Chris Mayhew –the Navy Minister – ruined them on this.') and
believes that Mayhew was over-confident about the carrier
issue: 'He thought we would never actually cancel. So, instead
of putting a moderate case, and trying to meet the real issues
involved, they presented their case badly.' But the cards were
stacked against Mayhew, who was not allowed to put his case
to the Cabinet.

Top Navy men, however, confirmed Healey's impression that
Mayhew was over-confident. One asserted that – 'the Navy
Minister played a disastrous game. He didn't seem to realize
that the case for the CVA-01 couldn't be made, and that the
case for the mini-carrier, which should have been re-examined,
would have given us a better chance of winning the day. He

thought he could defeat Healey on the big carrier issue – but the Navy had to pay the price.'

But Mayhew had fought hard for the CVA-01. 'His case was deployed with power and vigour,' said another Navy man, 'but by its very nature it played straight into the hands of the R.A.F., who were our major competitors for funds.'

This was critical, because 'pound for pound, the carriers gave smaller returns than the bombers'. The R.A.F.'s case centred on this.

Four basic arguments were deployed by the airmen. First, that out of a three-carrier force only two were ever active, given the need for overhauls and refits. As Healey said: 'We could never have more than one carrier in one place at a time with a three carrier force. Five carriers would have made sense, but would still have been too expensive.'

Second, the carrier needed two-thirds of its aircraft for self-defence, which made it an expensive way of providing air power with minimal effect. One senior naval planner admitted: 'One carrier, H.M.S. *Hermes*, could carry only seven bombers, plus twelve fighters, and, as Healey was fond of saying, even if she carried Buccaneer Two-Double Stars they'd have the capability of only three land-based F-111s.'

A distinguished air marshal further developed this point by saying that 'the carrier force that we actually have available is not really up to the task of giving air cover in an amphibious operation in the face of sophisticated air attack. The pongos on the ground would be chewed up unless land-based air cover could be quickly provided.'

The air staff also maintained that land-based aircraft had much better range and pay-load. Healey confirmed that this argument was put to the test. 'We did an incredibly complex study, taking an extremely rigorous East of Suez scenario, namely, how you could give continuous air cover to a naval task force travelling from Australia, round the North of Sumatra to Singapore, for a period of three months against sophisticated air attack,' he said. 'We learned that even in this situation we could do the job cheaper without the carrier.'

A member of Healey's Programme Evaluation Group who took a close interest in the carrier issue said that 'the Navy Board accepted that continuous air cover would have to be provided for a naval task force steaming round Australia and had always seen the logic for the purchase of the F-111'. This was an important concession to the air staff because, as another adviser in the forward planning section of the Ministry – D.S. 22 – said: 'There was nothing like a choice of "either/or" between the carrier force and land-based air power.' This meant, in effect, that the carrier force was expendable, but given the East of Suez commitment the need for long-range aircraft (like the F-111) was essential. And a close adviser to Healey said: 'The carrier was considered as an addition to land-based air power not a substitute for it.'

Finally, the airmen contended, land-based aircraft, whether committed to NATO, or elsewhere, could in emergency be deployed anywhere on the globe in forty-eight hours or less.

This was a devastating case in favour of land-based aircraft; but what of the Navy's side? The carrier was a very versatile weapons system, well adapted to service in the nuclear missile age, replied the Navy Board. Even in the nuclear age it could survive, they argued, but its real justification lay in its role in intervention operations. Its formidable presence gave Britain a capacity to deter; and to fight if necessary in local situations needing a quick response.

One admiral said: 'The carrier can hit surface targets with impunity within 1,000 miles, give air cover continuously over a radius of 400 miles, and provide protection against submarines up to 100 miles. It's the perfect ship for a role East of Suez.' In intervention operations the carrier was very successful, and had performed its task in Malaysian waters (and at the time of the 1961 Kuwait operations) with little trouble and risk.

A general with experience of the Malaysian operation said: 'We could always rely on the Navy. They flew their helicopters in Borneo irrespective of the weather, and gave excellent ground support where it was needed. The R.A.F. were most selective and cautious when it came to support for us on the ground.'

Admiral Sir Frank Hopkins, then Deputy Chief of Naval Staff, and a leading supporter of the carrier, remembered the scenarios the Secretary of State set for a number of situations which Britain could face in the 1970s in areas like the Far East and Indian Ocean:

'The job could be done with the existing carrier force and

naval aircraft, but to show that the carrier force could be dispensed with and replaced by shore-based aircraft proved more difficult.

'Many devices had to be resorted to in order to do so, such as assuming the existence of bases that were not there, and never likely to be; crediting the F-111 with a performance in which even its most ardent supporter could scarcely believe, and in the event never materialized; assuming almost super-human achievements in logistic support by the R.A.F.; assuming over-flying rights of countries in Europe, Africa and Asia which were unlikely to be allowed in the event; and even, in one study, moving Australia 600 miles to the North-West in order to bring certain targets within range of the already elastic radius of action of the F-111.'

This has been strongly denied by the Ministry of Defence; but the belief that the R.A.F. and the Secretary of State cheated over the scenarios, and fixed them to discredit the carrier was still widespread among top naval men when Healey left office. A high-ranking naval serving officer alleged that 'the R.A.F. was allowed to gerrymander its case with the connivance of the Secretary of State in order to demonstrate that the F-111 was a jack-of-all-trades'.

The inter-service bitterness over this controversy persisted with the R.A.F. gaining from the phasing-out of fixed-wing naval aviation. And, inevitably, all Defence Ministers are accused of a bias towards one service or the other. On this occasion, according to a top defence planner, the Minister of Defence was biased – favouring the Navy. 'Healey insisted throughout that the Navy Board should be allowed to make the best possible case for the carrier, even if it meant that the scenarios were weighted in their favour,' he said.

Healey himself said he had 'no prejudice one way or the other'. The trouble with the Navy was 'bad advocacy', according to one of Healey's aides. 'Then they tried to blame the jury when they lost the case.'

Healey believed the Navy lost because 'they argued on the wrong grounds, trying to defend the carrier, not as a protection for the Fleet, but for strike on land targets where it was ludicrously ineffective compared to land-based aircraft. You can't keep a carrier operating at full load for more than ten days at a time – and we could never have more than one carrier in one place at a time.'

Admiral Hopkins disagreed with Healey's assessment. He believed that the Defence Review studies were biased in favour of shore-based aircraft.

'They did not cover unusual or unexpected situations nor were we allowed to assume that intervention could ever be needed outside areas that could be covered effectively from friendly shore bases. . . .

'The great virtue of an entirely self-supporting seaborne force is that it can operate anywhere in the world with equal ease. It does not require overflying rights and it can remain poised in threatened areas for extended periods without infringing territory. It can be deployed quickly to any part of the world, and so take care of the unusual or unexpected situations which, history tells us, are the ones that occur far more frequently than those covered by contingency plans.' Such a capacity does represent a considerable asset. It appears, however, that the Navy lost its new carrier because, as an air vice-marshal said: 'They rejected a more cost-effective carrier, and opted for the CVA-01.'

A pro-carrier admiral admitted the logic of this (and pointed unconsciously to the central contradiction in the Admiralty's case) by asserting that 'we never took the view that the R.A.F.'s bombers should be sacrificed – we argued the case for the F-111 – but the sacrifice of P-1154 and TSR-2 ought to have released sufficient funds for the building of the CVA-01'. But once the Navy conceded the case for the F-111 in its projected role East of Suez it sank its own boat. This becomes obvious when the two principal aims of the Defence Review are recalled: to continue to meet Britain's obligations East of Suez for an indeterminate period; and to reduce the nation's spending on defence to £2,000 million at 1964 prices by 1970.

But Admiral Hopkins, supported by Lord Mountbatten, former Chief of the Defence Staff, takes the view that 'the Government were already quite determined to arrange that never again would British forces be deployed overseas against opposition in support of friends, allies or interests of any kind, except possibly as a token addition to a United Nations force.'

The publication of the Defence Review gave quite a different impression. Healey's public and private assurances to Commonwealth leaders would also appear to contradict it.

The real reason for the cancellation of CVA-01 lies not in the duplicity of the Labour Government's declared and actual policy, but in the badly-argued case made out by the Navy Board. A more modest carrier based upon the expected developments of the short take-off and landing principle (STOL) might have won Healey's support – but this was never attempted.

Healey was confident that his decision to cancel the aircraft-carrier was the correct one. He felt reassured that those for whom he had the most intellectual respect supported him most. He was impressed with the intellectual candour of the R.A.F., and felt that the Navy had been obscurantist and excessively traditional in its attitude. He confesses that 'the interesting thing was that the Navy conceded the case for the F-111 whether they got the carrier or not. But the Air Force wouldn't concede the case for the carrier. The Navy felt this was breaking a log-rolling tradition – that if I scratch your back, you must scratch mine. But the R.A.F., under Sam Elworthy, took the view: "No, I must follow where reason leads; I am grateful for your support on the F-111, but I'm not going to support you on the carrier because you are obviously wrong!"'

Healey's decision to cancel settled an issue over which there had been years of wrangling. As Sir Henry Hardman explained: 'The carriers had been an area of indecision for years. After months of debate Denis came out against the carriers.' He added: 'He had Mountbatten and Solly Zuckerman – the Chief Scientific Adviser – against him.'

Mountbatten's Silence

The silence of Earl Mountbatten of Burma throughout this struggle remains a mystery. He must have seen the fighting. Lord Mountbatten, moreover, was the chief architect of Britain's carrier task force and principal proponent in the Ministry of a continued role East of Suez. His brilliant career gave him unrivalled power and prestige; and had he spoken up on the carrier issue – as he appeared willing to do in retirement – then the decision may perhaps never have been taken. Conceivably if Lord Mountbatten had fought this decision, and resigned rather than retired – as Admiral Sir David

Luce decided to do – then Healey might have been forced himself to resign, particularly as Mountbatten's enlightened views on Indian independence had won him a great deal of Labour support.

The truth is that Lord Mountbatten, due to retire in June 1965, was not disposed to fight. His final six months were spent quietly, and this is understandable after his exhausting years at the Ministry of Defence forcing through his great contributions – the naval task force and an integrated Ministry. But Healey freely admitted: 'He could have been difficult on the carrier decision, but he knew he was leaving and felt it wasn't right to interfere.' Admiral Luce explained that he 'argued alone for the carrier for about six months', but he was clearly no match for Healey, who could be devastating in close combat.

Had Healey decided to keep Lord Mountbatten on as Chief of Staff, as Mountbatten wished, it could have been very awkward for a new Minister struggling to get and retain the confidence of the services in a period of withdrawal and retrenchment.

Healey's initial decision not to ask Mountbatten to stay beyond his retirement was therefore fateful: 'I told Dickie that he was leaving. It was one of the first decisions I had to take, and I talked to people throughout the Ministry about whether to keep Dickie on or not.' The advice was unfavourable to Lord Mountbatten, and Healey accepted the widely-held view that he should make way for another man. Healey recalled that once Mountbatten knew his fate 'he took a relaxed attitude'.

Cost Effective

The CVA-01 was also sunk because the Ministry of Defence began to use new techniques to establish what sort of value for money they were getting when buying weapons. When Healey arrived, the department was already beginning to use management techniques that McNamara had introduced into the Pentagon. Sir Henry Hardman was influential in promoting 'programme budgeting', with 'functional costing', and 'cost effectiveness'. These techniques, begun under Thorneycroft, were refined under Healey.

The Review was the first attempt to evaluate the cost of a

policy. As Healey put it: 'For the first time in British history – and machinery didn't exist for this earlier – the Cabinet was told what it would cost to adopt certain policies.'

The basic idea behind programme budgeting was to make decisions after rational and explicit reasoning. It involved planning, defining objectives, breaking down a programme into its constituent parts, then working out what each would cost, and finally estimating its efficiency.

When a certain plan was being costed Healey and his advisers would go along to 'Peck's Cavern' – the office of Tony Peck, Deputy Under-Secretary – to work it out.

But when it came to working out how 'efficient' the Ministry of Defence was, it became almost impossible. In business, efficiency can be worked out in terms of profit, and whether a target can be reached. In defence the most desirable result is never having to use your weapons. As Healey said: 'Determining efficiency, once you get away from a simple criterion, like how many bombs you can drop in a given area in a period of time, becomes very difficult.' As his department soon found, the most cost-effective weapon is the fist, and the next is the bayonet.

The cost-benefit analysis of Britain's East of Suez role showed that to keep one carrier on station three in all would be needed. When building and maintenance costs were added to running costs over ten years it was realized that keeping a carrier East of Suez was going to cost Britain £1,000 million more than having fifty F-111s. On economic grounds the carrier was rejected.

World Reaction to the Review

Consultations with allies began as the Review neared completion. Healey had discussed its major conclusions with NATO ministerial colleagues in December (a few days after the announcement that he was to get a new residence at Admiralty House, where he was to live for the next five years) and they were satisfied that Britain intended to remain committed to the defence of Europe, even if she had decided to cut expenditure on defence and reduce her disproportionate share of the cost of helping to defend Europe. The problem of B.A.O.R. support costs was a factor which determined the British attitude.

At the beginning of the New Year Healey was ready for his

14

crucial Washington visit to explain Britain's new definition of its role East of Suez. On 27 January he arrived in Washington for talks with Defence Secretary McNamara. An American official said of these talks: 'They went well. Healey explained that Britain's stay in Asia would continue, but when Confrontation ended the number of British servicemen in the Far East would be substantially reduced. He stressed that in future they would be committed only if certain political conditions were met. The carriers would go – and military opinion in Washington was that this was a sensible decision since the F-111s could carry out this role perfectly well.' Another official said: 'The only doubt was about how many F-111s Healey would buy. He decided on fifty but this wasn't confirmed for three weeks or so.'

After Washington came Canberra on 2 February. The Australians heard Healey with concern and interest. They had two questions: How long did Britain expect to stay, and in what strength? Britain, emphasized Healey, intended to remain a world power and would never abandon Australia. She would have a sea and air presence in the area, and with Indian Ocean 'baselets' would be able to come to Australia's aid, as well as to Malaysia's, should occasion arise. But he did warn that Britain's terminal date might be accelerated if economic circumstances made this necessary.

He then flew to Singapore where he explained to the Prime Minister, Lee Kuan Yew, that Britain would not be leaving Singapore for the time being, but that the future could not be guaranteed. Britain might base a naval squadron in North Australia and F-111s in Singapore, but she could no longer afford to sustain costly fixed bases overseas. The expansion of R.A.F. Transport Command (as it then was) with its VC-10s and American Hercules, the C-130, and the alternative route across Canada and the Pacific, would ensure that Britain was ready to help Singapore in an emergency.

Three days later he was in Kuala Lumpur, reassuring the Prime Minister of the Malaysian Federation, Tunku Abdul Rahman, and Defence Minister Tun Abdul Razack, that while Confrontation continued Britain would remain committed. Britain, he told them, would stay East of Suez until 1970 at least, and even beyond.

Confrontation

Confrontation was an almost unknown war to the British people, although officially 119 British servicemen were killed and 182 wounded before it came to an end in August 1966.

The conflict arose when the Federation of Malaya, Sabah – formerly North Borneo – and Sarawak was established as Malaysia on 16 September 1963. The Indonesians, whose territory adjoined, initially welcomed the idea of it, but after the Central Committee of the Indonesian Communist Party (representing 3,000,000 Indonesians) had denounced ' the formation of a new concentration of colonial forces on the very frontiers of our country' President Sukarno took action.

With the aim of acquiring all of Borneo, Indonesia began to 'confront' the Federation. Trade with Singapore stopped, British businesses in Indonesia were taken over, and diplomatic relations broken off. Raids were made into Sabah and Sarawak by Indonesian guerrillas, and paratroops were dropped across the Straits of Malacca. When Malaysia took the issue to the Security Council of the United Nations in September 1964 it voted 9–2 in favour of a Norwegian resolution deploring Indonesian landings, and calling for respect of territorial integrity.

When Labour came to power in October 1964 Gordon-Walker explained: 'We continued the succour of Malaysia without question.' Healey said: 'A new Government cannot just change things and retain any credibility – unless it does it under *force majeure.*' The way the Government were handling the economy it sometimes looked as if circumstances were *not* under control.

There were two different schools of thought on how to end Confrontation – which the Chiefs of Staff were urging on politicians because they were overstretched. Following the dropping of ninety-six Indonesian paratroopers in September 1964 at Labis – of whom thirty-two were killed and sixty-two captured – military advisers on the spot advocated a more offensive strategy. They wanted to escalate the conflict until the Indonesians gave in. Healey's arrival at the Ministry of Defence brought the short struggle between the hawkish military commanders in Malaysia and the doves in Whitehall to an end.

One commander engaged in Sabah said he 'very nearly

succeeded in persuading the Conservative Government to escalate the conflict'. His secret memorandum argued that 'a real show of force would certainly force General Nasution to overthrow Sukarno in a military coup'. Healey, however, rejected the idea of escalating the war.

The élite Special Air Service patrols, however, ventured many miles into Indonesian territory, and were highly successful at disrupting Indonesian operations. The Indonesians themselves did not like to admit that they could not control their own frontier. It is not known how many of the twenty-five soldiers who disappeared in action were killed by the Indonesians as they generally 'disappeared' in circumstances such as explosions, where bodies could not be recovered.

But the task was enormous, as Healey explained when he said that the British army 'held a difficult land border almost 1,000 miles long, and Commonwealth naval and air forces controlled over 3,000 miles of coastline and the air space above it, in a brilliantly-conducted inter-service and inter-allied co-operation'.

Admiral Luce paid tribute to the soldiers: 'The people who really won the war in Borneo were the soldiers on the ground, in their small packets. The Navy played its part on the Borneo coast, and in the Malacca Straits; it helped the Army wherever it could with patrol craft.'

It was not, as Healey explained, in any sense an imperial war. 'It was just an inconvenient war.' It was impossible to break even 'inconvenient' promises, although he did consider the possibility of withdrawal when the Federation started to disintegrate: 'I was very tempted when, in the middle of Confrontation – in the summer of 1965 – the Tunku and Harry Lee gave us an opportunity of getting out, by breaking their own Federation behind our backs. But you just couldn't do it. There wasn't a political solution as long as Sukarno was there.'

Britain was stuck with a military operation that looked politically increasingly embarrassing. She had put 50,000 troops into the Borneo territories at some risk and at great financial cost, especially in precious foreign exchange, and more than fifty ships of the Royal Navy were on patrol. The military risks were not negligible, and the war could always escalate like Vietnam. Indonesian aircraft had, for example, machine-gunned a settlement in Sarawak in early September 1965, the first air incursion since Confrontation, and more than 10,000 British and Commonwealth troops were rushed forward to defend it.

Healey was only too aware that the major threat in Sarawak came from the underground Chinese insurgent movement that had its roots among 16,000 rural Chinese families. This raised a critical internal security situation with the Clandestine Communist Organization claiming the support, according to military intelligence, of 5,000 to 7,500 Chinese, mostly farmers, and it was looking more and more like Vietnam in miniature.

Healey knew that the weakness in his Defence Review was in accepting these open-ended commitments on a semi-permanent basis. He wished to convey to the Tunku his anxieties about future British commitments. Under Article 6 of the Defence Agreement with Malaysia Britain had the right to make use of the British bases in Singapore and Malaya, not merely for Malaysian and Commonwealth defence, but also 'for the preservation of peace in South-East Asia'. This vague right, coupled with British membership of the South-East Asian Treaty Organization (SEATO) represented a considerable global commitment.

However, the main difficulty in considering whether or not to leave Malaysia was, as Healey said, 'when you are in the middle of fighting you can't think realistically about the post-war environment, because A. you don't know how and where the war will end; and B. if you are not losing the war you can't really say it isn't worth fighting it.'

Aden

In Aden and the Persian Gulf there was no war, but forces stationed there to keep the area stable were having the opposite effect. The large fixed base had become a target for local resentment.

Cost-benefit analysis showed that the area which meant most to Britain economically was the Gulf. But the British troops there were possibly counter-productive. When Healey suggested Britain should pull them out by the end of 1966 the Foreign Office overruled him.

As the Defence Review neared completion, however, Aden, with its huge internal security problem (and the Cabinet's growing conviction that it was strategically unnecessary) could be quietly dropped. Britain decided to pull out by the end of 1968.

Healey was aware that in July 1964 the Conservative Government pledged 'to retain her military base in Aden for the defence of the Federation and the fulfilment of her world-wide responsibilities'; but changed circumstances made the preservation of that pledge absurd and unnecessary. He decided to redeploy forces to the Persian Gulf where they were necessary for the maintenance of British interests.

He was aware that this sudden decision might cause difficulties, and that terrorist acts against the British Army in Aden might multiply (which did occur after the publication of the Review on 22 February) but it was a calculated risk that was well worth taking. A Ministerial colleague said: 'His Aden decision was correct. We had considered the possibility that Colonel Nasser might claim it as a victory – as he did a few days after the announcement – but it was really a victory for British commonsense.'

Healey was adamant that Britain's stay in the Gulf was unaffected by this decision, and that the importance of her economic interests in that area – as well as those in Western Europe – meant that a total British withdrawal would have been irresponsible. But one policy planner admitted: 'Healey wasn't frightfully keen on our commitment to the Persian Gulf rulers, who were in his book a pretty unattractive bunch of reactionary fellows with no thought beyond the cash register.' Yet he clearly recognized that orderly change in the Gulf needed British troops to stand guard against violent upheaval.

With these thoughts in his mind Denis Healey returned home. Ten days later he was in Washington for a NATO ministerial meeting. In nine days' time his Defence Review would be published. He was uncomfortably aware of a mounting crisis in the Ministry of Defence over his review of policy. But with typical aplomb he told a TV interviewer at London airport: 'I do not expect any resignations on the Navy side because of the Defence White Paper.'

On 23 February, six days later, the First Sea Lord and the Navy Minister resigned.

Britain Stands Down

Concerning Britain's application to join the Common Market:
'*We talked absolute tripe about a change in the French attitude.
There was no change.*'

DENIS HEALEY

Devaluation: '*We were forbidden to talk about it. We were not
even allowed to know the opinion of the experts.*'

LORD LONGFORD

Chapter Ten

THE decisions announced in the Defence Review gave Healey a rough passage in Parliament. The carrier issue caused as much consternation amongst Conservative M.P.s as had the cancellation of TSR-2. There was a widespread feeling that somehow the Royal Navy was being singled out for attack and Britain's claim to be a world power put in doubt at a time when countries like Indonesia and Egypt were prepared to challenge her interests by military means.

The Defence Review came out in favour of phasing-out the remaining carriers in the mid-seventies, since without the air-craft carrier CVA-01 they could not credibly continue for much longer. The death of the Fleet Air Arm by White Paper seemed an ignominious end to a proud service. The Navy Board had been intellectually out-gunned by those unable to discover a credible political rationale to support the contention that Britain would be mounting major amphibious operations against a sophisticated opponent in areas beyond the reach of land-based aircraft.

In the passionate Commons Defence Debate that followed, much was heard about the all-round usefulness of the carrier in dealing with likely threats to British interests in the Indo-Pacific theatre.

The Navy Board certainly felt the need to make a symbolic gesture of protest. As Healey put it: 'The Board felt that there had to be some kind of sacrifice – and they nagged David Luce into resigning.'

The position of the Navy Minister, Christopher Mayhew, the protégé of Ernest Bevin, was almost pre-determined. According to Healey, 'Chris was going to resign anyway; he'd more or less nailed his colours to the mast, and said he'd resign. I warned him not to be a bloody fool'. But Mayhew's attitude was already clear, because he imagined that the threat to resign would be enough to prevent the carrier decision ever being taken. His decision later broadened into an attack on the Government's entire East of Suez policy. His dislike of the Prime Minister, Harold Wilson, increased, according to one colleague: 'Chris hated Harold, and could see no good in him whatever. He was determined to make a stand against him at the first opportunity, and calculated that the Government would shortly be forced to turn to Europe and put an end to its role East of Suez. Chris felt he could pioneer the way and win the political affection of the pro-Europe faction in the Party, which was bound to win through in the end.'

Another colleague confirmed this impression by remarking – 'Mayhew was upset because Harold put him under Healey, whom he regarded as junior to himself as he (Mayhew) had served in a junior capacity under Bevin in the Attlee Government.' A left-winger said: 'The Mayhew resignation was one of the greatest non-events of recent times. He resigned looking in both directions at once. He was both for and against increased defence expenditure!'

An ex-Cabinet Minister described Mayhew's decision as 'a personal blunder that only looks good because now he can claim to have been right all along. In fact he was wrong over the CVA-01 issue and made a highly contrived resignation speech.'

Despite the resignations Healey thought the decision to cancel was right. Now he had the problem of persuading the Commons that the Defence Review was right, and that the carrier decision made absolute sense. With the General Election in the offing, the need to gain quick and sympathetic approval for his sixteen-month-long Review was essential.

The Review

On 22 February, Healey made his long-awaited statement to the Commons about the contents of the Review. He revealed that having achieved three-quarters of the planned £400 million reduction in the projected defence spending of the previous Government, substantial reductions in force deployments could now be achieved.

The Aden base would be relinquished in 1968, and Britain would confine her presence in the Middle East to the Persian Gulf. In the Far East Britain would cut the level of her forces as soon as Confrontation ended.

No British forces would in future be deployed in the Caribbean or Southern Africa. And Britain would not accept commitments overseas that might require her to undertake major military operations without the co-operation of allies; nor would attempts be made to maintain defence facilities in any independent country against its wishes.

Healey then announced major decisions on Forces' equipment. The Canberra strike/reconnaissance aircraft must be replaced by 1970, and since the Anglo-French variable geometry aircraft would not be available until the mid-seventies the Government had decided to buy the U.S. F-111 with a 2,000-miles ferry range.

The foreign exchange cost of the F-111 would be met by sales of British equipment to the United States and other countries. The V-bombers would be released from their current strategic role when the Polaris submarine force was fully operational. They would also 'supplement' the F-111 in the strike/reconnaissance role.

He announced that Britain would keep the existing carrier force as long as possible into the seventies, but that a new carrier would not be built.

He quickly explained to a restive Conservative front bench, and to the powerful naval lobby on their back-benches, that this decision was taken in the light of the operational tasks foreseen by defence planners. And that the question of operational returns was critical in this assessment, because the new carrier would cost £1,400 million over ten years. The new carrier could not become operational until 1973, and by then the remaining carriers would be in the final phase of their useful life.

But by the mid-seventies Britain should be able to provide the necessary elements of the carriers' capability more cheaply by other means: namely, the F-111s supplied by America. These aircraft were available on favourable financial terms under which Britain would sell equipment to the United States and join with her in joint sales to other countries. The Government had set ceiling totals for sales which together would cover the total cost of the F-111.

Healey argued that alone in the world British manufacturers would be able to tender for sales of British equipment to the United States free from the fifty per cent differential which hitherto applied under the temporary balance of payments regulations of the United States – and free also from the twelve per cent and six per cent differentials imposed by the Buy American Act.

The much-awaited Review seemed a typical compromise between the need to perform the same sort of military activities as in the past, and the manifest need to do it for less money and at less risk.

Rear-Admiral Morgan Giles, M.P., an ex-President of Greenwich Naval College, pointed to the patent contradiction that in Part II of the White Paper the aircraft-carrier was defined as the most important item in the Fleet for offensive and defensive action – but that in Part I the Government asserted that the cut-back decision had been made without any loss of military efficiency.

Several others had noticed the apparent contradiction, or indeed ambivalence in the Government's attitude to the carrier. A serving admiral observed that 'given Harold Wilson's sentiments, which he expressed in March 1964, that "we must effectively fulfil our commitments in Europe, but our contributions will be more and more in Africa and Asia", the decision to abandon the carriers was inexplicable!' And, as Mayhew lamented to the Commons, in his personal statement: 'I would like to make it clear that my position throughout the Defence Review has been that if the Government insists on a world role East of Suez in the seventies, then carriers are essential, and that my duty as Navy Minister was to fight for them.'

But whatever the strategic case for a British role East of Suez, the carrier question had been decided in terms of what the situation would be in ten years' time – that was, by 1976. Hence the apparent contradiction between Parts I and II of the Review. The former referred to the mid-seventies, and the latter to the immediate years ahead, during which period the whole shape of the Fleet would change. Britain was clearly looking forward to a sea and air presence in the Indian Ocean and South-East Asia, which could be provided by surface fleets and land-based air power in the shape of the F-111s (with their radius of 2,000 miles in either a conventional or nuclear role) flying from those Indian Ocean 'baselets', as foreshadowed in the Defence Review.

Britain's role East of Suez, as Paragraph 24 of the Review admitted, was in an area in which might lie the greatest danger to peace in the next decade.

If the Foreign Office had had its way Britain would have kept all her commitments until the country became insolvent and every outpost of empire was inadequately manned. In the Whitehall battle between the Ministries, Treasury and Defence were for pulling out, while the Foreign Office and Ministry of Power wanted to stay, to safeguard their own interests at any cost.

Sir Henry Hardman explained that in approaching the Defence Review two basic questions had been formulated: 'One, given these resources, which are all we can afford, what kind of defence can we procure? Two, how best can it be done?' Because of Foreign Office intransigence the Review had begun as a review of means, and not ends. By cutting expenditure on equipment, and on the Reserves, Healey got two-thirds of the way towards his target, but there was still a gap. The Foreign Office was then forced to look at commitments.

'The Foreign Office were compelled to take decisions on priorities,' said Healey. 'Until the Labour Government got in I don't think there was ever a serious attempt to cost foreign policy, of which defence costs are a very important part. In some way I think this forced the Government to take decisions on priorities they'd always managed to avoid in the past.'

In 1966 the electorate were asked to give the Government a vote of confidence to carry on the work they had begun.

Clash of Ideas

On 30 March, the electorate returned the Wilson Government with a vastly increased majority. The new House of Commons was inclined to question the rationale of Britain's role East of Suez, but the Government still insisted that its attitude was a contribution to local stability.

A Cabinet colleague described Healey's position as one 'based on a clear perception that whatever the faults of colonialism – and they were many – the gravest error lay in believing that in the granting of independence, Britain could, or should, wash her hands of her former subjects.' The Prime Minister of Singapore, Lee Kuan Yew, put it in a slightly different way:

'Healey always made it clear that the presence of British troops marked the true nature of Singapore's independence because they were there on request, and not as symbols of the domination of Whitehall.'

Before the Prime Minister's speech to the Parliamentary Labour Party in June 1966 it was an open secret that Healey and Wilson were at odds. Healey had abandoned the idea that the Commonwealth could be a power base for Britain, a third bloc in international politics. An ex-Cabinet Minister confirmed that 'Harold had an obsession that he could settle the war in Vietnam, and Britain could play the role of a major power at the conference table. He was convinced he could prove to be the great peace maker – the honest broker'.

Another Ministerial colleague said that the Prime Minister 'regarded the Labour Government as uniquely endowed to bridge the gap between America and Russia over a Vietnam settlement, provided British military power in Asia remained fairly considerable'.

Wilson's speech to the Parliamentary Labour Party on 15 June 1966 went a long way towards reasserting the traditional view that British presence East of Suez was essential to world peace. Healey was privately sceptical of this argument because he felt that while Britain might contribute to local stability, it was clearly beyond her to accomplish much more. He did feel, however, that Britain's capacity to induce local stability was considerable and made his attitude clear in the Commons Defence Debate on 8 March, when he said that – 'We shall be able to carry out a large range of peace-keeping tasks like that in East Africa two years ago, entirely on our own, while maintaining a powerful deterrent against intervention by others, and we shall also be able to make a powerful contribution to allied operations if we so decide.' With America pressing Britain to send a token battalion to Vietnam as the conflict escalated, the reference to 'a powerful contribution to allied operations if we so decided' had rather a hollow ring to it in Washington.

A Presidential aide said 'Lyndon Johnson couldn't understand the British attitude, and privately believed that Healey would have liked to have sent some troops into Vietnam but that "Peacemaker" Harold was too timid of left-wing reaction.'

He added that 'urgent consideration had been given by the British Foreign Office to the diplomatic need to consider sending in British troops to fight alongside the Australians and New Zealanders.'

Canberra was known to have pressed Harold Wilson for a response to the American request and, of course, added its own request for British military intervention. The response was an emphatic No. Indeed Wilson angered the Americans and confused the Australians by his famous June P.L.P. utterance that Britain 'had to take account not only of theoretical strategy but of what our partners in that area want, and I am thinking here of Australia and New Zealand as well as Singapore.' Yet instead of offering the ANZACs material support in Vietnam, he asserted a doctrine that angered L.B.J. when he roundly declared: 'There is a need to neutralize the Asian trouble spots and potential trouble spots.' Yet not, it appeared, by standing with America, Australia and New Zealand, but by preventing India from having 'to choose between Russia and America to protect her against China'.

Britain's presence in Asia was seen by Wilson as a means of preventing polarization; a slick way of getting left-wing support for the contention that his moderating influence over America might prevent nuclear disaster. Healey was discomforted by this analysis. He himself was utterly opposed to British intervention in Vietnam, but was appalled by the idea that Britain could help defend India from the Chinese; and the reported suggestion that the British Prime Minister had suggested deploying the Polaris force to the Far East in order to deter China seemed to him to be nonsense. An Indian diplomat said: 'Britain's stock in India wasn't high after the 1965 Indo-Pakistan war, and Wilson was regarded as responsible for Britain's neutral attitude to this question. Therefore whatever happened if China attacked, we would have turned to Washington and Moscow, not to London.'

A defence adviser said: 'Healey sensed that Britain's stay in Asia had nothing to do with keeping India free of external domination, but of keeping a kindly police presence in South-East Asia, where local rivalries might lead to outright aggression that would involve Britain – and only Britain – in a deeper and more protracted conflict.' In other words, Britain had to outface President Sukarno's policy of Confrontation on her own, and on her own assessment of what an Indonesian domination of the Federation of Malaysia might involve for Asia and the Commonwealth.

This was an implicit recognition that America regarded some of Britain's military pre-occupations East of Suez as the sole concern of Britain, and conducted in her own economic and political interests. British operations in the Borneo territories had been regarded in Washington with mixed feelings. A Presidential aide revealed that it was widely felt in the White House 'that Britain's rather large military effort to prevent Sukarno annex territories, which she had some right to claim, contrasted with her reluctance to put troops into South Vietnam.' And that the President had noted 'that when it came to opposing the real Communist threat to the whole of Indo-China, instead of lining up with us Wilson sought to undermine our position by talking claptrap in Moscow'. (This was a reference to the Prime Minister's second trip to Moscow to discuss Vietnam in July, a few weeks after his so-called eyeball-to-eyeball speech to the P.L.P. at Westminster.)

Clearly Britain's role East of Suez was, for Healey, an essential and inevitable part of the process of de-colonization. It had nothing to do with combating Chinese aggression nor with the struggle in Vietnam; although a possible military set-back for Britain in the Borneo territories had strategic implications for the whole area, because of the Jakarta/Peking axis that Sukarno had forged. Wilson's attitude was close to this, but he tended to see Britain playing a role between America and Russia in order to prevent either from facing China in a war which he was certain could become global. Such a role Healey regarded as fanciful and misplaced.

B.A.O.R. Costs

As the great national debate on defence unfolded, Britain's economic situation worsened considerably. It was clear that the loans the Chancellor was forced to borrow from abroad must lead to further cuts in defence expenditure. Britain was already seeking to save essential foreign exchange by getting the West German Government to finance the entire costs of B.A.O.R. This crisis with Germany coincided with the growing crisis in

NATO over the French decision to withdraw from the integrated structure of the alliance.

Healey faced problems with gritty determination. Britain, still heavily committed to Malaysia, and to NATO Europe, was in need of a more rational distribution of effort within the alliance.

In the autumn of 1965 the Special Committee of Defence Ministers had been set up. This new NATO committee delegated its work to a five-nation group to work out nuclear plans for the alliance. Rapid progress was made, and after eleven months of consultations a report was ready for consideration by NATO Defence Ministers meeting in Rome. The Defence Ministers agreed to form a Nuclear Planning Group (N.P.G.) which first met in April 1967. This group consists of seven members, five of whom are permanent. But in the meantime the Anglo-German defence cost row threatened the very fabric of the alliance.

Towards the end of June West German Chancellor Erhard made a four-day visit to London in search of compromise. Britain was forced to press the West Germans for an increase in B.A.O.R. support costs which hitherto West Germany had offset by about half. Britain now wanted West Germany to carry the entire cost of B.A.O.R.'s stay in Rhine-Westphalia.

Bonn itself was in difficulties because Washington had also demanded that West Germany buy arms worth £500 million in the United States by the end of 1966. This was to help offset the cost of the 300,000 American troops in Germany, and help spread the burden of Vietnam. Britain's request, however, was more modest. Jim Callaghan, the British Chancellor, wanted West Germans to buy additional goods worth £90 million a year, which would cover the whole of the Rhine Army's foreign currency costs.

The Erhard visit ended in a modest agreement to set up an Anglo-German Commission to investigate ways of overcoming the foreign exchange burden on Britain of keeping B.A.O.R. at the level of 51,000 troops and 12,000 R.A.F. members.

A summer of crisis bargaining followed, and that it was finally settled owed much to Healey. A defence planner said: 'The Treasury was all for bringing the lads back home – perhaps a cut of 30,000 in the size of B.A.O.R., but Denis disagreed and bluntly told the Chancellor that a way must be found round the problem.' The West German Government, alarmed by the Treasury's attitude, quickly agreed to increase its cover for foreign exchange costs of the Rhine Army to DM380 million (almost £32 million) and promised to make substantial increases in this amount by the end of the year. These concessions were announced in October talks between Britain, America, and Germany on the whole question of support costs.

These discussions were to include strategic issues as well, and it was on this score that a final compromise was made possible. Just before Christmas the United States Government decided to assist Britain with the problem. Healey had created the conditions for this compromise agreement, under which America and NATO accepted that Britain had assumed a heavy and disproportionate financial burden in maintaining B.A.O.R., and that in future the scale and size of forces in Europe should be related to three major conclusions that the Special Committee of Defence Ministers thought necessary.

This planning group, later superseded by the N.P.G., consisted of Denis Healey, Robert McNamara, and the Defence Ministers of Italy and Turkey. They agreed that in the event of invasion of Western Europe NATO would be compelled to 'go nuclear' within a few days; that tactical nuclear weapons might slow up an advance but not eliminate the Soviet Union's advantage of greater numbers; that the Soviet Union might use tactical nuclear weapons from the outset and then NATO would be faced with the choice of using strategic weapons or surrendering.

Large numbers of reserves were therefore irrelevant, and what mattered was the number of troops actually deployed before hostilities began. The size of Rhine Army was therefore of secondary importance, and would be determined by the offset in foreign exchange that West Germany might make available.

As a British general in the Rhine Army put it: 'What Healey was suggesting to West Germany was that if she wished to lower the nuclear threshold in diminishing the size of the Rhine Army by failure to help finance its present numbers, then she should be prepared to face the battlefield consequences.' In the event, neither West Germany nor the United States was prepared to face a substantial lowering of the nuclear threshold.

15

And such a development would have been dangerous, and quite inconsistent with Healey's belief that sufficient ground forces were required to deal with sizeable local incidents that might escalate dangerously. But with France virtually out of NATO, the Healey strategy for the defence of Europe was inevitable.

The Far East

Healey now turned his attention to the Far East where his strategy was still evolving within the limitations set out in the Defence Review.

In early July Healey and his wife visited the Far East, by way of Aden. On the eve of his departure it was quite clear that Confrontation was coming to an end. Inevitable defence savings would follow. This would give Healey a chance to produce a more coherent defence policy, free of the constraints of a full-scale emergency.

In Hong Kong on 13 July Healey explained to a press conference, according to the *South China Morning Post*, that the announced 'cut-back in defence was solely one of finance, and he denied that it was prompted by any political reason'.

An officer on the staff of Lt.-General Sir John Worsley, Commander of British Forces in Hong Kong, admitted to having received the impression 'that the Secretary of State was frightfully keen on our staying in the Far East'. But quite a different impression was gained by a senior R.A.F. officer who said: 'Mr Healey was quite frank about the situation . . . After the ending of Confrontation the British military presence would be run-down, and eventually the whole commitment reassessed.'

This analysis had been confirmed on the previous evening on Hong Kong television by Michael Stewart, the British Foreign Secretary, who appeared in an Australian TV programme, 'Four Corners', in which he suggested that U.K. defence policy did not envisage the retention of troops in any particular area as a part of a kind of 'welfare policy'.

An official who flew with the Healeys on this trip said, 'Denis was playing it cool. He couldn't suggest publicly the nature of the defence cut-backs in the Far East, but he knew pretty well the magnitude of those cuts. They were roughly calculated by Healey as in the region of between 10,000 and 20,000 men in the next eighteen months, including the 3,400 due home by November.'

The ending of Confrontation could bring a rich dividend in defence savings. Another official of the Hong Kong administration said, however, that 'Healey wasn't counting his chickens too soon, and though he often referred to force withdrawals from Sabah and Sarawak, he was emphatic in denying that the commitment to defend the sultanate of Brunei was affected by the end of Confrontation'. Until and unless the Indonesian–Malaysian agreement was ratified Healey remained anxious about the question of a British withdrawal from the area. As a brigadier serving in Sabah said later: 'Had there been a really serious escalation of the conflict the balloon might have gone up, because Healey and the entire Wilson Cabinet were ardent theoretical defenders of the Commonwealth.'

Retreat, not advance, became the order of the day. It is clear that on this visit to the Far East in the summer of 1966 the Secretary of State had mentally programmed the extent and pace of withdrawal in the post-Confrontation period – withdrawal which foreshadowed an even bigger decision to pull out altogether.

Confrontation formally ended with the ratification of the Bangkok Agreement in August 1966 by Malaysia and Indonesia – now under the control of General Suharto. While Sukarno was still nominally in power, however, Healey's military advisers did not think it would have any effect on Confrontation. But the Malays, who knew the area better, were certain it would make a difference.

'I had an awful period in July 1966, when the Tunku was pressing us to take our troops out of Borneo, and the military were very much against it,' said Healey. 'I agreed to take them out and gamble, but both Michael Stewart and I warned them that once we had taken our troops out it was unlikely that we would agree to send them back.'

Within eight months, more than 10,000 servicemen had returned to Britain, saving £8 million a year in foreign exchange. The move from Asia to Europe was gathering momentum.

Common Market

In November 1966 the Government announced that it would

examine again the prospects for British entry into the E.E.C. On 2 May 1967, the application was announced.

Healey was far from enthusiastic. He was no Europeanist, and had been closely identified with Hugh Gaitskell's opposition to British entry to the Common Market.

A Ministerial colleague said that 'Denis was sceptical of the move since he was convinced that de Gaulle would veto the application with gusto'. Another friend said that 'Healey hadn't really seen the move towards Europe made sense even if de Gaulle did say "Non", because Britain's strategic interests would have to be centred on Europe in the seventies'. But one defence planner has denied this: 'Healey was looking towards Europe, but realized that a fully-fledged Eurocentric policy could come only after a final decision had been made about the East of Suez policy, and that the French veto had hardly affected that.' Economic constraint would put an end to the role East of Suez rather than the decision to identify the economic interests of Britain with a group of European nations operating a customs union.

Healey admits to this attitude, and confesses to having been too preoccupied with the practicalities of European defence to worry about the metaphysics of the Treaty of Rome with its supranational goal.

But a conflict of purpose did exist in the country's foreign and defence policies, which the application to join the Common Market highlighted.

The Government statement *Membership of the European Community* proclaimed 'long-term potential for Europe, and therefore for Britain, of the creation of a single market of approaching 300 million people, with all the scope and incentive that this will provide for British Industry'. Yet a few paragraphs later it conceded that the economic case could not alone be decisive, and that the case for entry was essentially political. Political unity of Western Europe was now to be put above either Anglo-American alliance or even the much-vaunted world role.

A Cabinet colleague observed that 'Denis didn't approve of the political implications of the Treaty of Rome – few of us actually did, despite all the rant and cant – but he recognized that Britain's economic future looked bleak indeed without access to a larger market for our exports'.

A junior minister said that 'Healey felt that George Brown and Harold Wilson were wasting their time tripping round European capitals in search of support for a British application when the French President had made his attitude to the question so plain'.

Healey led the opposition to any British application to join the Market after Wilson and Brown had made their tour of European capitals. 'We talked absolute tripe about a change in the French attitude. There was no change,' he said. Yet his opposition was voiced in Cabinet only. In public he remained loyal to the group's decision – although he did not speak in favour of the application.

The Parliamentary Labour Party were given different reasons for Britain's application from those announced publicly. One that many found acceptable was that if Britain did not join, who, after de Gaulle, would be able to control the rising power of Germany? Another, later voiced by Michael Stewart as Foreign Secretary, was that the mere fact of applying would slow the growth of competitors. They would quarrel to delay the implementation of such schemes as that for agriculture, hoping for better agreements later.

The surprising thing, to outside observers, is that there seems to have been no attempt by the Cabinet to link Britain's Foreign and Defence policies in a coherent strategy. As Gordon-Walker has admitted, in his book *The Cabinet*, even after the end of Confrontation 'the Cabinet remained as reluctant as ever to abandon its East of Suez policy'.

The Defence White Paper of February 1967 stated: 'The continued presence of British forces can help create an environment in which local governments are able to establish the political and economic basis for peace and stability.' Following a back-bench rebellion in the Defence Debate, when sixty-three M.P.s abstained, the Prime Minister made his scathing 'dog licences' speech justifying the East of Suez policy. But, as those in favour of withdrawal gathered strength, and as the Cabinet was deciding to re-apply for entry into the Common Market, there was no attempt to take a wider strategic view. 'The two things were not directly or intellectually related,' said Gordon-

Walker. 'Each policy was being separately considered in the Cabinet.'

The Six-day War

Less than a month after Britain had applied again to join the Common Market the weakness of British diplomatic and military power was convincingly illustrated. Dramatic decisions were on the way, as were some shattering events. Throughout May 1967 tension increased in the Middle East, culminating in Soviet-inspired rumours that Israel was about to attack Syria. The U.A.R. mobilized its forces on 15 May. Other Arab states followed. On 18 May President Nasser called for the withdrawal of the United Nations Emergency Force (UNEF) from Egyptian territory, where it had been patrolling the Egyptian–Israeli border since 1957. The U.N. agreed to withdraw its forces immediately. On 22 May the U.A.R. closed the Gulf of Aqaba to Israeli shipping.

The British Cabinet met to discuss the crisis, and formulated a tough policy. They urged international support for a naval task force ready to force the blockade of the Gulf of Aqaba. The Royal Navy would take part.

George Thompson flew to Washington on 24 May, followed by the Prime Minister on 2 June. George Brown went to Moscow on 23 May. Britain's allies were not at all interested; and her proposal to intervene with an international fleet collapsed. In angry discussions the Cabinet's inability to prevent the war, affect its course, or do anything about the Arab ban on sending oil to the West, showed the Government that much of Britain's Foreign and Defence spending East of Suez was wasted.

Israel attacked Egyptian forces in the early hours of the morning of 5 June. Six days later Israel had settled the matter by seizing control of the Sinai peninsula, the West Bank area, east Jerusalem, and the Golan Heights. Egypt, Jordan, and Syria had been humiliated.

As a British defence planner said: 'The Cabinet's proposal was an excellent one, and if enough naval support had materialized the June war would never have occurred.' There was never any intention, however, to go it alone and force the Gulf of Aqaba in defiance of Egypt. Such a policy made sense only if America and France joined with Britain in a joint enterprise. A former Egyptian diplomat said: 'Only the British Navy could have forced the Gulf and got away with it, because President Nasser wanted precisely that to happen. It was a way of getting off the hook, and only Britain was intelligent enough to see this.'

British impotence was, however, dramatized by the events in the Middle East when some Arab states took reprisals in the shape of oil sanctions after Cairo Radio on 6 June had broadcast an allegation that British and American aircraft had taken part in the Israeli attack on Egypt. Britain's troops in the Gulf were seemingly powerless to prevent this action.

The crisis in the Middle East helped cause another run on the pound, which continued throughout the summer. Britain moved inexorably towards devaluation, so consistently opposed by the Prime Minister since October 1964.

At the height of the sterling crisis a supplementary White Paper on Defence was published just before the Parliamentary recess in July. It announced that by 1971 Britain would withdraw half her troops from Malaysia and Singapore, and the rest some time between 1973 and 1976. Because of the state of the economy, it said, there was 'a more pressing need to reduce overseas expenditure'. British forces would, however, remain in the Persian Gulf. The need for permanent bases was declining as Britain slowly reduced commitments.

The White Paper foreshadowed a distinctly Europeanist strategy, largely forced on the Government by its inability to cope with the economic crisis.

France also had economic problems. On 29 June 1967 Healey and John Stonehouse, Minister of State for Technology, were told by the agitated Pierre Messmer, French Minister for the Armed Forces, that the economic axe had fallen on the Anglo-French variable geometry aircraft project. It was in an advanced state of planning, but the French, he explained, would have to withdraw. Other aeronautical projects, he stressed, need not be affected, and the three men signed a supplement to the memorandum authorizing the second stage of the supersonic training and tactical support aircraft, the Jaguar, of which Britain and France each ordered 200 the following January.

France's withdrawal from the A.F.V.G. project, however, was no great surprise. 'It became pretty obvious fairly quickly that they would get out of it if they could,' said Healey. The French had indicated in May 1966 that there were difficulties in the phasing of expenditure, and, a defence aide said, 'Healey worked at the problem for nine months so that the French might remain committed to the A.F.V.G.' An understanding had been reached in January 1967, but the March elections for the French National Assembly left the Gaullists in a minority – although still the largest single Party – and civil and military expenditure was subsequently cut. 'It was an irritating experience for me,' said Healey. 'But seeing Messmer kept me in touch with France's general problems.'

The end of the A.F.V.G. project, however, meant that Healey needed a replacement aircraft to supplement the F-111 in the late seventies. Consultations with friendly governments led to agreement with European allies to build the multi-role combat aircraft (M.R.C.A.), but the difficulties in controlling a project under more than two governments have yet to be surmounted, and the problem of building an aircraft which is more than either fighter/strike, or purely for reconnaissance, have taxed designers.

Devaluation

British economic difficulties increased throughout the second half of 1967. Wilson seemed unwilling to delegate power and responsibility on foreign affairs, strikes, or the economy, grasping the headlines as he heroically struggled to deal with domestic and international crises on his own.

The decision not to devalue the pound had been his own. On the Saturday evening of 17 October 1964, he told Callaghan and Brown that there was to be no devaluation. From then until the crisis in July 1966, as Lord Longford said: 'We were forbidden to talk about it. We were not even allowed to know the opinion of the experts. Until the summer of 1966 it had been thought too dangerous to discuss.' So wage freeze, deflation, and international loans propped up the pound.

Unfortunately Wilson's senior colleagues did not challenge him. Gordon-Walker and Stewart stoutly put the official Foreign Office view, and sought to keep British influence from declining. Callaghan, an astute politician, was out of his depth at the Treasury where he had to work doggedly to grasp the problems presented to him by some of the most able brains in the Civil Service. His refresher course in economics at Oxford was little help.

Healey was preoccupied with the Defence Review, and he later admitted: 'If the situation was such that we had to devalue we should have done it as a rational act earlier. In those days I wasn't particularly interested enough in economics myself to press this point.' Brown was working hard to put some life into Britain's antiquated union and business organization. Jenkins, initially Aviation Minister, was not in the Cabinet, and had turned down the offer of the Education Ministry. In December 1965 he had, however, joined the Cabinet as Home Secretary.

Wilson, who could turn from one subject to another in Cabinet and seemingly remain master of all, kept power for himself. As an expert in getting and keeping power he had no equal. He decided that he did not want the collective advice of the Cabinet on whether or not to devalue. While Callaghan wavered, Wilson stood firm.

Economic experts were, and still are, divided on the merits and demerits of devaluation. Devaluation makes a country's goods cheaper to other nations and theirs dearer to it. Whether a country can sell enough exports to cover the increased cost of imports, and then add some – or there will still be a deficit on the balance of payments – depends largely on the state of world trade. If it devalues just before a boom in world trade things should get better. If the economies of countries which buy its goods begin to stagnate, however, or if its own salesmen just sit back hoping that lower prices will do the trick, then devaluation fails.

Wilson, a brilliant economist, knew that devaluation was not bound to work. But when it came, on 18 November 1967, it was bungled so badly that there was no plan for immediate curbs on the British public's spending, which would reduce the demand for imports. Seemingly the Government wanted its domestic manufacturers to have time to readjust to the idea that more of their products would have to be sold abroad than before.

Following devaluation, Healey became engaged in a battle with the Cabinet over whether arms should be sold to South Africa to help the export drive, and over the size and nature of the cuts needed in defence spending. But in November he assured the Commons: 'We must above all keep faith with our forces and with our allies in making these cuts. We can have no reversal of the July decisions which revised Britain's overseas policy over the next decade, and fixed in broad terms the role, shape, and size of the forces required to support it.'

Three weeks later it was announced that the whole of defence expenditure was being reviewed again. Devaluation forced the reluctant Cabinet to reconsider Britain's world role.

Chapter Eleven

Britain Turns to Europe

F-111 Cancellation – '*I nearly won on the first discussion in Cabinet. Cancellation might never have taken place if Harold hadn't won over two weaklings.*'

DENIS HEALEY

'*Britain's defence effort will in future be concentrated mainly in Europe and the North Atlantic.*'

Defence White Paper, February 1968

Chapter Eleven

HAROLD WILSON took over the Department of Economic Affairs on 28 August, as the economic crisis worsened. On 3 October the Treasury announced that gold reserves had dropped for the fourth consecutive month. The half per cent increase in Bank Rate that month did little to relieve pressure on the pound. On 5 November the pound reached its lowest level in ten years. Nine days later the trade figures, reflecting recent dock strikes in Liverpool and London, showed a huge deficit, and the pound had its worst day ever.

The Cabinet finally decided that Britain had had enough. On Thursday, 16 November, the decision to devalue the pound by 14·3 per cent was taken. It was announced two days later. It added £50 million to the annual cost of defence immediately. But defence expenditure was to be cut by a further £100 million in the coming year, abruptly forcing the Government to announce that it would be giving up its East of Suez role by the end of 1971.

The shift towards a European-orientated defence policy was at first perversely rebuffed by France, however, when de Gaulle vetoed Britain's application for membership of the Common Market, at a press conference on 27 November.

Arms for South Africa

Meanwhile, the Cabinet was reconsidering its attitude to the question of selling 'defensive' arms to South Africa. It began with the commercial question of arms sales to help the balance of payments, but the strategic issue of the presumed importance of the Cape sea route had to be considered after the June 1967 Six Day War. South Africa had raised the issue with the Foreign Office, and indicated that the British Government should decide whether to sell her a wide selection of naval hardware – Buccaneer aircraft and frigates – as a matter of urgency. A formal reply was wanted by 31 December.

South Africa indicated that the whole question of the Simons-town treaty was at stake. A South African diplomat conceded that 'We approached the British Government because we knew they might have a financial interest in selling us what we genuinely required for defensive purposes'. This was essentially a correct analysis of the position. About nine months earlier the British Prime Minister had agreed that the Foreign Secretary, George Brown, should put up a paper examining the question of the sale of 'defensive' arms to South Africa. They wanted to see what difference this might make to the need to cut back social services expenditure.

South African military intelligence learned of this move (as the result of a casual remark made by George Brown at a diplomatic reception) and informed Johannesburg that the deal might go through. Dr Vorster, South Africa's Prime Minister, responded by suggesting that Admiral Heinrik Biermaan should visit London in mid-December to discuss the matter with British Chiefs of Staff. On Friday, 8 December, the Cabinet's Defence and Overseas Policy sub-committee met to discuss the matter.

As usual the Prime Minister was in the chair. The committee considered George Brown's document which Wilson had earlier asked for, but about which he now had serious misgivings. The sub-committee was divided. Those present included Roy Jenkins, the new Chancellor (who replaced Jim Callaghan on 27 November), Tony Crosland, Richard Crossman, Michael Stewart, Lord Longford, Denis Healey, George Brown, George Thompson, and several junior ministers.

A member of this committee later recalled that both 'Brown and Healey were keen on selling certain arms to South Africa, and said so'. And another one confirmed that this was so – 'within the context of the difficult economic position'. The D.O.P.C. were fairly evenly split at their meeting on 8 December, with Wilson against the sale of arms, supported strongly by Stewart, Crossman, and Longford.

The meeting took place against a disturbed background. The D.O.P.C. must have been aware of the Party unrest. The idealistic Left were making clear their distaste for any sales on pragmatic economic grounds.

Wilson was aware of his weak position as leader. Following

devaluation his standing was low; and supporters of both Callaghan and Jenkins were engaged in trying to rally support for an alternative leader. The sale of arms therefore became the question over which the issue of the personality and style of leadership was decided.

It is difficult to sort out the myths from the facts, but it is clear that Brown, the Foreign Minister, had been discussing the question with the South Africans for more than a year on behalf of the Government. Wilson had agreed that he should put up a paper for the Cabinet to look at. There seems little doubt that the main pressure for this came from the Foreign Office, which was anxious to get the South Africans to help put pressure on the illegal Smith régime in Rhodesia.

Brown left for a NATO ministerial meeting in Brussels on Monday, 11 December, without a firm decision having been reached by the Cabinet; but they had agreed that the South Africans seemed to be rushing things, and should be asked to postpone their deadline. By the time he returned, on Thursday, 14 December, he was convinced that Wilson was organizing a campaign against him. It seems more likely that Wilson was safeguarding his own traditional left-wing support to maintain his position as leader.

Mr Kevin McNamara, an M.P. close to Wilson, has said that following a dinner on 11 December at which Callaghan was the principal guest, and where the question of the change of policy was freely discussed, 'John Ellis and I agreed to put down an Early Day Motion to test the water'. He added that this 're-affirmed our support of the declared Government policy'. It was this motion, which received the approval of the Whips' Office, that was thought to be Wilson's bid to outflank Brown. Callaghan, unaware that the matter was before the Cabinet, had said to Labour back-benchers, in reply to a question about it, that it would be necessary to weigh the economic advantages against the political disadvantages.

Richard Mitchell, a back-bench supporter of Healey and Brown described it as 'the dirtiest business imaginable'. His view is typical of a number of right-wing Labour M.P.s who saw the whole affair as a deliberate attempt by Wilson to organize support: 'The first thing I knew was that I had a motion presented to me and was asked "Would you sign this?", and I did, because I don't believe in the sale of arms to South Africa – but John Silkin, the Chief Whip, organized it for the P.M. I found out later that this was an officially sponsored motion being used by Harold as part of an intra-Cabinet squabble. I was asked by one junior minister why the hell I had signed.'

It was similarly believed that a letter signed by junior ministers, including Shirley Williams and Dr Jeremy Bray, who reaffirmed their support for the policy of withholding arms sales, was part of Wilson's attempt to manoeuvre Brown and Healey into an awkward spot.

The Cabinet meeting, held against this background of confused suspicions on Thursday, 14 December, left the question unsettled. The battle continued over the weekend with such highlights as the Frost television probe in which Alan Lee Williams and Reginald Paget were two Labour M.P.s supporting Healey and Brown against Ben Whitaker who opposed the resumption of sales. The Party was torn between those who would be prepared to sell the arms to avert the possibility of cuts in the social services, and those who thought it was necessary to take a moral stand against any gesture of support for a régime that prospered on the moral evil of apartheid.

Lord George-Brown later wrote that 'during the weekend the press publicity, the leaking and the briefing continued, and by Monday morning it was pretty evident that it was no longer possible for a balanced argument to take place. Mr Healey and myself, who had jointly submitted the original memorandum and recommendation, and those others who were originally in favour of supplying these limited arms, had become a pretty small minority, and we were no longer able to carry our colleagues with us.'

Whatever the pros and cons of the decision itself, the most dramatic effect that resulted from it arose from the way in which the matter had been discussed, and the manner in which the Cabinet reached its final verdict. It has been suggested that Cabinet Ministers who shifted their position during the month were persuaded to do so by Wilson, who argued that arms sales would have to be dropped for the sake of the Party. It was an argument that was acceptable to men like Gordon-Walker.

Leading Cabinet Ministers, however, saw the whole question as being 'more about leadership' than as an attempt by a minority to foist an unpalatable policy on the Government in a bid to stave off such unattractive domestic measures as the reintroduction of charges for medical prescriptions – the issue over which Wilson had ostensibly resigned in 1951.

The arms to South Africa fracas focused attention on the real struggle in the leadership of the Labour Government, and the need for government by consent, and with the support of certain sectors of the Parliamentary Labour Party. A distinguished London-based American commentator saw it as – 'The time that Denis really hammered Wilson. He was the leader of a movement to keep Wilson in check.' But the support which Healey was able to assemble to force Wilson to seek the collective advice of his senior colleagues drew its strength from their dislike of Wilson's autocratic tendencies. Healey himself, however, lacked widespread support among the rank and file, and only his personal ability enabled him to get so many of his policy decisions accepted by his Cabinet colleagues.

Labour's Back-benchers

The only thing the Labour Party expected of Healey was that he would reduce defence costs. The Labour Whips had no doubt that this was the view of nearly all Labour M.P.s. They left the timing of these cuts to Healey, and it was a measure of his standing and intellectual dominance that he was able to take them so gradually.

Without Healey there would have been drastic cuts, probably less intelligently made. At a meeting several months later between Roy Jenkins, the Chancellor of the Exchequer, and his junior ministers, Jenkins confided that if the Minister had not been Healey he would have exerted much more pressure for rapid cuts in defence expenditure.

Healey's weakness lay in the aims of the Party. The Left were against all defence expenditure, and the right preferred cuts in defence to cuts in social services. The argument was emotional, not intellectual as P.L.P. defence group meetings showed. Michael Foot, leading left-wing critic of Healey, never attended, for Healey's intellectual dominance and arrogance almost always ensured that his critics were humiliated.

As a Minister, Healey became more of a lone wolf than before. His lengthy poorly-presented speeches grew shorter. But he was able to play at baiting the Opposition as he did in the 1970 Defence Debate with the arrogance of a man who had all the information at his finger-tips. He appeared to have intellectual contempt for most back-benchers. They neither knew as much as he did, nor did they care as much. And the Tory cries of 'What Army? What Navy? What Air Force?' that punctuated his speeches infuriated him.

To intellectuals on both sides of the House he showed no mercy, although he concedes that Enoch Powell could occasionally sniff out weaknesses in the Defence White Papers. The less pretentious, however, he believed had a right to speak; because their experience, as union organizers on his own side of the House, or as serving officers, on the Opposition side, qualified them to put the views of important sections of the community.

He acquired an *élite* group of supporters in spite of his detachment. When fellow Leeds M.P., Charles Pannell, told him that his prestige as Minister of Public Building and Works depended on keeping the agreement that all building for the services would be done by his department, Healey took note. Every time the matter was raised at a meeting Healey threw it off the agenda. 'He knows what his word is worth,' said Pannell. 'He is a man of principle.'

Healey's own attitude to issues other than defence, however, showed him to be an authoritarian with a permissive streak for individual behaviour. Thus, he staunchly sided with the Prime Minister in 1969 over the question of trade union reform as other colleagues deserted him. He wanted firm control of wages and prices, even if this meant three or four per cent unemployed. But the simple shorthand labelling of 'right-wing' or 'left-wing' is inadequate if applied to his attitude on personal behaviour. 'He is the most permissive parent I have ever met,' said his wife. In the House his liberalism showed itself in his support for such measures as homosexual law reform, and the Bill to make divorce easier.

In the political fighting within the Cabinet, however, Healey was almost outflanked by McNamara's motion which Silkin and his aides carried round Labour M.P.s. One hundred and thirty signed; only six of those who were lobbied refused. But some who signed had no idea of the motion's background until it

16

was too late. An M.P. who supported Healey on this issue said: 'It was Wilson at his worst. It shook the confidence of his Cabinet colleagues. The result was that they had a blow-up, and the P.M. more or less promised there would not be a repeat of it.'

On 28 December the Frost Show returned to the South African arms theme, this time with Healey as the programme's main guest. This episode sparked off a public row which culminated in the Prime Minister demanding a transcript of the Frost–Healey encounter. Healey is a formidable television performer, as Frost quickly discovered.

The show produced an explosive encounter over Frost's allegation that the Downing Street publicity machine had revealed the names of Ministers who allegedly supported the sale of arms. Healey hotly denied that this had been done, and refused to admit the belief he held.

In the course of the interview he advanced the case both for and against the resumption of the sales. He stressed 'the potential benefit to employment in Britain of sales', and 'the political damage to Britain in going against an undertaking it had made in the United Nations'.

On the Frost Show Healey publicly defended the Prime Minister, and denied attempts to displace him as Premier. He fiercely declared: 'There's nobody in the Party who wants to replace Wilson or thinks he can be replaced as Prime Minister – infinitely the best we could have.'

A Parliamentary colleague subsequently remarked that – 'Denis protesteth too much. He was publicly telling Harold that there was no plot to unseat him. He knew that Harold would be watching the programme, sitting in his Scillies bungalow – Harold avidly followed the TV appearances of his colleagues – and he was right. Harold saw it, but pretended he hadn't by sending for a transcript. That always looked good.'

Healey's Frost Show appearance was deliberately used to help him in the Cabinet. 'Being in my job, out of the public eye, people had forgotten about me. I accepted the invitation to go on the Frost Show, in spite of the obvious risks, because I thought I could establish a set personality in the country, which would strengthen me in the internal battles; I was in a very weak position in the Cabinet at that time,' said Healey. 'I did another TV show the following week with Robin Day, and they both did me the world of good.' Healey's constituents remembered his performances on television with admiration. Few remembered what he said. All remembered how he said it.

Wilson's performance during the consideration of the arms sales question is understandable if his weak position as leader at that time is taken into account. He appeared, however, to have a paranoid streak. He was considerably influenced by his Paymaster General, George Wigg. Wigg had organized the campaign which got Wilson the leadership of the Party. Wigg's incessant burrowing and questioning had unearthed the Profumo scandal which seriously affected the image of the Conservative Party in the early 1960s. Wilson also felt he could talk freely to Wigg, since he did not fear him as a rival. Wilson's relations with senior Cabinet colleagues was never as close.

Under Wigg's influence Wilson had over-reacted to the alleged misuse of D notices (by which the Press voluntarily agreed not to publish certain matters considered by the Government to affect national security).

Wilson deliberately ignored the collective advice of his senior colleagues. He organized the Cabinet committee system so that he alone knew all of what was happening.

Through his contact with junior ministers Wilson was able to keep a close eye on what their chiefs were doing. He also placed his own men as juniors in the important Ministries, often against the wishes of the Minister, so that he would receive reliable reports. By knowing all, and keeping his top colleagues ill-informed, Wilson hoped to divide and rule.

By his behaviour over the question of arms sales, however, he antagonized important Cabinet colleagues, and they organized themselves so that Wilson was forced to listen. His senior colleagues demanded a greater say on economic policy. Ministers with a knowledge of economics, and – like Healey – able to master a brief, wanted more control over strategic economic policy. Wilson now had to agree to have a more powerful version of the Steering Committee for Economic Policy set up after the economic crisis of July 1966.

When Wilson later went to Nigeria, in a bid to settle the civil war there, boosting his image as international statesman and peacemaker, Crossman, Healey, Jenkins, and Peart organized an inner Cabinet, because they thought there was a need for a more effective strategy on such measures as the Constituency Boundaries Bill and industrial relations. Upon his return Wilson accepted this.

It was too late to be of practical value, however, and the introduction of the Industrial Relations Bill was hopelessly out of touch with the mood of the House of Commons, as lobby correspondent Peter Jenkins showed in his book, *The Battle of Downing Street*. Douglas Houghton, chairman of the P.L.P., organized the opposition to the Bill, and tried to rally support for Healey as an alternative leader of the Party if Wilson fell.

Robert Mellish, the Chief Whip, told the Cabinet that their Bill would fall if put to the vote in the Commons. Wilson's colleagues deserted him, although Healey continued to support him, believing that it would be demoralizing to drop the Bill at this stage. The time for drastic institutional reform had passed, however, and the weaknesses stemming from the delayed devaluation left Wilson with no option but to await the promised economic miracle.

As a necessary part of that 'economic miracle' Chancellor Jenkins sought to restrain public spending in December 1967/ January 1968. In the battle over the cuts in Government expenditure Healey nearly left the Cabinet.

F-111

The struggle over the proposed cancellation of the F-111 was almost unrivalled in intensity and importance during the Labour Government's period in office.

The F-111 was to be sacrificed in a package deal, partly so that the left wing of the Party would accept swingeing social service cuts, and partly to help cut total Government spending. As one Member put it – 'They went round the table saying "What can you give?" If somebody said "I am not offering anything" then the others would say "I am not unless you are". You had to have a sacred cow from every department – school-leaving age, for example, from Education.'

The decision to defer raising the school-leaving age was important for a number of reasons. Lord Longford resigned in protest from his position as Leader of the House of Lords. The decision represented the defeat of a policy many Labour supporters felt was an important social advance. It was a measure at the heart of socialist philosophy – to help the less privileged members of society.

The change had been pressed by Crosland, an important philosopher in the Labour movement, when he had been Secretary of State for Education. He was thus strongly in favour of the proposal, as being essential to the programme of any socialist government. The Labour Party did, in fact, emphasize in later propaganda that one of their major achievements was to spend more on education than on defence.

The attitude of other members of the Cabinet, however, was illuminating. Crosland's supporters included Callaghan, Brown, Stewart, Marsh, and Gunter. The opposition included some of the better educated members of the Cabinet: Castle, Wedgwood Benn, Healey, Crossman, and the Education Minister, Gordon-Walker, who thought it the least harmful cut.

Stewart was so convinced that there should be no question of going back on the earlier commitment to raising the school-leaving age that he nearly resigned. Only the intervention of a Cabinet colleague seems to have dissuaded him.

George Brown described the decision to postpone the extra schooling as being made for 'a ludicrously small and highly dubious saving of money'. In his memoirs *In My Way* he states: 'I thought it was one of the greatest betrayals a Labour Government so overwhelmingly composed of university graduates could make of the less privileged people who, after all, had elected it.'

Healey, who found himself arguing against Stewart and Brown, did not see it as a matter of principle at the core of Labour's political philosophy, but thought that the priorities in education were in other areas. He was no theoretician out of touch with education, for his parents were educators, and his daughter Jennifer had followed her mother into the teaching profession. 'I thought it was more important to prepare for the introduction of the new measure by firstly, training more teachers, and secondly, thinking more carefully about what we were going to teach them,' he explained.

Other Ministers, fearing cuts from their own departments, also voted with Healey. For Brown it was the high point of a series of Cabinet setbacks, and he resigned from his position as Foreign Secretary and Deputy Leader of the Labour Party two months later, on 15 March. In his memoirs he writes that he was less affected by the decisions which the Government had taken, than by the way in which they were taken.

Wilson's influence over such men as Gordon-Walker, the Education Minister, who had put up no fight when the proposal to scrap the raising of the school-leaving age was discussed, showed also in the debate on the cancellation of the F-111. Healey fought for it, not as a 'sacred cow', but as something he needed for the newly-envisaged European role. Although the R.A.F. had concentrated on the immense ferry range, the F-111 was a low-level advanced strike aircraft, and had always been suitable for use in Europe.

The fight within the Cabinet, however, as Taverne said, 'was really a battle between Roy and Denis'.

Healey himself said: 'I nearly won on the first discussion in Cabinet. Cancellation might never have taken place if Harold hadn't won over two weaklings.' Healey argued that the F-111 was vital to Britain's defence needs. His opponents, led by Wilson and Jenkins, said that for economic reasons alone it had to be cancelled.

After the first meeting of the Cabinet, where Healey lost by only one vote, he decided to raise the subject again. Taverne explained: 'Denis saw Frank Pakenham (Lord Longford) as the weak member. He arranged for him to be visited at the House of Lords. He was swung round in favour.

Longford saw Air Chief Marshal Sir Charles Elworthy, to find out if it was really important to Britain's total defence effort. He explained: 'I had very little information on which to make up my mind – we did not have very much information in Cabinet – so I asked to see an expert.' Though he had voted for ending the role East of Suez, Longford was satisfied that there was a case for the F-111, but he added: 'After a three-quarters of an hour's talk you can't pretend that your knowledge is very big.'

In the second vote he supported Healey because 'defence spending was coming down', and Healey had convinced him that Britain would be virtually naked without the F-111. A Minister said that that – 'The vital vote was taken on a totally inadequate basis', and added that Wedgwood Benn, for example, after examining all the technological arguments in favour, had exclaimed – 'I will probably vote against it', without explaining why.

In spite of winning over Lord Longford, Healey was out-flanked. The economizers had won over Patrick Gordon-Walker and Cledwyn Hughes. The case had been carried at the Chancellor's push. Healey explained: 'Roy was brilliant in presenting his case. He staked his reputation publicly at the beginning of post-devaluation to A., ending East of Suez, and B., dropping the F-111. He always had it in for the F-111 because he had fought to keep the TSR-2. And he took the line, "I don't mind cancelling TSR-2, providing we don't replace it." '

What had amazed Healey at the outset of the review of policy was the Press story that the F-111 was about to be cancelled – put about by the Prime Minister well before the Cabinet had taken a decision on it. Healey therefore campaigned hard for support against the Prime Minister and very nearly won the day.

Healey's attempt to reverse the first F-111 Cabinet meeting decision took place over a hectic weekend. David Fairhall of the *Guardian* recalls that 'at this point Denis realized some of his friends were quite capable of sniping at him behind his back, and that perhaps he had better try and establish where he stood – so he talked to the journalists'. He explained to a largely sympathetic Press the case for the F-111 and, as one journalist said to another – 'Do you know, that is the first time that Healey has ever bothered to ask me along to discuss a difficult situation. Other Ministers let their views be known every time they see a situation on the horizon. Denis has never done this before. This was a political occasion.'

Healey's relationship with journalists was generally frank. In his briefings for them he was noted for clear presentation and fairness. If he thought one of them had something wrong he would tell him off in front of other journalists. As one said: 'He is very blunt, but charming.' Even journalists whom he often criticized had to admit he made them work harder at mastering defence issues, because, unlike many of his predecessors, he read everything they wrote.

East of Suez

Yet the cancellation of the F-111 did not surprise either the

American Embassy in London or McNamara, the U.S. Defence
Secretary. Britain had bought the F-111 because she thought
she had a need for it, not because of super-salesmanship by the
Americans. McNamara was grateful, because it helped him
defend his policy against critics. But he was doubtful whether
Britain had the resources to stay East of Suez, and said so to
close friends – although he argued with the British throughout
that they should remain in the Far East, and suggested that
American support for sterling would be dependent on Britain
staying there.

The 1964–5 review of Britain sent by the American Embassy
in London to the State Department said it was unlikely that
Britain could afford to stay East of Suez; and if Washington
wanted them to stay then they should offer some kind of pay-
ment. On the F-111, an American diplomat explained: 'The
Embassy said it might not be a viable deal.'

The decision to withdraw from East of Suez by the end of
1971 was far more damaging to Britain's relations with the
Americans than the F-111 cancellation. 'Britain's influence declined from the moment the decision was announced', another
American said.

'This was immediate – there was no need to wait for the
actual withdrawal. What Britain thought didn't dictate but
had influence. There are two sayings Americans think important – one, don't kibitz, get in the game; two, put your money
where your mouth is.'

A decision to withdraw most of the forces in the Far East,
leaving only a token force, had been taken by the Cabinet in
the spring of 1967. Because Americans feared the effect this
would have on their own position in Vietnam they persuaded
Wilson to hedge the announcement. But devaluation was the
traumatic shock, and in the Defence White Paper of February
1968 the Government said: 'Britain's defence effort will in future
be concentrated mainly in Europe and the North Atlantic.'

The timing of the withdrawal had been debated in the
Cabinet, with Healey wanting a later deadline, but it was
quickly agreed that Britain should pull out in 1971.

Healey's defeat over F-111 was his worst moment as a Minister. The day before the decisive Cabinet meeting he had told
his mother – 'I think I will just pull it off.' But after the

Friday meeting he returned home, and Edna told Mrs Healey, 'It's the first time in my life I've really seen him broken.' Tim Healey, an Oxford undergraduate (at Balliol College) described the week as 'like living on the edge of a volcano. Every time he came in we wondered if he was going to resign.'

The Chiefs of Staff were also contemplating resigning; but, as Healey said, 'I was very much against any of them resigning.' He added: 'Although I had told the Press in advance that I wouldn't, I was very depressed, and I considered it. But I wanted to carry the department through the difficult period that was bound to follow these decisions.'

Healey had become very attached to the services, and did not resign 'because I thought they would be worse off. The risk that someone unsuitable might have replaced me kept me there.' The fear that a more left-wing colleague could destroy all that he had achieved, and make much more drastic cuts, was widely felt by Chiefs of Staff and other senior officers.

Healey explained his decision to stay: 'I do not think that you should resign unless you can improve the situation by doing so, or unless it is beyond improvement.

'If I had been politically ambitious I would have resigned then, broadened the issue, and been in a very good position to come back a year later.'

This seems difficult to accept, because as Richard Mitchell trenchantly observed – 'The P.L.P. don't like resignations. I can't remember anybody who resigned in the last Parliament who got any sympathy at all – Gunter, Mayhew, Brown . . . You just don't achieve things. Had Healey resigned he would have been out. There is a tradition in the Labour Party that once a majority decision is taken you all stick by it. Anyone who re-signs is accused of rocking the boat.'

Many people thought that Healey should have resigned, on principle; but, as the pragmatists explained, the collapse of his policy was not his fault. It was caused by a failure of economic policy, which others had brought about. Those who thought he should have resigned pointed out that Britain had told the Australians she would not pull out unless they agreed, and then withdrew without consultation. Healey's decision to stay in office could be accepted only if he was merely a defence man-ager, rather than a politician with principles.

It is interesting to note that one of Healey's favourite books on political behaviour was Kennedy's *Profiles in Courage*, in which the heroes are men who act in ways that appear morally wrong because they believe the public good requires it.

Healey's private agonies were cushioned by his wife. She recalled that 'it was a time when he was under great strain', and he returned to Admiralty House absolutely deflated and emotionally drained. She realized it was pointless asking him whether he intended resigning because 'this was his decision, so I deliberately held back. We didn't discuss it.' She sought to provide 'an intellectual armchair' to take away external strain and help him relax and concentrate.

Healey had much to think over since the publication of the Defence Review in 1966; but he was convinced that he was right to accept his Cabinet colleagues' demands to accelerate withdrawal from Singapore and Malaysia, to withdraw from the Gulf too, in 1971, and maintain only a general capability to operate East of Suez, as well as cancel the F-111 and rephase part of the naval construction programme, together with a larger and speedier run-down in the size of the Army.

He explained on television on 16 January that what had disturbed him essentially was 'the pledges the Government and I myself have made to the forces that the Defence Review we carried out in July 1967, only six months ago, would be the last in the life of this Parliament. I believed it at the time. The whole Government believed it. But devaluation came and we turned out to be wrong.'

He accepted that the Cabinet had the right to decide ultimate policy, and that economic constraints had in any event imposed a severe limitation on defence policy. He decided against resignation and routed his critics in the 25 January Defence Debate by declaring that the Conservatives 'invented a brilliant technique' for dealing with their continuous series of somersaults on defence policy that took place when they were in office. They switched their Defence Minister to another job before the somersault. That is why they had nine Defence Ministers in thirteen years and why our defences were in such a mess in 1964.'

Healey has never taken the view that the decisions of January 1968 marked as dramatic a departure from previous policy as many in the House, Press, and television claimed. He made this abundantly clear in a lecture at the Royal United Service Institution on 22 October 1969, when he declared: 'It was only when we brought Confrontation to a successful conclusion in the summer of 1966 that we were able to make detailed plans for the reduction of our commitments and capability in that area.

'The planning of those cuts took a further eighteen months and was hastened by the economic consequences of devaluation. But since we were anxious to give time for the governments in the areas concerned to make an orderly adjustment to our decisions, this accelerated our final withdrawal from South East Asia by only twelve months compared with the earliest date envisaged immediately after Confrontation.'

Mayhew, who had lost the fight to build another aircraft-carrier, had at least the satisfaction of seeing the Government accept the policy which he originally advocated. A Cabinet colleague who heard Mayhew give the speech in which he said 'No white face will be seen on the mainland of Asia' called it 'a terrific speech'. He added: 'I have never heard a case so powerfully deployed before the Cabinet. It visibly impressed Jenkins and a few others, and from that moment the skids were under the Healey policy.'

When the decision to leave the Far East was taken by the Wilson Cabinet, however, it was a milestone in British foreign policy, only slightly dimmed by the decision of their Conservative successors to retain a token force East of Suez with Commonwealth allies. One close friend of Healey's thought it was 'as historic and important as the decision of Mr Attlee to grant Independence to India in 1947'. Professor Lawrence Martin, however, believed that the logic of the policy had been fashioned in the Defence Review of 1966, and Michael Howard, the former Professor of War Studies in the University of London, and now a Fellow of All Souls, Oxford, agreed that this assessment was correct. Howard, an admirer of Healey, believed that his great merit lay in a capacity to adapt policy to 'the profound changes in the political, economic, and military position of the country. When he realized that these changes had fundamentally affected British defence capability he faced up to them with candour.' But Howard also believed that Healey should have tackled the significance of Britain's changed position a little sooner. A British general with NATO agreed: 'Healey's basic misunderstanding of defence policy from the mid-sixties to mid-seventies stemmed directly from his excessive interest in the Indo-Pacific area.'

The advice of academic strategists and historians was valued by Healey. Under one of the reforms begun by Thorneycroft there were five lecturers in Higher Defence Studies – examining the sea bed and outer space, defence organization, economics, as well as maritime and Soviet strategy.

He was perhaps less enthusiastic about the advice from the House of Commons, but it helped keep him on his toes. Perhaps the most spectacular example occurred over the suggestion that the Indian Ocean island of Aldabra should be made into a military base. Tam Dalyell, alerted by naturalist Peter Scott, put down 120 questions to be answered by Ministers during Question Time. The naturalists' paradise was reprieved. 'It had an effective lobby in the sense that one had to take notice of it,' said Healey. 'I had to argue the case more fully.'

But, as Alan Lee Williams explained, 'Denis was already shifting his own opinions when Tam created all the fuss, and was annoyed that he could not say so'.

As Healey was such an expert, surrounded by M.P.s who were relatively ignorant, pressure grew for a Commons Select Committee to keep defence under permanent review. Supporters of the committee system, however, put it low on their list of priorities. As M.P. Richard Mitchell said: 'To get worthwhile information it would mean vetting.' Healey thought this problem was almost insuperable. 'A good spy is always going to get through vetting,' he said. 'It can only ensure that if a chap is vulnerable to foreign agents, and is prepared to admit to vices that make him vulnerable (or his friends tell you about them), then you must leave him out.'

Healey's no-nonsense approach made him friends in the services. When he explained the 1965 White Paper (his first) to senior officers 'he charmed the whole audience', according to one man. The personal touch went right down through the ranks – as was shown during his visit to troops keeping the peace in Northern Ireland.

David Fairhall of the *Guardian* summed up the attitude of

many senior officers he had spoken to: 'Over and over again they said "We know that we have been hammered, but we think that in Healey we have had a man in there fighting for the best deal." He convinced them that the Labour Party took defence seriously.'

Air Vice-Marshal Paddy Menaul noted why Healey was such a success with servicemen: 'He always impressed audiences by One – his detailed knowledge of weapons systems; Two – the ease with which he could tackle detailed and complex problems; and Three – his sincere and genuine interest.'

Without Healey's support one of the most important 'think tanks' on defence would now be either extinct or Government controlled.

The Royal United Service Institution (R.U.S.I.) is an organization centred on London where serving officers (and now lower ranks and the professions) can meet, discuss, and analyse defence problems. Under its director, Menaul, it has begun to produce research studies to help improve policy. A series of top-level seminars, open to all members, has broadened knowledge of service and strategic problems. Most of its funds have come from industry, largely as a result of Healey writing to more than 100 friends in important positions. 'Healey kept R.U.S.I. alive,' said Air Vice-Marshal Menaul. 'It would not have existed without his support.'

The Ham in the Sandwich

Healey was Minister of Defence for almost six years. His service advisers spent short, two-and-a-half year, terms with him. Naturally, he knew much more than the people who flew in and flew out, and this discouraged the less-experienced new arrivals.

One of his problems was to work out what the advice of the Chiefs of Staff and his permanent officials was really worth. As he said, on policy questions 'you don't get a single recommendation, so you must have a private office which can filter, organize, and manage the mass of information pouring from the machine'.

Within a few months of taking over, Healey had his private office working as a top-level filter. He brought in an Assistant Secretary as his assistant.

The private office of the 'S. of S.' included four secretaries, and another outside to deal with Parliamentary Questions and letters from the public. The main policy issues were looked after by the Assistant Secretary, and the slightly less important issues by a principal grade civil servant. The third man looked after Healey's programme, and the fourth – usually a high-flying junior – was dealing with miscellaneous matters and getting an insight into work at the top.

The Assistant Secretary's position might be described as 'the ham in the sandwich between the Minister and the Department'. His relatively senior rank enabled him to act as go-between 'on more or less equal terms with what is called the "two-star" level. He thus had the necessary authority to keep in touch with the V.I.P.s, making sure policy went through smoothly, and repairing any weaknesses in advice given to Healey.

Two key men for the Private Secretary were the Deputy Secretary (Programmes and Budget) and the Secretary to the Chiefs of Staff Committee. Most policies affecting the services would eventually have to be approved by the Chiefs, so it was important to know what they thought on any matter, and how they were likely to react to proposals.

Besides advising Healey on whom he should see, and which questions to ask, the Private Secretary was mainly responsible for organizing the Secretary of State's paperwork. Healey wrote about ninety per cent of his speeches himself, using his private staff only to get factual data and critical information. Of the rest of the paperwork, the drafting in ninety-nine cases out of a hundred would be the Private Secretary's, though all minutes and letters went out under Healey's signature.

When papers reached the private office, they would be photographed, and within twenty-four hours the Private Secretary would try to give Healey an analytical note on them. Most of the administrative work arising from meetings, and from discussions with Healey, was also handled by the private office staff.

In running the department Healey set the pace. A senior member of his staff said: 'He raised the standard of work more than anyone else in twenty years.' Healey's impact had been immediate. Before he arrived, it was said, the Minister was likely to ask for a report on a problem within three weeks, and then agree with its conclusions without argument. Healey usually wanted the report within twenty-four hours, and would then send it back, drawing attention to its weak points, flaws in analysis, and questions unanswered. 'A strong Minister like Healey sets the tone for the whole department,' his Public Relations Officer, John Groves, said.

Healey created the small Programme Evaluation Group (PEG) as another critical group to provide him with an independent assessment of issues coming through the formal machine.

A special organization for co-ordinating policy, planning, and procurement was a relatively recent idea. Apart from the Committee of Imperial Defence set up in 1904, and the Chiefs of Staff Committee in 1924, it was not until 1946 in Attlee's Labour Government that a Ministry of Defence, under a Minister with major responsibilities for policy, emerged. Twelve years later the Chief of Defence Staff job was created, and in 1964, the main structure of the unified Ministry of Defence came into being. All the top people were now on the sixth floor of one building. As Sir Henry Hardman observed: 'The Secretary of State in the M.o.D. is thrust back on himself. In Aviation or Agriculture, for example, the whole machinery reports through the Permanent Secretary. In Defence there are three: 1. Scientific side. 2. Military. 3. Civil personnel. The Secretary of State is working with all three, and has three separate channels feeding him information, asking for decisions.' Healey added that there were four service channels to make the job more difficult.

PEG served a vital purpose because it enabled the Secretary of State to be better informed and to decide between the policies coming from the three channels. The head of PEG, Cliff Cornford, who was Chief Scientist to the Army, agreed that was his main job, but also recalled Healey's detailed grasp of policies, issues, and recommendations that PEG was able to present and clarify: 'He's intensely curious about all that goes on, about the details of the substance that's presented to him, so he felt the need for something akin to the French Ministerial Cabinet, with a group of independent advisers whom he could charge with the inspection of any issue, either current or otherwise.'

PEG had a chairman, who was a leading scientist, another scientist, representatives of the three services, and an economist. Its chairman had access to Healey through the ordinary executive machinery, and by direct link. He also had to report to the Permanent Secretary and Chiefs of Defence Staff, although he admitted: 'I didn't need to expose precisely what was going on.'

The rest of the M.o.D. did not like PEG. A member of the Chiefs of Staff observed that – 'PEG was an irritant because it was particularly well-informed, and inflamed feelings because it was obviously used by Healey to sharpen the questions he might put to those of us in the normal official machine.' But PEG did not always receive all the information it wanted. This undermined the whole experiment, because, as PEG's chief recalled, Healey 'had a feeling that he was only seeing the top of the iceberg'. So, PEG was regarded as a fifth column by Chiefs of Staff and a large part of the administration. But having direct access to Healey made people take notice of them, and help them.

A new planning system was later drawn up largely on the basis of PEG's recommendation. 'The new policy staff inherited the kind of role that had been assigned to us in programme evaluation,' said Cornford, of the Policy Planning Staff. Cameron, the airman on PEG, thought PEG had achieved a lot in the short time it existed. He said: 'Our direct contact with Denis Healey meant that we could inject into defence planning a detached and objective input that could intellectually satisfy Healey.'

The top official who succeeded Pat Nairne as Healey's Principal Private Secretary, said: 'Setting up of a Deputy Chief of Defence Staff (operation requirements), and A.C.D.S. policy (study staff), and the greater use of the Defence Operations Analysis Establishment (D.O.A.E.) at Byfleet, as well as the whole budgetary system, were developments pointing in the same direction.' That direction was to find 'better tools for central management that wouldn't interfere with the way in which the three services ran themselves once the decisions were made'.

Healey's real contribution in the field of defence planning came in 1968 with his decision that forming defence policy had to be separated from the task of operational and contingency planning.

Operational and contingency planning came under the Assistant Chief of the Defence Staff (Operations) and the Assistant Chief of the Defence Staff (Policy). Under him the Defence Policy Staff (D.P.C.) replaced the old Planning Staff.

The Defence Policy Staff got two separate jobs: to prepare draft papers on policy issues, and to advise on policy aspects of day-to-day business involving British forces.

Healey found able young men in the Ministry of Defence and promoted them to positions where they could be of more use, much to the annoyance of less-gifted civil servants waiting their turn on the promotion ladder. A senior official said: 'Denis recognized integrity and intelligence in his officials, and made certain that they were promoted rather more speedily than is normal in a vast department like the M.o.D.' It was the same with senior officers. General Sir John Hackett, former Commander of NATO's Northern Army Group, now Principal of King's College, University of London, remembered that 'Healey found that the generals, very early on, were very much more stupid than he was. Healey made no friends with the straight soldier type. The more reactionary generals didn't like him, but a lot of us did.'

A serving general, and admirer of Healey, believed that 'part of the dislike that a few of the generals had for him was really an extension of the rooted suspicion amongst military men that all intellectuals – which means all university graduates – are arrogant, and in some way, even unpatriotic.'

One retired major-general explained why he regarded Healey as a security risk: 'The fellow civilianized the Ministry of Defence, didn't he? Most civilians are pacifists when it comes down to fundamentals. I say – restore real power to the War Office and let the professional military men run the Ministry of Defence.'

The blimps of Whitehall are now fewer in number. Today most senior officers are both better informed and more intelligent than ever before.

Nuclear NATO

Healey needed all the military, civil service, and political

17

advice he could get on the question of how nuclear weapons should be used, if at all. It was potentially the most politically explosive issue he faced, but it became perhaps the most important success of his whole period as a Minister.

Ivor Richard, the able former Under-Secretary of State for Defence (Army), found that when he succeeded Dick Taverne as Healey's P.P.S. in April 1966, his main preoccupation was NATO's nuclear strategy. The need was for controlled escalation as a part of deterrence. The Nuclear Policy Group of NATO was largely Healey's brainchild, even though it was known as the McNamara Committee. It was this committee that laid down guide-lines for the use of nuclear weapons in NATO. Ivor Richard claimed that 'Denis was undoubtedly the most influential Defence Minister NATO had ever had – he was the longest-serving Defence Minister and commanded respect because of his experience and knowledge'.

On the nuclear question he was brilliant, said Richard, a view endorsed by Sir Henry Hardman: 'He used to infuriate the military by the vigour of his comment, and he would ask, "Can you really have tactical nuclear weapons? Are two or three needed before you have a holocaust?"' But Healey's contribution was not made without difficulties. 'He had a bitter dispute with the French Foreign Minister, Couve de Murville, over the future of NATO strategy.' The French resisted the strategy of the 'flexible response', and rejected the notion that the American nuclear guarantee could be made effective now that the Soviet Union had reached parity with the United States at the strategic-nuclear level. Healey vigorously rejected this defeatist notion.

West German Chancellor Willy Brandt, who saw Healey in action, said 'I have the greatest respect for the clarity of his thoughts, the strength with which he stands for convictions and the statesmanlike way in which he dedicates himself to his tasks.

'I have been most aware of this at the sittings of NATO ministers, not least at a closed meeting in May 1969 in which a dialogue between President Nixon and Denis Healey took place that was very fruitful for the rest of us.'

Healey rebutted the French case against NATO at every opportunity, but he was also the first Defence Minister of any standing since the Belgian Foreign Secretary, M. Spaak, to examine the strategic implications of NATO's main aim – to prevent war in Europe.

Speaking to the North Atlantic Assembly in Brussels on 20 October 1969, Healey declared that 'the essence of effective deterrence is the prior commitment of forces to the alliance in peacetime'. He also said that effective action in a crisis depended on a command and control system 'thoroughly tested in normal times' through constant exercises by the allied armies.

He declared emphatically that NATO's purpose was 'to prevent a war rather than to fight and win one'. Healey referred to the arguments advanced by Alain Enthoven, in an article in *Foreign Affairs*, in favour of attempting to match the conventional strength of the Warsaw Pact. He said: 'It is not wholly clear why he aims at conventional equality with the Warsaw Pact, since he admits that nuclear weapons enhance the deterrent against all forms of attack . . . like any reasonable man, he wants to avoid the use of nuclear weapons in any but the most extreme circumstances, but I fear this has led him substantially to exaggerate the relative conventional capability of NATO at the present time. And I think he flies in the face of both psychology and experience when he assumes that the European powers would respond to a major reduction in America's NATO forces by making good the resultant deficiency in conventional power, rather than by insisting on greater reliance on the nuclear element in NATO strategy.

'Of course, Mr Enthoven is right in suggesting that a crude comparison between the numbers of divisions in NATO and those in the Warsaw Pact exaggerates the Soviet preponderance, since Soviet divisions are much smaller,' he said.

'It is quite unrealistic to compare the forces of the two sides world wide . . . the British forces in Hong Kong can hardly be regarded as a potential reinforcement in Central Europe. What is critically important is the forces readily available on the spot.'

Healey added that he was 'reminded of a British soldier who fell in love with a girl in Singapore. His sweetheart in England wrote to him asking "What has she got that I haven't got?" "Nothing," he replied, "but she's got it here." '

Getting the generals to plan on the basis of the troops they had there, instead of the imaginary force levels they wanted,

was the first thing Healey had had to do when he became a
Minister.

Playing at Make-Believe

NATO's military chiefs, who were very much in charge of
policy when Healey became the British Minister of Defence in
1964, were planning to defend the NATO countries for about
thirty days against a large-scale Soviet attack before having to
resort to nuclear weapons. To do this they needed all the
divisions that the politicians had agreed they should have.
The trouble with this was that the level of divisions needed,
agreed at such meetings as the 1952 Lisbon Conference, had
never been approached. The generals had less than two-thirds
of the troops promised, yet they planned to defend Europe with
those, plus the make-believe armies they had been promised.

'I got NATO to adopt a more realistic policy after 1964,'
said Healey. 'This was tied to actual forces instead of just planning from force goals.'

The argument which the military leaders put forward was
that they were not prepared to accept the low level of troops
that their member states were offering, and that the NATO
countries ought to provide more of them. But the politicians
knew that they were not going to get any more. The pragmatic
British generals accepted this, although they stressed the dangers inherent in such a policy.

'There was always a strong view among the American and
Continental military that unless they asked for twice as much
they would not get as much as they could,' said Healey. 'The
whole thing was totally unrealistic.'

Healey set about transforming the NATO set-up, in a bid
to make it more efficient. His efforts reflected his earlier thinking, particularly in his emphasis on closer relations with the
Germans.

He personally cultivated the German civil servants and military leaders as well as political spokesmen. 'We already had
some halting bilateral staff talks, and I got the level of these
raised,' said Healey. 'I got them to discuss the really big questions of strategy, and not the piddling little things which they
had previously been discussing.'

This enabled the Germans and the British to get at the

heart of each other's thinking, and begin to build up a good relationship which was crucial to the formation of a worthwhile European Defence policy. The important personal role played by Healey was summed up by German Defence Minister Helmut Schmidt, who said: 'Denis Healey is one of the British personalities who is most popular in Germany. He has frequently visited the Federal Republic of Germany and knows and speaks our language. At one of our most popular carnival events he was awarded the highly reputed "Order against Beastly Seriousness" (Aix-la-Chapelle, 1970).'

Healey's crowning as European joker seemed inexplicable to many of his British colleagues. But his two-hour television spectacular, seen throughout Germany and the Low Countries, was earned by his NATO performances. 'He was the first NATO Minister to crack a joke at a ministerial meeting,' one permanent official said. 'Until Healey changed the style of things it was just a ritual where each Defence Minister would read out a statement that had probably been written by some civil servant,' he added.

With his regard for de Gaulle as 'the greatest French statesman of the eighteenth century', and his frosty relations with France's NATO Minister, Couve de Murville, which had begun with a row at their first meeting, it was not surprising that Healey concentrated on forming good relations with the Germans, whom he thought to hold the political key to the future of Europe. Schmidt summed up his success: 'The population of our country appreciates his abilities, his personality, and his charm.'

European Caucus

The close links with the Germans were more than just personal, however, for they had at their root a different approach to European strategy. Until the French withdrew their troops from NATO command in March 1966, they discouraged any discussion of NATO strategy, believing that there was little need for a concerted strategy, and that each country should make up its own mind on what it should do if war broke out.

The British approach was summed up by Healey: 'It is impossible for Britain to make sense of defence on a purely national basis; it's no use us having a NATO strategy if nobody else agrees with it, and won't supply the forces for it. What we do only makes sense in so far as it is part of a wider set-up in which other people are doing their bit too.'

The major difficulty Healey faced with his NATO ministerial colleagues, however, was that they were afraid to say anything to the Americans, who held the nuclear umbrella that protected them against Soviet invasion.

In 1964 he found NATO committed to a policy of 'forward defence' with non-existent armies. To contain aggression therefore meant a fairly rapid escalation to 'massive retaliation', involving American nuclear weapons. The Europeans, doubting whether America would, in fact, use its nuclear weapons in the light of the Soviet nuclear build-up which threatened the American homeland, began to think that there was a lot of sense in the French 'go-it-alone' approach.

With the Kennedy/McNamara 'flexible response' strategy (intended to give more options to deal with different types of conflict) the Europeans got even more worried about whether America would help them if the Warsaw Pact forces invaded.

When Healey arrived at the NATO Ministerial meetings he warned the Americans that if they reduced their nuclear commitment to NATO then the European reaction would be to start producing more nuclear weapons, not to build up the conventional forces which the Americans wanted them to do. Healey explained that after his speech – 'Every European Minister came up to me and said "I am so glad you said that. I would have liked to say it myself." So I said "Why the hell didn't you?"'

A Ministerial aide explained that the reason was that 'they were never prepared to say anything to the Americans'. Later, however, other Defence Ministers, such as the Italian and Belgian Ministers, spoke up.

Healey's relations with the Americans who, preoccupied with Asian and internal problems, seemed to regard NATO as a strategic afterthought vis-à-vis the Russians, were often strained. The formation of the Nuclear Defence Affairs Committee, and its subsidiary Nuclear Planning Group, although attributed to McNamara, in fact owed much more to Healey, who pushed them into existence and made them work. They gave the Europeans more say in how nuclear weapons might be used in a future European war. A NATO official said that 'Healey appeared to be the major European spokesman in the N.P.G., and fought hard to get the Americans to face the facts.' He successfully dissuaded McNamara's successors, Clifford and Laird, from shutting down the N.P.G. Healey explained: 'The Americans don't like being faced with some awkward realities, and with alliance problems in this form.'

Healey's performance in the N.P.G. helped edge the Europeans into forming a separate European grouping or caucus within NATO. A friend described his task as being 'like rowing a boat through treacle', and added that he was able to get changes like this 'because he was the only one who seemed to take the job seriously'. Until Schmidt became a Defence Minister there was none to match his hard work and professionalism. Even the American Robert McNamara, who had formulated the McNamara doctrine, became preoccupied with Vietnam. 'He made totally disparate speeches on strategy just six months apart,' said Healey.

The idea of having a separate European caucus was put forward by Healey in 1968 in a bid to set up a group that would show that they took defence seriously, thus discouraging the Americans from making troop withdrawals further and faster than they needed to.

Italy, which had a large Communist Party opposed to NATO, thought it would be easier to sell defence on a European basis, and supported him.

The Germans, with Schröder Defence Minister from 1966, were more wary. 'It took a long time to persuade him that we wouldn't be encouraging the Americans to withdraw from Europe by meeting on our own – even for dinner in an evening,' said Healey.

The British efforts were finally accepted, however, and the first all-day meeting of the European Defence Ministers was held after Healey left office, in September 1970. But Healey's contribution was appreciated, as Schmidt explained: 'He made great efforts to extend European co-operation in the field of defence. His share in the development of common European concepts on important questions of the Alliance – for example, on the doctrine for a potential tactical use of nuclear weapons – has without doubt been very great.' His contribution to the

formulation of a policy using nuclear weapons quickly to defend
NATO countries, however, came under fire from critics in his
own party at home.

Wigg's Attack

Lord Wigg, one of Healey's former colleagues and member
of the Defence and Overseas Policy Committee, criticized a
lecture which Healey made on 3 February 1969, in Munich,
when he wrote in *The Times* on 20 February.

Wigg felt that Healey had been more frank with the Germans than with his fellow countrymen over his strategy of
nuclear deterrence by controlled escalation. Healey had argued
that a low nuclear threshold, though not desirable, had effectively deterred war by presenting the Soviet Union with the
unacceptable risk of an uncontrolled escalation to outright
strategic nuclear war. What was now needed was to present
the Soviet Union, in effect, with a more credible threat of controlled nuclear escalation by NATO if the Soviet armies invaded.

Healey had been advocating this policy since he first entered
the Ministry of Defence. Wigg argued, however, that this doctrine of controlled nuclear escalation expected too much of the
Americans, and relied too heavily on the Soviet Union playing
the game. He wrote: 'If Healey is right, and the Russians are
afraid to take the risk [of initiating war], well and good. If, on
the other hand, they decide to face that risk we shall, as Mr
Healey rightly points out, have no choice between surrender
and nuclear war.' The best way to avoid such a dire possibility,
Wigg argued, was to increase NATO's conventional forces –
'both in formations deployed in a state of genuine combat-
readiness, and in reserve capability'. This would involve,
according to Wigg, additional troops 'in the order of eight active
divisions, with proportionate reserves', and these would have
to be provided by the European powers themselves.

It was natural that Lord Wigg's verbal assault on Healey in
The Times, in which he charged him with intellectual arrogance and with living in a world of bizarre fantasy, should
appear more important than the issues he actually raised. But
Wigg had raised a number of important points about the nature
of Healey's local NATO strategy that required refutation.

Appearing on television on the evening of 20 February 1970, Healey dismissed the view that, if Russia attacked, NATO would either have to give in or launch an all-out nuclear war. He said: 'The whole purpose of NATO strategy is to deter aggression, to see that a war never breaks out. Now, to do that, you have to have enough nuclear strength to make a war not worthwhile. You also have to have enough conventional forces to ensure that you don't need to use nuclear weapons in situations where their use wouldn't be justified. We have enough now and I hope we shall keep enough.'

Later that evening Lord Wigg and Michael Howard, the war historian, also appeared on television's '24 Hours'. Wigg renewed his attack. Kenneth Allsop, the interviewer, asked Howard to comment on Wigg's contention that 'the situation is about to move from the serious to the deadly dangerous'. He replied: 'I don't think the situation is worse in principle than it ever has been. It's been the same for about ten years past, that we have been dependent on tactical nuclear weapons because we are not willing to, or are not prepared to, put up a total conventional defence of Europe. And also we do not think that that in itself would be an adequate deterrent against a Russian attack – in the extremely improbable eventuality of the Russians wishing to attack.' This was Healey's argument in a nutshell.

But Wigg, and *The Times*, legitimately doubted whether, if deterrence failed, it would actually be in the interests of the West to use large-scale nuclear weapons. Moreover, NATO strategy relied on a rational Soviet reaction after the West had used nuclear weapons. If the Soviets actually attacked, NATO policy could then be irrelevant, since it was geared to preventing war, not waging one.

Healey worked very hard in the Nuclear Planning Group of NATO to make its policy of deterrence by nuclear escalation more credible.

The N.P.G. dealt with the possible tactical use of nuclear weapons and decided that Europe's 7,000 were enough. The essential problem was their possible use, because, as Healey insisted, deterrence was only credible if the Russians were convinced that NATO would use them if attacked. This needed prior agreement on plans and procedures for their use within the 'flexible response' strategy – NATO's response to a Soviet move at any level. This was difficult to achieve, but after studying a number of possible Soviet moves the N.P.G. formed political guide-lines for the use of tactical weapons.

America, Germany, and Britain prepared discussion papers. Britain looked at the use of tactical nuclear weapons at sea; and America, tactical nuclear weapons as a warning signal; while West Germany examined battlefield usage. Britain and Germany together worked out guide-lines from these, and after further amendments, they were approved by the Nuclear Defence Affairs Committee and Defence Planning Committee (D.P.C.) in December 1969.

Talk of close Anglo-German nuclear collaboration in NATO (together with co-operation over the development of nuclear energy for peaceful purposes) led to difficulties for Healey with back-bench left-wing critics – but less than he expected.

Healey strongly repudiated the suggestion that substantial conventional forces would resolve the problem of whether to use nuclear weapons or not, because, as he said in the Commons on 4 March 1970: 'Military arithmetic dictates that if there were a major invasion by the Red Army . . . Western Europe would either have to surrender without a fight, or use nuclear weapons.'

There was, however, a third way out, and that was the 're-introduction of conscription in an attempt to provide an all-out conventional defence against an attack'. This he regarded as politically remote, and militarily irrelevant. There was no alternative to controlled nuclear escalation. This was also the view of the entire N.P.G., and of almost every military adviser in NATO.

Healey's main aim had really been to achieve political solidarity in NATO, and this had been achieved, turning a 'paper tiger' into an effective political and fighting machine.

But Lord Wigg had the support of The Times and Lord Mountbatten, who, a year later, revealed his attitude in a letter to The Times. Mountbatten wrote that while he was on NATO's Military Committee he never lost an opportunity to warn against the use of tactical nuclear weapons because they would end in escalation to 'total and global nuclear destruction'.

These attacks greatly irritated Healey. He felt that Wigg

ignored the realities of the situation in Europe, where the will
to deploy massive conventional forces simply did not exist. A
Cabinet colleague felt that 'George was out of touch' and was
making in public 'the same silly and irrelevant contributions
that he made before the D.O.P.C.' Healey suggested that what
Wigg ignored was the basic strategic facts of Europe – especially that since the Soviet invasion of Czechoslovakia the local
military balance at the conventional level had moved against
the West.

In thirteen hours, on 21 August 1968, more than twenty Warsaw Pact divisions, with 250,000 men, weapons, and supplies,
had invaded Czechoslovakia from three flanks and advanced as
far as its border with West Germany.

As Healey said: 'The Soviet Union and Warsaw Pact countries had a substantial superiority over NATO in conventional
forces. The Soviets had a two-to-one advantage in infantry and
aircraft on the central front, and three-to-one in armour. It was
clear that NATO could not cope for more than a few days with
a Soviet attack by conventional means. And it made no sense
to attempt a massive Western rearmament with conventional
forces, since the Soviets were equipped for nuclear confrontation as well. The only strategy that made sense in this situation,
Healey told the North Atlantic Assembly in Brussels on 22
October 1969, was for NATO to prepare to *prevent* war in
Europe rather than prepare to *fight* one. Which meant spelling
out a credible nuclear policy so that the Soviet Union could be
in no doubt about it.

Healey was puzzled by Mountbatten's letter. 'He expected it
from George Wigg, whose strategic thinking was still rooted in
the mid-fifties, but Dickie knew better,' said an aide.

Lord Mountbatten had advised the retention of the British
deterrent at the Chequers meeting in November 1964, on the
grounds that Britain's capacity to influence the strategic nuclear
response NATO was committed to would depend upon it.

He made it plain that NATO forces could not fight a general
war, but only assist in keeping the nuclear threshold high
enough to prevent the automatic use of nuclear weapons.

Healey took the unusual step of telling the Commons on
3 March 1970 that Mountbatten had given very different advice

to him – 'in view of the gross misinterpretation of Lord Mountbatten's views, that arose from the publication of his letter
to *The Times*, which purported to given an account of the
views which, as Chief of Defence Staff, he made to the military
committee of NATO'.

European Security Conference

The best hope for continuing peace, however, lay in the
efforts to negotiate an agreement between the NATO allies and
those of the Warsaw Pact. If general disarmament was difficult
to achieve (as Lord Chalfont, the Minister for Disarmament,
found when he took up his job) then the answer lay in a more
limited agreement. A consistent part of Healey's thinking on
European security has been concerned with the possibility of
mutual reduction of forces in Europe. This was endorsed at
the 1968 ministerial meeting of NATO in Reykjavik, and proposals were made to the Warsaw countries. No response came.

With the Soviet invasion of Czechoslovakia, however, the proposal looked irrelevant, or even dangerous. Yet in the wake of
the rape of Czechoslovakia the Soviets and the Communist states
of Eastern Europe proposed a European Security Conference.

Healey was suspicious. He declared that 'they (the Soviets)
do not yet seem prepared to discuss at such a conference the
real problems of European security'. These problems related
to 'the overwhelming case for both sides seeking to maintain
security in Europe with a lower level of forces and at a lower
cost'. He hoped that the Warsaw powers would view mutual reductions in Europe more favourably. He hoped that the U.S./
U.S.S.R. strategic arms limitation talks (SALT) which were in
progress could show the way.

SALT

Healey said that he believed that the attempt to limit the
deployment and development of certain weapons, which
America and Russia seem anxious to achieve, could be a mixed
blessing for Western Europe. Unless such an agreement between the superpowers carried the support of their respective
alliance systems, the agreement would either be temporary or
not worth making.

He believed also that an agreement between America and Russia about offensive/defensive missiles must be achieved in such a way as to avoid forcing Europe to become a nuclear power in its own right. Any suggestion that the American nuclear umbrella had been removed from NATO Europe, or any fear that America no longer had a credible nuclear deterrent, must force Europe to go it alone.

The failure of the SALT negotiations, argued Healey, would result in a vertical proliferation between the superpowers, in which pressure for more offensive missiles to swamp the anti-missile defences would grow.

The last domestic storm Healey had to deal with was over the question of what should be done about C.S. gas. Lord Chalfont, the Minister for Disarmament, had tried to get a treaty banning the use of biological weapons accepted at Geneva, but had been thwarted by the Soviet Union which tabled a treaty to ban both chemical and biological weapons. The Foreign Office tried to persuade the Cabinet to accept this, believing it had much to commend it.

Healey, leading the Defence Ministry team, successfully fought to keep C.S. gas out of the proposal, believing it was a humane means of dealing with internal riots like those facing his soldiers in Northern Ireland. He opposed the Foreign Office's attempts to include C.S. gas, which they felt ought to have been covered by the 1930 amendment to the 1925 Geneva Protocol. Following a heated and lengthy debate Chalfont and the Foreign Office were overruled.

Under Healey, Britain adopted a defence policy that was more in line with her economic and strategic position. This was not to the liking of the Conservative front bench – at least in public – nor to the liking of 'traditionalists' and the well-orchestrated band of ex-officers always anxious to get more money and resources to fight the last war all over again.

Britain had turned towards Europe. Both her defence and foreign policies were in line. As the global strategic scene changed, with America and Russia in strategic nuclear deadlock, and with NATO becoming uncertain of how America would respond to a Soviet move in Western Europe, the need for a European defence caucus became the central issue of strategic analysis. Healey was the best-equipped Defence Minister in the whole of NATO to think through the implications of this new challenge. But it was a task he was not to finish, and one that he had hardly begun when Labour went out of office after the 1970 General Election.

Chapter Twelve

Summing up Healey

'If defence policy had been determined by the needs of foreign policy, and not by budgetary constraints, Healey's gifts could have been used to better effect.'

THE AUTHORS

'Horrible Healey . . . the atomic maniac.'   PRAVDA

Chapter Twelve

HEALEY was an important – if controversial – Minister. His long apprenticeship was thorough; but it was biased towards foreign affairs rather than towards defence.

His career, checked at the age of fifty-two by the 1970 General Election, has been markedly affected, perhaps even retarded, by his five and a half years at the Ministry of Defence. No Labour politician has been as competent a defence specialist, nor any as consistent or intellectually honest.

His short spell as an Oxford Communist has not been a real handicap, even though it could have gone against him as a civil servant, or as a regular member of the armed forces. One legacy of the period is his love of over-emphatic and frank comments.

Even during the thirties his inevitable interest in Marx, and understandable but misplaced sympathy for Russian communism, had fewer roots in the great slump than in the rise of fascism. In Hitler's Germany, fascism, with its excessive and romantic adulation of power, authority, and political order, added the sickness of active anti-semitism.

To the young Healey fascism was an absolute evil, alongside which Stalin's Russia appeared to be a country with wholesome ideas leading to true social equality. It was a myth widely shared by Western liberals, intellectuals, and leftists.

Donald Maclean, Guy Burgess, and Kim Philby, the upper-class Oxbridge traitors attracted to communism during the Depression, never outgrew their political immaturity, and became dangerous enemies of the state. Healey was never an establishment figure like them. His Bradford Grammar School and Balliol background gave him an anti-Establishment attitude that was critical, but free of contempt. He wanted an Establishment run by his type of meritocrat in an open and enlightened democratic-collectivist society.

In different ways his extreme left-wing period, his Oxford

friends, his time in the army, and not least his period as a back-room boy at Transport House helping true socialists against the Communists in Eastern Europe, all contributed to his authoritarian character and libertarian temperament. Intelligent, often insensitive, essentially self-reliant, and self-centred, he stands as a gifted 'loner'.

Healey is an outstanding example of the sort of man the old Labour pioneers hoped a reformed, mainly collectivist, state would produce. The grammar school boy who made good: natural intelligence, a fine education, financed by scholarship and public funds, and then service for the people both in the armed services and the socialist movement.

'Horrible Healey'

Labour's left wing has always been less committed to the idea of a mixed economy and a liberal democratic state. Its members did not believe that Britain was threatened by the Soviet Union, or that British political institutions were worth defending in all circumstances, or that anything could justify the use (or planned use) of nuclear weapons. In the Labour Party's Defence Debate Healey successfully challenged their beliefs.

Healey fought them with ferocity, and got his Party to accept the nature of power politics in world affairs, and the need for the military alliances that Bevin and Attlee had helped create. As a result he became an object of abuse and derision to the Communists.

In the Soviet Union the caricature of 'Horrible Healey' – the 'atomic maniac' – were prominent in *Pravda*, which, judging by its continuous flow of lampoons, regarded him as the Defence Minister most to be feared in Western Europe. A deluge of uncomplimentary remarks followed his comment that the Soviet Fleet in the Mediterranean could be obliterated by NATO aircraft within minutes. The British left were also upset when they learned the 'horrible' truth, presuming (incorrectly) that this meant the use of nuclear weapons.

Healey's attitude and his experience in office showed that some Labour politicians were interested in defence policy, and could even outflank professional exponents in their own field. But it also showed how difficult it was for a Labour Defence

18+

Minister to achieve the right policy. The ignorance of the
P.L.P. on defence made the job difficult.

As a Defence Minister Healey was more of a success than a
failure.

A realistic assessment of his term in office must begin with
the Labour Party's belief that defence matters less than social
and economic advances. In its simplest form defence is the insurance policy for the family of the state. Inadequate provision
for it can have appalling consequences.

Everyone would rather spend a greater proportion of the
gross national product on education, social services, and welfare. This is short-sighted only if the nation later has to rearm
quickly, and at greater expense, to deter or fight a war.

Top Priority

In October 1964 the top priority of the Wilson Government
was to save money on defence. With the economic situation
that then existed, and the cost in foreign exchange resulting
from Britain's global role, this was sensible.

When Healey began his major Defence Review however, the
first question posed was – 'What is the best policy we can get
for less money?', rather than the more fundamental 'What
must we spend?' This emphasis on economy and efficiency, reflecting the mood of the nation and of the politicians, preoccupied defence planners throughout the period of the Labour
Government. It was an emphasis on means and not ends.

Defence expenditure could have been reduced once Britain's
role for the seventies had been decided. If the answer to 'What
sort of defence policy do we want?' had been – 'a European-
orientated one', then Britain could have had both a coherent
policy to match her foreign policy, and a policy she could have
afforded. But the formulation of policy became more difficult
when expenditure was arbitrarily fixed before a serious review of commitments and capabilities had taken place.

When Healey became Secretary of State for Defence in 1964
he had the most complete grasp of policy of any Minister since
the war. Yet he had no substantive programme, apart from the
vague and contradictory policy thrust on him by the Labour
Party's Annual Conference and its Executive Committee.

The policy set out in the 1966 Defence Review could, however, have been afforded if the Government had succeeded in running the economy. The Prime Minister's decision not to devalue in 1964–5, and the collapse of the National Plan, however, sealed the fate of the Government and of its attempts to stay East of Suez.

Had an attempt been made to cost defence requirements, rather than what defence would be allowed from the Treasury, Britain could have had a coherent policy, and money saved for social services.

The important question, on which the Defence Review should have been centred, was how much was required to pay for an adequate policy based on a balanced assessment of national interests and commitments. Interests must shape commitments, not the other way round. A policy more in line with British interests was achieved – by a process of trial and error; mainly error.

Healey, because he was a Labour Minister and personally lacked a strong power base within the Party, found himself in a situation where the Foreign Office simply refused to re-examine commitments; and there was little that he could initially do about it. He thus tried to underpin the numerous existing commitments with a substantially-reduced military capability.

In 1966, following the publication of the Review, Britain gave the uncomfortable impression of being a country with a global role forced on her by commitments that were a legacy of her history and tradition. De Gaulle had known when to cut his losses. He ended the economically exhausting war in Algeria, and then increased the pride of the French by reaching a position of strength following a less ambitious policy.

Healey is fond of saying that the key factor in politics is the timing of a decision; in defence that means knowing when to withdraw. The Labour Government seemed to lack the necessary political judgement. They did not show they had mastered 'the art of the possible'.

If Britain's defence policy was to match her interests there should have been a rigorous examination to find out what they were in the late sixties, and what they were expected to be in the seventies and eighties. It never took place.

The Review had all the signs of excessive British pragmatism
– that preoccupation with 'means' rather than 'ends'. It was no
doubt easier with the Foreign Office in a state of intellectual
paralysis.

Despite the contempt with which Enoch Powell is often regarded by intellectuals, he did, during his period as Shadow
Defence Minister, force the Conservative Party to re-examine
its romantic attachment to Britain's world-wide 'empire'. He
rightly questioned the relevance of having British forces in the
Far East. His emphasis was first on 'ends', and then on the
'means' to achieve them.

Clearly the Foreign Office was largely to blame for the banal
nature of the Defence Review, because it refused to establish
a more realistic foreign policy, or even to examine it thoroughly. This alone could keep defence policy its faithful servant.

But the Cabinet compounded the mistakes of the Foreign
Office by pretending that economic facts alone should determine policy. The main error of Harold Wilson's Government
was the prior and absolute commitment to unrealistic goals,
which became more and more unrealistic as attempts to manage the economy collapsed. Politicians are by nature optimistic.
Wilson's Government, however, attempted too much with too
little, and failed to find the extra resources needed.

It is difficult to alter policies moulded by hundreds of years
of tradition and history, but the Foreign Office had failed to
consider Britain's declining economic position. It would have
been irresponsible to drop everything outside Europe – like
Confrontation – immediately, but the consequences of having
to adjust to crisis changes as events got beyond control were
worse than the possible effects of more considered planned withdrawal. If the job of politicians is to decide between alternative
values and policies, and to decide when to do what, then the
Wilson Cabinet must be criticized for its inept performance
during the first three years of office.

Dodging the Issue

In the crisis following devaluation the Defence Minister was
told to cut all existing commitments except the 'irreducible'
commitment to NATO Europe.

This policy was chosen by men in a difficult position, faced by the problem of how best to salvage what they could, and, of course, to remain in power. The Cabinet must keep its non-defence cohorts sufficiently loyal. Their mismanagement of the economy had left them weak, and it was the moment when the left wing of the Labour Party had most power in affecting defence affairs.

But the real question was still avoided. What were the irreducible limits of military effort required to uphold the nation's interest? Merely to reduce defence expenditure avoided this. Saving money on defence is a virtue only if the essential job can still be done. Yet it must be admitted that under Healey substantial savings were achieved, and defence resources were often more efficiently used. Under a weaker Minister the cuts would have been even greater.

With benefit of hindsight it is possible to claim that if the Government had devalued sooner – for example, in 1964 or 1965 – then the swingeing defence cuts would not have been necessary. And if substantial reductions had occurred in Britain's defence commitments and capabilities in 1966 devaluation might perhaps have been averted, or postponed to a time chosen to suit the Government and the interests of the British people.

Britain's efforts East of Suez were at last reluctantly abandoned by the Labour Government in February 1968. As from 1971 Britain said she would have no further strategic interest in the area east of the Persian Gulf.

The claim advanced in the Review of 1966 and the White Paper of July 1967 that Britain could make an indispensable contribution to peace and stability East of Suez ended when the Government found that the price was too high. Britain had made some contribution to stability by her modest military presence. But that was altering as growing nationalism and the changing pattern of economic and commercial affairs made this of declining value. The policy cost more, and achieved less. For the British at least, it no longer seemed worth the money.

Britain should have announced her decision to withdraw when Confrontation ended. Aden, together with the Gulf and the Far East, should have been abandoned in 1966, with total withdrawal by 1970 or 1971. This would have given the Gulf and Asian Commonwealth rulers one to two years more in which to cope with the consequences of withdrawal.

Into Reverse

Healey fought and lost the battle to keep the F-111, and was doubtless right not to resign over it. He was an extremely loyal member of the Cabinet, and believed in the central principle of Cabinet government: that decisions, once taken, reflect the collective will of the Cabinet, and must then be accepted. But there comes a time when the Cabinet may be wrong, and vital interests may be at stake. It is then the duty of a dissenting Minister to say so.

The F-111 should not have been cancelled. There was, and is, a strong case for using it in Europe. The American decision to deploy the F-111 in Europe, and the Soviet deployment of a remarkably similar aircraft indicate a useful role for a machine with a deep-strike and reconnaissance capability in Europe. Given the economic circumstances then prevailing a smaller number of F-111s than the fifty ordered might have been purchased – say, twenty-five.

For Healey, who had always sought a close understanding with the U.S.A. and influence over her, the sudden decision announcing the withdrawal from East of Suez, followed by the cancellation of the F-111, were more than a reversal of policy. They were a rejection of two decades of thinking and personal commitment.

After the F-111 decision he worked harder on getting a viable Eurocentric policy, which may yet form the basis for renewed influence over the U.S.A. But this is tied to the question of how nuclear weapons may be used in Europe, and the relationship to conventional forces available there.

Nuclear Strategy

Healey's view of NATO's nuclear strategy cannot be refuted as easily as Lord Wigg seems to believe. It can be said, however, that it depends too much on the notion that governments will behave rationally in a crisis – and with all the relevant facts before them. Healey himself has said that 'crisis management' really means deciding the best possible course of action with something like fifteen per cent of the necessary facts. In a

European crisis the governments of East and West may not behave rationally; and probably will not have all the relevant information. Even when the information is available – as it was to Western governments when Czechoslovakia was invaded in August 1968 – information can be misinterpreted. In the event of a situation possibly leading to war, however, the crisis is more likely to remain under control if there are enough local conventional forces to defend the area for more than a few days.

But there are not enough troops facing the armies of the Warsaw Pact countries, as Healey has admitted.

He knows no NATO government is likely to agree to a massive increase in ground forces that may never be used, and cannot be proved necessary – like short-term life insurance. On the other hand General Sir John Hackett, a former commander of NATO forces, said: 'I detect here a lack of intellectual integrity.' He added that Healey's policies were similar to those of the 1957 White Paper, 'where you take what is the cheapest course, or politically the most saleable, and offer it as militarily the most desirable'. Nuclear weapons are cheap but dangerous.

Healey's brilliant work on NATO's nuclear planning reveals the position. It also shows the blind alley into which British defence policy has got itself on the nature of war in Europe.

Under Healey the position became marginally better. By emphasizing, for example, a nuclear riposte to a sudden Soviet move, and planning for it in some detail, uncertainty – an essential psychological factor in deterrence – and credibility were restored to a position of prominence.

It is doubtful, though, if Healey was right to emphasize the British contribution to the flanks of NATO. It appeared more to be a way of taking up the slack caused by withdrawal East of Suez.

Britain, although well able to play a role on either the northern or southern flank, still needs a big say on the central front (still the most likely place for unintended or accidental war) where the question of when it may be necessary to use nuclear weapons would most probably be decided. The nuclear threshold is still too low, and Britain has done little to raise it.

The Strategic Reserve – 20,000 soldiers, comprising the Third Division – are inadequately equipped for action on the central front. They are better suited for the southern flank, in the politically unsettled Eastern Mediterranean.

With the Third Division Britain can provide naval strength and tactical air power; but her efforts ought to be concentrated on the central front, with larger, more mobile, and heavily armoured ground forces. B.A.O.R. should be substantially reinforced.

Before the Soviet invasion of Czechoslovakia Healey argued that, while Soviet military capability remained more or less the same, its intentions had become benign with the strategic nuclear deadlock. Much of his thinking about deterrence was based on this belief. Yet his distinction between 'capabilities' and 'intentions' is facile and misleading.

The Soviet Union has the capacity to inflict overwhelming damage on Western Europe much faster than a change in her intentions can be noted by those who monitor her outward political behaviour.

Intentions may not equal capabilities, but the will to use that capacity can change without much warning, and in certain circumstances without any warning at all. On the morning of 23 June 1941, for example, the Germans allowed trains carrying raw materials and supplies from the Soviet Union to cross into the lands occupied by them, before launching their attack on the Russians. (And this was less than two years after the Russo-German Pact had been signed!). On 7 December 1941 Japan attacked Pearl Harbour at the same time as her negotiators were working out a treaty of friendship with the U.S.A.

It is the forces in being that matter, and they must remain even though the opposition's intentions appear to change. It is difficult to equip a modern army in a short time. The Chieftain tank took seventeen years to get from the drawing board to the battlefield. The average time taken to design and build a weapon in Britain is ten years.

Britain still needs more of the type of armed forces that Healey substantially achieved; that is, regular professional soldiers – trained and equipped for the three most likely contingencies confronting the alliance. These are:

1. A Soviet probe to test intentions.
2. A medium-scale, non-nuclear push over a small area.
3. An overwhelming Soviet assault, either with or without

nuclear weapons, in a vast land campaign from Norway to Greece.

Britain needs to contribute more regular divisions to NATO to help cope with the first and second of these three. Although Healey stressed this, it tended to be obscured by the emphasis on nuclear deterrence by controlled escalation.

Finally there is the question of the British deterrent. The Labour Government continued the programme they inherited, and built four Polaris submarines.

The Labour Government never re-negotiated the Nassau agreement.

Labour's reluctance to discuss the matter has discouraged a public argument on the future of the deterrent. Healey's cancellation of the fifth Polaris submarine is questionable. With only four such submarines in service this tiny force is disquietingly small, and potentially vulnerable.

Basic issues about Polaris have never been discussed – at least in public. How vulnerable to detection and attack will they be? Can their missiles penetrate the anti-ballistic missile defences that the Soviets have, or are likely to have? Are there enough? In so many wars Britain has staggered to its feet after early set-backs. If another war occurs there will be no time to remedy mistakes.

Achievements

In spite of his shortcomings Healey remains the most outstanding Defence Minister since 1945. He can claim five substantial achievements.

His first was to dominate the Ministry of Defence. He 'civilianized' policy, and forced the military to become more professional in the preparation of policy. He was most strongly identified with that policy. He drafted White Papers, and wrote large parts of the Defence Review.

His second achievement was to sustain the morale of the Ministry of Defence and all three services, at a time of bewildering changes and innovations forced by economic stringency.

Had he resigned at the height of the F-111 row, when Britain was renouncing her world role, the Chiefs of Staff might also have resigned, and the impact on service morale would have been the most dispiriting since the fall of Singapore in 1942.

18*

He was regarded as the last line of defence in the Cabinet; and if removed or humiliated, then, it was felt, his passing would mark the end of British military power. This feeling, though exaggerated, expressed the dismay and frustration caused by successive Defence Reviews. Military men are bad at accepting defeat; and it is a question of honour that when defeated by the politicians senior service chiefs resign. To threaten resignation if the Secretary of State himself resigned, to deter him from actually resigning, was a remarkable tribute by the Chiefs of Staff to their political boss.

Healey's third achievement was his ability to take the big decision: the cancellation of the TSR-2, HS-681, P-1154, and the CVA-01 carrier. Considering the dither over weapon systems that had plagued defence policy in previous decades, the capacity to take even essentially destructive decisions was welcome. The cancellation of the TSR-2 and the CVA-01 were major decisions that basically affected British strategy.

Healey was able to play a part in the implementation of policy through the unique grasp of detail that virtually made him a superior permanent official. With the help of the Defence Council, composed of senior political, civilian, and military figures, he hammered out a new defence policy, which the Cabinet finally approved. He therefore took the big decisions, and had the capacity to direct, implement, and inspire an adjustment of policy. His analytical ability helped him to see what was essential. If defence policy had been determined by the needs of foreign policy, and not by budgetary constraints, Healey's gifts could have been used to better effect.

He has been accused of failing to bring about radical administrative reforms, but his decision not to pursue this course was deliberate. Imposed on top of far-reaching policy changes it would have damaged the morale of the services. As Healey was fond of saying, 'You don't take out someone's appendix when he's moving a grand piano.'

Important administrative changes did, however, occur in the Ministry of Defence after 1964, based on the Thorneycroft/Mountbatten reforms.

As Secretary of State for Defence he had two 'functional' Ministers under him, responsible for Administration and Equipment – in place of three single service Ministers.

Between 1964 and 1970 a more efficient machinery was created. Healey showed a real interest in cost-benefit analysis and modern management techniques. He was directly involved in the work to achieve better personnel management, job evaluation, and productivity agreements.

Healey also saw the importance of 'cost-effectiveness', budgeting in workshops, and analysis of maintenance and repair data. The number of Commands in each service had been reduced by amalgamation. The reorganization of the Ministry had resulted in the number of Whitehall civil servants being reduced from 24,000 to 16,000 by 1969. This saved £20,000,000 a year.

Healey also took the big decision on service pay and conditions. He fought Cabinet colleagues to implement Prices and Incomes Board recommendations that the old pay structure should be scrapped, and substantial pay increases introduced. The total increase which the services received was four times as great as under the previous method of pay calculation, and was already showing in the recruiting figures when Healey left office.

His fourth achievement was to improve defence thinking and planning through such things as the University Defence Lecturers scheme, support of the Royal United Service Institution, and the encouragement of forward defence planning in DS22 of the Ministry of Defence, and of the Defence Operations Analysis Establishment (D.O.A.E.) at Byfleet.

The University Defence Lecturers scheme and the service fellowships involved financing academics interested in defence who were anxious to publish work that might help the Ministry in thinking through defence policy and organization. It was first introduced in 1965 at five centres: Oxford, London, Aberdeen, Edinburgh, and Southampton.

Healey kept in close contact with the lecturers there who were successfully developing Strategic Studies. Serving officers were also encouraged to study at British universities. Healey strengthened the Ministry's forward planning work and separated it from contingency planning and operations work. Forward planning became the responsibility of DS22 under Peter Nailer, now a Professor at Lancaster University. At Byfleet the work of D.O.A.E. involved analysing the costs and benefits of equipment, and how best to cope with a range of tactical operations.

Healey saw the importance of being better informed and of thinking about defence over the next twenty years, as necessary for a more rational policy. He realized he needed a relevant political and strategic framework to help predict what weapons might be needed to deal with future conflict.

His fifth and most important achievement was the contribution he made to NATO's nuclear thinking. His work on the Nuclear Defence Planning Committee (N.D.P.C.) and in the Nuclear Planning Group (N.P.G.) was brilliant and original. He achieved three things here:

He fostered the feeling that in nuclear planning the European members of the alliance were important. He closed the gap between nuclear and non-nuclear members of the alliance, created by the distinction between having an independent national nuclear capacity, and sole reliance on the U.S.A. This was important because of dwindling faith in America following the abandonment of 'massive retaliation', with its automatic reply to a Soviet invasion. The strategy of the 'flexible response' was adopted by NATO in 1967 following the decision to abandon the old 'trip-wire' strategy with its immediate nuclear response.

He also helped to shape the means of producing a new NATO strategy to prevent war by controlled nuclear escalation. He played a major part in adapting the McNamara Committee to the needs of its European members.

Finally, he helped draft the new NATO strategy, avoiding automatic use of nuclear weapons against anything but a major attack. He worked out how conventional forces could be used both in the defence of Europe and to win time for negotiations.

The biggest unresolved problem, of course, is whether NATO's present level of conventional forces is sufficient to deter war, or to cope with its consequences for long enough to allow diplomacy a chance to achieve results.

Healey may well be remembered most for his major contribution to making nuclear deterrence effective. But his impact was considerable in all directions.

Index